PRAIRIE TALE

PRAIRIE TALE

a memoir

MELISSA GILBERT

G

GALLERY BOOKS

New York London Toronto Sydney

G

Gallery Books
A Division of Simon & Schuster, Inc.
1230 Avenue of the Americas
New York, NY 10020

First Gallery Books trade paperback edition February 2010

GALLERY BOOKS and colophon are trademarks of Simon & Schuster, Inc.

For information about special discounts for bulk purchases, please contact Simon & Schuster Special Sales at 1-866-506-1949 or business@simonandschuster.com.

The Simon & Schuster Speakers Bureau can bring authors to your live event. For more information or to book an event contact the Simon & Schuster Speakers Bureau at 1-866-248-3049 or visit our website at www.simonspeakers.com.

Designed by Jaime Putorti

Manufactured in the United States of America

8

Library of Congress Cataloging-in-Publication Data is available.

ISBN 978-1-4165-9917-3 (pbk)
ISBN 978-1-4391-2360-7 (ebook)

For Sam, Lee, Dakota, and Michael,
the four chambers of my heart.

And for Bruce William Boxleitner,
my true companion.

Do you know how fine you are to me?

I will not die an unlived life.
I will not live in fear
of falling or catching fire.
I choose to inhabit my days,
to allow my living to open me,
to make me less afraid,
more accessible,
to loosen my heart
until it becomes a wing,
a torch, a promise.
I choose to risk my significance;
to live so that which came to me as seed
goes to the next as blossom
and that which came to me as blossom,
goes on as fruit.

"Fully Alive"
Dawna Markova

Contents

A Brand-New Start of It

Exactly Where I Need To Be

FOREWORD
By Patty Duke

My friend Melissa and I met when I was a so-called grown-up and she was a so-called kid. This happened shortly after my agent phoned and informed me that Melissa's company was producing a television version of *The Miracle Worker*, in which Melissa would play Helen Keller and I would play Teacher Anne Sullivan. Some twenty years before, I had played the role of Helen Keller, opposite Anne Bancroft as Teacher, and the experience had an enormous impact on my life and career.

Two decades later, my reaction to the remarkable opportunity to play Teacher was a cacophony of feelings: thrilled, flattered, and not a little apprehensive. How would it work, having a thirteen-year-old actress be my boss? Not to mention the fear of trying to fill Anne Bancroft's extraordinary shoes. As I child I had longed to play Teacher, and here I'd been presented with the chance to fulfill that dream.

I took a deep breath and said yes, and with that, negotiations were under way. In the meantime, however, there was something my heart insisted I do. With a good deal of anxiety, I called Anne Bancroft. There was no way I could do the movie if it created any discomfort for her. But my anxiety was quickly dispelled; Anne was excited for me, and she couldn't have been more supportive. As had been the case as long as I'd known her, her generosity of spirit and her demonstration of unconditional love were inspiring.

Once I'd secured Anne's blessing, it was on to the task at hand. What I knew of Melissa Gilbert going into the movie was this: she was the adorable Half Pint on *Little House on the Prairie,* and her talent was real and had kept growing over the years. What I didn't know was that we were almost exactly the same size. *The Miracle Worker* is very physical; the characters go at it in no uncertain terms, and often. After I'd sized her up (literally), my biggest fear became: *She could take me with a couple of moves or less.*

But my biggest obstacle had yet to be revealed. It came to light on the first day of rehearsal, when the director pulled me aside and exacted a vow from me not to influence Melissa's performance. No tips, no critique.

This agreement didn't feel right to me. In rehearsal we are supposed to explore each other and delve into each other's psyches. If I wasn't such a people pleaser, I would have never taken that vow. But I would learn that a desire to please people was just one of the many characteristics Melissa and I have in common.

As we rehearsed, the vow was an intrusion in the process. Finally, I couldn't stand the secrecy anymore, and I became determined to reveal the director's instruction. Rehearsals were coming to a close and we'd soon be off to Palm Beach for a two-week run of the play prior to filming.

During the flight to Palm Beach, I imposed on our friend Charlie Siebert, who would play Captain Keller, for his insight and advice. He aimed me in the direction of trusting my instincts. Melissa and her mom were in the seats in front of us, and I leaned forward and tapped Melissa on the head and said, "We need to talk." She popped up, looked back, and grinned a mile wide.

I rushed into sharing insights about playing Helen, and called up directions from Arthur Penn (the original director of the 1959 version) from memory. The relief was enormous for our new and energized team. With the barriers gone, our work was able to breathe free and our personalities were falling in love with each other. Melissa's confidence grew in leaps and bounds, and she absorbed and delivered Helen Keller.

Since Melissa had never been onstage, it was important for me to also teach her theater etiquette and superstitions (she actually picked her nose during one of the first curtain calls). I emphasized discipline so often, I sounded like Anne Sullivan both onstage and off. We both learned a lot during the run and became tighter than ticks. Our trust in each other didn't waiver and hasn't since. We made our movie with determination, joy, love, and some good performances.

It wasn't until years later that we found the time to fill each other in on the dark sides of our lives: The early deaths of our fathers. The pressure to be perfect kids and actors. The responsibility of being breadwinners. The search for love and respect. Like most folks, we had family issues, career issues, and just plain girl issues. Watching Melissa grapple with these challenges was like looking at a younger version of me, walking the same tightrope.

As is typical in show business, our paths took us in different directions for some time, but to this very day, whenever we catch up, it's as if we'd talked yesterday. And thankfully, over the years we were teamed again in two more television movies, and both times we luxuriated in our symbiotic and solid friendship. Even our age disparity fell by the wayside.

Later, was I surprised when Melissa ran for Screen Actors Guild president and won handsomely? Nope! My only advice, having held that office, was "Stay tough" and "Don't let them get to you." She did, and they didn't. For decades I've been getting all puffed up with pride as I watch her mature. You'd think she was my daughter. And I'm prouder still of her for this book, her latest accomplishment. In the following pages, she presents herself, warts and all, and allows insight into one woman's emotional roller-coaster ride.

Once again, she makes me proud to be (as she calls me) her teacher/friend.

REVELATIONS AND REALIZATIONS

Fairy Dust

My mother was nearly a month past her husband's funeral when she turned her attention back to my desire to write a memoir. It wasn't just a desire; there was an actual book deal, and she was against it. If the book were on any topic other than myself, she would've already been circulating word that "Melissa is writing the best book ever." But this was different. It was about me. Which meant it was also about her. And she was against telling *that* story if she wasn't the one doing the telling.

She had tried numerous times to talk me out of it, but her efforts were interrupted by the death of my stepfather, Hollywood publicist Warren Cowan. Now she was back on point.

She showed up at my house one afternoon carrying a large box packed with news clippings, ads, letters, and diaries of mine. She set it down on the kitchen table with a thud and announced with a smile as deadly as a pearl-handled Derringer that the contents would be helpful.

"For your *book*," she said, pronouncing the word "book" as if it were a petrie dish containing the Ebola virus that I was going to let out in the world.

I marveled at her gamesmanship—and at her. She looked a decade younger than her age, which, if revealed, would be taken as a bigger crime than revealing Valerie Plame was a CIA agent. Her hair was blond and coiffed. It's sufficient and necessary to say she was strikingly attractive. She looked great whether going to her weekly appointment at the hair salon or to movie night at the Playboy mansion, which she and my stepfather had attended for years.

I also cringed at the layers at play here in my kitchen. I thought, thank goodness I have four sons. The mother-daughter relationship is one of mankind's great mysteries, and for womankind it can be hellaciously complicated. My mother and I are quintessential examples of the rewards and frustrations and the joys and infuriations this relationship can yield. By and large, we are close. At times, though, she could render me speechless with her craftiness. Now was one of those times.

While I sifted through the box packed with sacred bits from my life, my mother offered sly commentary and full-on reinterpretations of the contents. Ah, the contempt and fear and anger she hid behind her helpful smile.

To me, at forty-four years old, my book was a search for truth and identity. To her, it was—if only you could have seen the look on her face, you'd fully understand—the ultimate betrayal.

I moved on. I made tea. We talked about some of the condolences about Warren that continued to stream in. We mentioned which friends checked on her, the dinner invitations that kept her busy as ever, and of course the latest comings and goings of my husband, Bruce, and my sons. Finally, after we had caught each other up on everything, she returned to the book.

"You can write the book if you want," she said with a nonchalant shrug.

"Thank you," I replied. "I'm looking forward to it."

"I can understand why you want to write it," my mother said. "You write it and get it all out of you."

"Thank you."

"You have my blessing."

"Thank you again."

"But," she said, "the classy thing would be to burn it after you're finished."

My life was a mystery even as I lived it.

Several months earlier, I had called my mother and asked if I'd ever had a conversion ceremony to make me officially Jewish. Although I was raised Jewish, my upbringing didn't include any formal religious education or training. We celebrated Passover and other major Jewish holidays. But we also celebrated Christmas and Easter. It's why I always emphasized the "ish" in "Jewish."

As I got older, though, I grew more observant and intrigued by a more personal relationship with God. One day, as I discussed this with a friend who had converted to Judaism as an adult, she asked if I recalled my conversion ceremony.

"Huh?" I said.

My friend explained that adults wanting to switch to Judaism from another religion had to go through a conversion process. It included reading and discussion among friends; a deeper course of investigation with a rabbi; then study, immersion, and approval by a board, culminating with a public ceremony and celebration.

Even though I was just a day old when my parents adopted me, my friend explained my parents would still have needed a rabbi to perform a ceremony and a blessing to make me officially Jewish. That's when I asked my mother if she recalled doing the ceremony.

"Why do you need to know now?" she asked.

"Because if I never had a conversion ceremony, then I'm not really Jewish," I replied. "And if I'm not Jewish—"

"But you're Jewish," she interrupted.

"Who says?" I asked.

"I do."

"Mom, believe it or not, you are not the final authority on this issue."

"I'm your mother," she said. "And I'm Jewish."

"But my birth parents—"

"We adopted you at birth."

"Was there a conversion ceremony?" I asked.

"I don't remember," she said.

"You don't remember?"

"No."

"No?"

When it came to my childhood, my mother's memory was more reliable than the Apple-S command on my laptop, so I knew she had the information filed away somewhere. I switched tactics. I asked if she remembered what I did for my second birthday. She did, and described the party she threw me. I then asked if she remembered my first birthday party. She recounted that, too, including the flavor of the cake and the bakery where she bought it.

"Mom," I said with a dramatic pause worthy of the best courtroom lawyer, "you can remember my first and second birthday parties as if they happened an hour ago. But you can't remember whether you hired a rabbi and had a conversion ceremony for me. How is that?"

"Melissa!"

"Mom!"

"Maybe I didn't have one," she said. "I don't really know. What's the big deal?"

"It means I'm not Jewish," I said. "It means I'm not who I thought I was for all these years. It changes everything."

Okay, I exaggerated. It wouldn't change everything. When I hung up the phone, I was still going to be me: dressed in sweats, juggling car-pool duties, going to meetings, planning dinner, trying to wedge more into my day than twenty-four hours permitted. In one sense, my life would be fundamentally unchanged.

However, in another sense, my inner compass had already started to spin wildly out of control. Was there a conversion ceremony? That was a simple question. Was I who I thought I was? Not such a simple question.

Welcome to my not-so-simple life. My mother, whom I love dearly, has continually revised my life story within the context of a complicated family history that includes more than the usual share of divorce, stepchildren, dysfunction, and obfuscation, and I've spent most of my adult life attempting to deconstruct that history and separate fact from fiction, especially as the facts pertain to . . . me!

For example, my mother was at the helm of everything, including my career, my food intake, and how I dressed—my whole life. I never questioned her or rebelled. Speaking out against the family was the ultimate form of disloyalty, and disloyalty was not tolerated. It was like the mafia. Although I never feared getting whacked, I was always just a little afraid of being sent back to wherever it was I came from.

So in an interview back when I was ten years old, I'd likely have said that everything was wonderful, everyone in my life was fantastic, I was happy, and life was perfect. But most of that was untrue. Just as it wasn't true when I told a reporter in an interview three months after my mom's second husband suffered a brain hemorrhage that I had my crying moments, but I was pretty tough about that sort of thing.

The truth is that I never cried over my mom's second husband. I was never close to him. I never liked him. I didn't have any relationship with him. I was dragged to the hospital when he was sick to add cachet so the nurses would take better care of him. I know it was difficult for my mother, but I don't remember being upset about anything at the time.

Could I say that to the press? Absolutely not.

A large part of my life has been an illusion—not an illusion crafted through carefully controlled media; it's more like light going through a prism, in that there's one story bent in numerous directions. There's my mother's version, there's the one in the press, there's the one I lived, and there's the one I'm still trying to figure out.

However, there are some facts. For instance, I am a twice-married, now-sober former child actor and mother of four. I acquired those hyphenates by living the way I wanted to or needed to, hopefully with some grace and dignity. I made my share of mistakes, which I think of as the stones I stepped on to get to where I am today, and through luck, hard work, serious reflection, and a desire to face the truth about myself, I ended up at a place where I now enjoy the peace that comes from allowing myself to not be perfect.

Such was not always the case. My mother, beautiful, delicate, and deluded, saw me as the pillar of perfection—and told me that I was the world's best actor, the best wife, the best . . . at everything. I knew I wasn't, but I lived my life as though I had to be, lest I disappoint her.

Today, I just want to be *my* best, and I don't fear disappointing anyone other than myself and my family. I'm in love with a good man, and my children are brave, funny, and compassionate people. I love the lines around my eyes, but I hate the way my cheeks are falling; I'm carrying around an extra ten pounds and enjoying it (most of the time). I suppose I am truly fat and happy.

I play drums, surf, and meditate. I'm in a peaceful state of mind most of the time. Though I am lucky enough to earn a living at a job I love, I'm also thinking about going back to school to get my RN or LVN in end-of-life pediatric care. I'm much better going forward than backward or sideways. I have no real plan, just general dreams.

It wasn't always like this. I wasn't always at peace. I wasn't always content to let life happen.

For my first couple of decades, there was fairy dust sprinkled over everything in my life courtesy of my mother. According to her, and via her, through the press, everything was sparkly, beautiful, and perfect. Everyone was well behaved. We didn't have any problems. We never had colds.

In reality, things were quite different . . . and not okay. One of the first times I recall opening my eyes to this was when Rob Lowe and I were planning our wedding. Our plans were becoming ridiculously overblown and we were even talking about renting a sound stage. Oh, then there were the doves. *Doves? Oy!* It was a whole production.

One day my mother and I were in the car, going to meet the wedding planner and the florist. I was anxious about everything from the wedding details to the commitment I was about to make to Rob. I was a kid living a big life and growing up fast. Those years I spent in the "Brat Pack" (I really hate that stupid name) running with Rob, Emilio, and Tom, that was my equivalent to college. I didn't have the confidence of a bride-to-be. Nervous and near tears, I was a babbling river of anxiety and fear.

"I'm so scared about this," I told my mom. "I don't know, I don't know. Am I doing the right thing? Am I making a huge mistake? Can this work?"

My mother gave me a look full of calm and wisdom. "Sweetheart, don't worry," she said with total sincerity and earnestness. "Rob will make a wonderful *first* husband."

I heard that and something inside me clicked. It was my first allergic reaction to my mother's fairy dust. I thought, *That is a really tweaked way of looking at life,* and I knew something was not right. And such were our issues, my issues.

As with so many women I've met, my issues eventually caught up with me. I got to a point in life, somewhere into my second marriage and during my effort to get sober, where reality tapped me on the shoulder, demanding attention, asking questions I'd never stopped to consider: Who are you? How'd you get here? What does it mean to be a wife, a mother, a woman? What will make you happy? What does a peaceful life look like to you?

Sometimes life is like an uninvited houseguest. It shows up and refuses to leave until you deal with it. Call me a late bloomer, but I didn't feel eighteen until I was in my twenties, and I didn't start putting my life together until much, much later.

Furthermore, I still get letters from women whose lives were and often still are truly horrible, victims of physical and sexual abuse. These women say the one escape they had growing up was *Little House on the Prairie*. They wished they had Laura Ingalls Wilder's life the way I played her. What I don't ever tell them is that I'm also among those who wish I had Laura's life the way I played her.

For me, work was a fantasy where I was a happy-go-lucky kid with a larger-than-life surrogate father, Michael Landon. There were people I could talk to and count on, and horses and cows and other animals I could play with in an idyllic outdoor setting. In real life, I struggled with the mythology of my existence—the story of my birth grew from the fairy dust my mother sprinkled on the truth, whatever that was.

I always knew I was adopted. I was told that I was the child of a prima ballerina and a Rhodes Scholar; my mother was a beautiful dancer who wasn't able to give up her career, not just yet, and my father was in the middle of some project, and though I was the product of a loving relationship between two brilliant individuals, the timing was simply off, so they gave me up for adoption, this wonder child endowed with the gifts of both Margot Fonteyn and Stephen Hawking. My mother recognized in me the potential to be not just good but the most exceptional, and, well, that story was perpetuated over the years, told and retold like some sort of fairy tale or legend.

Finally, I reached an age where I was able to fact-check the story and found out my mother the dancer *was* in fact a dancer. What kind of dancer was never clear. She wasn't a prima ballerina, though. That much I figured out. And my father the Rhodes Scholar was a sign painter and stock car racer. They had both been married to other people. They each had three children. They ran off together, got pregnant, moved in together with their six children, and decided they couldn't afford a seventh.

So they gave me up for adoption, a child who would eventually end up wondering who she really is, who she's related to, if she has a predisposition for high blood pressure, heart disease, or diabetes, or any history of cancer or personality issues. If that's asking too much, I'm willing to settle for finding out who gave me the nose I disposed of at eighteen.

The latest twist in the story of my birth was brought to light a few days after my stepfather died. Close family and friends were at my mother's, and my godmother, Mitzi, started in about the day my parents picked me up at the hospital. She was hilarious as she described my parents and their first day with a newborn. Out of the blue my mother said, "Well, imagine what a shock it was for me!"

Everyone turned toward my mother, including me. She wasn't joking. She looked as if she was reliving that shock.

"I mean, we had no plans to adopt a child," she said.

As I had many times throughout my adult life, I cocked my head and flashed a quizzical look at my mother. *What?*

"We weren't even looking," she continued. "Then I got a phone call that there was a baby available and did I want it?" She turned to me. "I called your dad. He was on the road and he said, 'Yes, that's the one. Go get it.'"

"It?" I said. "You keep referring to me as an *it*."

"Well, actually, you weren't even born yet."

This was news to me. And I would have explored it further, except new people arrived at my mother's and she switched into hostess mode.

A few days later my mother came over to my house and we talked about my stepdad's death. I walked her through it because she didn't remember much; by contrast, I remembered everything in detail. I had brought in a superb hospice team and used my training to turn myself into a patient advocate, which allowed my mother and the love of her life to have a peaceful good-bye.

I told her who had come to visit in those final days, and then I described how she had spent Warren's last day alive lying in bed next to him, sharing her strength and comforting him through his final moments. I told her what I saw as I watched him take his final breaths wrapped in her arms. I thanked her for letting me be a part of something so private, so spiritual, and so profoundly moving.

After we had a good cry, I reminded her of the story she and Mitzi had started to tell about my arrival in this world. I still wanted clarification. Tired and vulnerable, she opened up and said that she and my father had been trying to have a baby and were actually going through fertility treatments when she got the call. The strange part was, until then, they had not spoken about adoption—or so she said.

A few weeks later I was replaying that conversation and realized something. My father had a daughter from a previous marriage. I'd met her once. And my mother was pregnant twice after me, once with a baby she lost at six months and once with my sister Sara. Both of my parents were fertile. So why couldn't they—

Obviously more was going on than I knew. Once again, the beginning of my life was defined by a question mark.

————————————————————

two

WITH PARDONS TO DARWIN, THE ORIGIN IS SPECIOUS

There was never a time when I didn't know I was adopted, but neither was there a time when my parents sat me down and said, "We have something to tell you." I just always knew.

I have a book called *The Chosen Baby* that my mother used to read to me. It's about a couple who adopt a little boy and then a little girl. My mother, a gifted artist, crossed out all of their names and put all of our names in it. She changed the little boy's name to Melissa and drew bows and ribbons on him to make him look like me, and made a sailor hat and shorts on the little girl to make her look like my brother, Jonathan, who my parents adopted a month before my fourth birthday. So not only did I know that I was adopted, I thought it was pretty special that someone had written a book about it.

Again, more fairy dust.

My earliest memory is of myself, at two and a half or so, standing on a chair in the back of a nightclub, watching my father doing his standup act. I was doing his act along with him. I adored my father. I wanted to be just like him.

I always say that I was born to perform, but he was literally born into performing. His father was an Irish vaudevillian, and his mother was a French aerialist. He was their only child. They lived together in Philadelphia, and then, at the age of eight or nine, he was shipped off to Buenos Aires and raised by a family of circus performers, who were aerialists like his mother. His parents died when he was in his teens. On his own in the world, he became an acrobat and traveled in a circus with his surrogate family. At eighteen, he fell from a trapeze, and although he survived, it ended his career in the circus. He returned to the United States and studied music and acting until World War II, then enlisted in the navy.

While in the military, he appeared in the George Cukor–directed war film *Winged Victory*, the upbeat story of young men joining the air force in the hope of becoming pilots. It was kind of like *Top Gun*, only the 1944 version. Edmond O'Brien, Judy Holliday, Lee J. Cobb, and Red Buttons were among the many stars appearing in the film. My dad's part was very small, but I have a hunch he was much better suited to acting than soldiering.

During my first term as president of the Screen Actors Guild, I received a letter from a man who'd served with my father. He said their job was to patrol the California coast. He reminded me this was not long after Pearl Harbor and people were pretty sure California was going to be hit next, either by another surprise air attack or by torpedoes fired from submarines. Everyone was on edge.

He and my father were on patrol one night when my father, looking off in the distance, saw something on the beach move in an unusual manner. They watched for a moment. My father was sure it was moving toward them. He raised his machine gun, opened fire, and . . . killed a cow.

Luckily for all the livestock in the state, after the navy, my dad went straight into show business. Which brings up an interesting sidenote about him: Paul Gilbert wasn't his actual name. When he went to join the Screen Actors Guild he was told there was already another member with his same name, Ed McMahon. I don't know where he came up with Paul or Gilbert, but it became his name and now it is mine. He was in a lot of movies, appeared on some very early TV shows, and performed on *The Ed Sullivan Show* playing a French horn and doing his comedy. He tap-danced and incorporated acrobatics into his act. In his nightclub act, he walked out onstage, tripped on his way to the microphone, did a front flip, landed on his back, and then got up and did his thing.

He costarred in *So This Is Paris,* a 1955 film with Tony Curtis and Gene Nelson about three sailors on leave in Paris and looking for women, or rather, looking for dames. It's one of Nick Clooney's favorite movies. Nick's son, George, is an actor like me. Well, not like me—he's a big movie star and I'm . . . well . . . not. But I digress. In it, my dad has a fantastic solo number called "I Can't Do a Single, but I'll Try." He dances and he sings. He was more than a triple threat; he sang, danced, acted, played five instruments, and juggled. In his forties, he made *3 Nuts in Search of a Bolt,* a silly comedy about three crazies who flee the nuthouse. I love the title of that movie.

At a certain point, he graduated from film and TV to touring full-time, taking his brand of entertainment on the road until the end of his life in 1976, when he passed away at age fifty-seven. I was eleven years old when he died. I learned most of what I know about him from reading the back of his record albums and hearing stories other people told me.

Here's one of the more interesting facts: my father was married thirteen times. Even he knew he exchanged I-do's a ridiculous number of times. In his act, he used to joke, "It's true I have had a number of wives. I don't believe in premarital sex."

My mother was born in Flatbush, Brooklyn, to a brilliant but struggling stand-up comic, Harry Crane, and his former Miss Brooklyn artist wife, Julia Crane. Extremely poor, they had one more child, another girl, my aunt Stephanie, before separating acrimoniously. I don't think my grandparents were ever in the same room together after that.

Growing up, we never spoke about my grandfather in front of my grandmother, which was difficult given his exciting life. And mention of my grandmother in the company of my grandfather was almost like a hanging offense. It wasn't done.

Following the split, my grandmother moved to Florida with my aunt Stephanie, and my grandfather and mother moved to Hollywood, where he began a legendary career as a comedy writer, first in the movies and then in television. Profoundly funny, prolific, and in demand, he wrote a movie for Laurel and Hardy, cocreated Jackie Gleason's classic TV series *The Honeymooners*, and worked with a who's who of stars, including the Marx Brothers, Red Skelton, Dean Martin, Jerry Lewis, Joey Bishop, Frank Sinatra, and even Robert Kennedy.

My mother was eighteen when they moved to L.A. She had her sights set on a career as an actress. She arrived in town looking to be a combination of Natalie Wood, Sophia Loren, and Merle Oberon. She moved into the Studio Club, an apartment building for young women, mostly actresses. There she met my future godmother, Mitzi McCall, who briefly dated James Dean. They ran with a cool crowd—funny, young, sexy, and talented.

My mom worked at Mannis Furs in Hollywood. Every day on her way in and out of the salon, she walked over my father's star on the Hollywood Walk of Fame, not knowing, obviously, that one day she would marry him. My mother was in her early twenties, acting in some Roger Corman movies (*Sorority Girl* and *Unwed Mothers*) and engaged to comedian Don Rickles when my father stole her away. He swept her off her feet and away with him to a gig in Houston, where they married.

Afterward, my mother called my grandfather and said, "Dad, I want to tell you that I just got married."

He asked to whom.

"Paul Gilbert," she said.

Without missing a beat and knowing my dad, he quipped, "Take a sweater." I'm not sure if that was because my dad was on the road so much or because it wouldn't be long before my dad moved on to the next wife. Either way, it's a damn funny line!

I understand her attraction to my father. He was a seriously handsome man. I have photos of him throughout my house, but two of them, which I keep on the wall beside my vanity, stand out as rather extraordinary. In one, he's on a beach someplace in Mexico, dressed in rolled-up khaki pants, no shirt, and standing next to a gigantic swordfish that he's just caught. In the other, he's in swim trunks, with scuba gear on his back, holding a spear gun that has a huge manta ray at the end.

He was the quintessential man's man adventurer, with a real movie-star style and elegance about him. You know those photos of men in the fifties and sixties that always feature a really handsome guy in a tux with the bow tie (a real one) untied, shirt unbuttoned, cigarette in one hand, drink in the other? That was my daddy. He had such panache, such style! He was particular about his clothes, from the way he organized them neatly and by color, to having his shirts, cuff links, and shoes monogrammed. He built furniture in his spare time. Even the work suits he wore in his shop were monogrammed.

He and my mother made a great-looking, dashing couple. He was twenty years older; she was radiant. They settled in a one-bedroom apartment in West Hollywood, which was where they lived when I arrived.

Old photos in my mother's albums show me in a bright wicker bassinet with hand-sewn lace and ribbon. I was dressed in adorable baby clothes. According to my mother, I never spit up or had even a crumb of food in the corners of my mouth. I was perfect. Everything was perfect.

Everything but the suddenness and surprise of the way I entered the scene. It didn't sit well with me. It was like a puzzle someone finished by forcing pieces to fit. The picture was nice, but the edges were off. My mother is not a spur-of-the-moment person. She plans and calculates. Like her artist mother, she treats life as a lump of clay she can shape and sculpt to suit her vision. Little is left to chance. So the revelation following my stepfather's death rattled me. So did the revelation that came soon after—that my dad had been stepping out on her.

I didn't know what to make of this new twist. Nothing was out of the realm of possibility. Years earlier I had gone through the process of finding my alleged biological family, and this latest wrinkle sent me scrambling for my phone book. I called my alleged biological older half sister, Bonné, the daughter of my alleged birth father, David, and stepdaughter of my alleged birth mother, Cathy, and through her, I found out that David and Cathy had split for a spell in 1963. When they got back together in early 1964, Cathy was pregnant. A few months later, her baby was gone.

During the period Cathy and David weren't together she may have met my father, gotten pregnant by him, and then arranged to have him adopt me. Considering the man was married thirteen times during his life, it's plausible. If it still doesn't make sense, though, all I can say is welcome to my life.

My personal "big bang" mystery aside, I was loved. That I know—and knew—without any doubt. My mother and father were entranced by the new addition to their lives. My mother was especially enchanted, and why not? I was pretty cute—chubby and freckly with the perfect little swirl of red Kewpie doll hair on top of my very round head. She would come home after a night out with my dad, wake me up, and play with me as if I were a doll, even changing my clothes, and then put me back to bed without hearing a whimper of complaint from me.

For the first three years of my life, I was the center of everyone's universe. I went shopping with my mom and I rehearsed with my dad. When people came to the house, I sang and danced for them, then bathed in their compliments about my red curls and freckles. My nickname was Wissy-do. I had a beagle named Sir Saul of Wissy, Saulie for short. It was all really very precious. Idyllic, even.

Not much time passed before I entered show business, which was like the family business. I was just two years old when I landed the first job I went out for, Carter's baby clothes. It was 1966, and my mom took me to the audition, where I met the director, who like many commercial directors of that era looked like an upscale hippie or artist, with long hair and a beard, which might have frightened most little children. Not me. The story goes that I ran straight up to the hirsute director, who was sitting cross-legged on the floor, climbed right into his lap, threw my arms around him, kissed him, and started singing songs and telling stories.

My mother was appalled at what she saw me do and heard me say. She feared the people in the room and the other mothers waiting with their little girls would think she'd told me to do that, but the truth was, she didn't coach me one bit. It was all me, my predisposition for the spotlight presenting itself in an irrepressible gust of enthusiasm and blur of red curls. I saw that my excitement was infectious. So, in later auditions, whatever the product was, I told the director it was my favorite thing in the whole world. I *loved* whatever brand of mustard they were selling! I only ate McDonald's! My daddy used that deodorant!

At home, life was like a giant nightclub date. My parents had parties all the time, filling the house with talented, funny people. I remember sneaking onto the stairs in my nightgown, my legs dangling through the railing, and watching the grown-ups downstairs as they sang and danced, played charades, told jokes, and regaled one another with great stories.

One time I was sound asleep when my mother came into my room and woke me up, urging me to follow her downstairs. It wasn't "do you want to come downstairs?" It was "you have to come downstairs now!" She'd been to the ballet and Rudolf Nureyev and Dame Margot Fonteyn, two of the greatest dancers ever, were in the living room. A few years ago, I told that story to my godsister, Jenny Brill. She responded, "Ruth Buzzi slapped me once."

I became a big sister when I was almost four years old. Jonathan arrived to great fanfare and to my even greater annoyance. I had no idea how my parents got him, where they got him, or, more important, *why* they got him. As far as I was concerned, he was an interloper relegating me, the headliner, to opening-act status.

Apparently I was pissed. According to my mother, we were in a rented house in Reno about a year later (my father had an engagement), and she set my brother up in a playpen and went to sit down nearby with my father while I ran around, seemingly content and happy. Moments later, she heard my brother screaming hysterically. She sprinted around the corner and found me standing beside the playpen, slapping Jonathan across the face. Right hand. Left hand. Right hand. Left hand. Just like I'd seen on the Three Stooges.

She yanked me out and yelled at me to stop, which I did immediately. Hey, I was a good girl.

My mom couldn't figure out what the hell was going on or why her precious little daughter would do such a thing. I think one can safely wager I was jealous of Jonathan and wanted to get rid of him.

As a little kid, I spent a lot of time riding in the backseat of the station wagon we traveled in when we accompanied my dad on the road, which we seemed to do frequently. I have quite a few memories of late nights on long stretches, headlights, and falling asleep with my head against the car window. It was always a delicious feeling to be carried from the car to bed, where I'd fall back into a deep, comfortable sleep, even if it was a new motel. It was the comfort that came from knowing a bed was waiting and both of my parents were there in case I woke up and found monsters in the closet. I felt safe and secure, like all was right in the world.

Even now I have a hard time with long drives at night because the lights lull me to sleep. My mother drove a white Cadillac Eldorado, with white interior. She got a new version of it every few years. Triple white. A cloud on wheels. By rolling up the windows, she could close herself off from the outside world. It was like being sealed in a luxurious living room.

So there I was one day, sealed in that living room, along with my brother, when my mother said something to the effect of "Your father is not going to be living with us anymore." I don't know about my brother, but my first thought was *It's no big deal, he's on the road again, and we can't go with him because we're in school.*

Then I realized what my mom had actually said—that he wouldn't be living with us anymore. I asked what she meant. She explained he was moving into a different house, adding as reassuringly as possible that it would be close by and that we didn't have to worry because "nothing is going to change."

What?

"It's going to be exactly the same," she said. "He'll be there when you get home from school. He'll stay to tuck you into bed. He'll be with us on all the holidays. It won't be any different."

And that was it. There was no hysteria, no crying, no grieving or even griping about the loss of what I believed was our cozy family unit. The pillars that held up my little world were splitting, but it was presented as something I shouldn't be upset or concerned about, so I wasn't. Which was weird. Because it was something to get upset about. Except I never did. My mother drove us home and life went on.

That was the emergence of the porcelain doll, the little girl who did and said everything she was told, didn't complain, and would learn to tell others that everyone in her life, whether at home or on a TV set, loved one another even when there were serious problems. The porcelain doll would wear outfits made of wool even though they gave her a rash. She would always smile, always have a perfect hairdo, and always say the right things no matter what else was going on in her life.

I still have no idea why my parents' marriage ended. It stayed between them. To their credit, they kept their promise. Family life was as close as possible to the way it had always been. If my dad wasn't on the road, he was at my mother's home, greeting us when we came back from school. We lived in a relatively new area in the hills above Studio City, and he moved nearby. We spent every other weekend at his house. He stayed with us when my mom traveled with her friends. At night, I still threw my arms around him and let him put me to bed. The lights went off and he or my mom said good night. I still knew I was loved. But it wasn't the same as before. All of us knew it, too. We just didn't acknowledge it.

three

SHOWTIME

My mother made sure there were no limits when I was growing up. Life was like a rolling field for as far as you could see: all open spaces rising into hills that descended into a lush valley, and so on for eternity. Her philosophy could be encapsulated in a single word: yes.

Bad news needn't intrude on her reality. She wanted her life to be a big flower garden, and she wanted mine to be even bigger and more beautiful. When I was a baby, she stayed up at night and ironed the lace on my underpants, the frilly ones that went over my diapers. Later, after we moved to Studio City, she decorated my bedroom as if it were out of a children's picture book, with a canopy bed whose fabric matched the room's delicate red rose wallpaper. It was perfect.

We got along well, much better than she got along with her own mother, with whom she had always had a contentious relationship, beginning when my mother was a very little girl and my grandmother was trying to feed her cereal, but she wouldn't open her mouth. After repeated attempts, my grandmother gave up and dumped the whole bowl over my mom's head. My mom laughed as she told me that and other, similar stories. Tossing her head back, she said, "It's because we're all Tauruses."

Indeed, my mom had a temper and could fly off the handle pretty quickly, but it was never unbearable, and she was pretty much the center of my universe, and in turn I was her quick-learning, quick-thinking protégé, especially as I got more into work. I was six going on seven when my curly red pigtails and slightly buck teeth began to charm one director after another, even if I had to lie (which I did, if it meant I got the job; I was often rewarded for my deceptions). Along with the lessons I'd learned from my mom and my own instincts, I was downright lethal at an audition.

I racked up a ridiculous number of commercials—Crest, Clorox, Butterball turkey, McDonald's, and many others. I continued to say whatever I thought would play well at the audition to the casting agents, and I never thought twice about it.

It was always the same group of girls at the auditions, there with their moms, who would do little corkscrew curls on their daughters as they waited. My mom picked me up from school and took me to auditions no matter what condition I was in that day. If I had food on my face or dirt under my horribly bitten nails, that's what the director and casting agent saw. I did have my interview outfit, though—a pair of overalls, a plaid shirt, and Keds. My hair was always in pigtails, too.

Dozens of girls would come in for each audition, and the group would be cut down to the same handful of girls. Typically that small group included Jodie Foster, Kristy McNichol, Dawn Lyn, and me, and one of us always got the job. It reached a point where I would walk into an audition and see the other girls and their moms turn to one another and groan, "Oh, she's here."

My mother was an unusual stage mom. She didn't help me read lines, make me change my clothes, or tell me to clean up. In the early 1970s, the country was rife with change and upheaval, and she understood how it was playing out in the world of commercials and TV. Casting agents, directors, and their clients wanted a new kind of American family, one more realistic than the perfectly coiffed people of the fifties and early sixties, and my mom realized that with my buck teeth, freckles, and one ear that stuck out farther than the other, in other words my imperfections—as well as my bitten fingernails and dirty knees—I fit the bill perfectly.

We were also a showbiz family. Between my mother, father, and grandfather, everyone in Hollywood seemed to be a friend, pseudo-relative, or acquaintance. Not much happened in town that didn't get discussed and analyzed as if it affected us personally, or as if we were part of it, too, which I suppose we were.

Even before I was old enough to understand who was who and what was what, I was absorbing information. I felt like a normal kid, but all around me, it was always showtime. The switch was flipped, the lights came on, and people did their thing. I was encouraged to show off whatever talent I had. My parents' friends provided the best entertainment right in our living room, and I squealed with laughter when my grandfather showed me off to my "Uncle Danny" (Danny Thomas), and when I entered my teens, my "Uncle Miltie" (Milton Berle) dubbed me "baby Ann-Margret."

In the late sixties and early seventies, my grandfather was the head writer for the *Dean Martin Show*, and I used to visit him on the set. I didn't know that my "Uncle Dean" was a superstar until many years later. To me, Uncle Dean was the slow-talking, very handsome man who had a great big tray of candy in his dressing room, which I loved since we didn't have candy in our house. I knew as long as I sat on Uncle Dean's lap and didn't get too close to my mom, whose hands were like Venus flytraps, I could eat as much candy as I wanted.

My first television show was a Dean Martin Christmas special. My grandfather put me in a number with a group of kids whose parents were in the cast and crew, and we sang a song with Dennis Weaver. It was preceded by a bit in which Dennis explained how the song was supposed to go. He listed how we would all play the instruments we had, and I realized he had made a mistake. Without hesitation I corrected him loudly, declaring, "No! The whistle first!"

The audience and Dennis laughed and I was hooked. Funny followed my grandfather wherever he went, as if his sense of humor was an extra appendage, and quite often he was around others equally funny, and I was lucky enough to frequently be along for the ride. Like the time when I was a little older and already on *Little House* and he took me to an NBC affiliates function, where, at one point, he pulled me away from the action and said, "Listen, I want to introduce you to someone."

The intonation of his voice when he said the word "someone" led me to believe this was someone special, but I couldn't imagine who could be more special than the man I'd only just met, Chuck Barris. So I was kind of grumpy as my grandfather escorted me into a back room and shut the door, closing us off from the din from the larger gathering. Across from us was a little old man in a beret with his back to us. My grandfather said, "Groucho," and the man turned around. I was stunned. It was Groucho Marx.

It was like encountering Abraham Lincoln, or Batman (hey, I was a sucker for Batman; still am, though I prefer my Batman in the form of Christian Bale these days), someone so legendary he couldn't possibly be real, except he was—and he was only a few feet away from me. He stood about five feet four inches tall, wore a gray suit with a turtleneck, and held a cigar. It was like seeing Leonard Bernstein with his baton or Claude Monet with his brush. Having grown up watching Marx Brothers movies, I recognized Groucho immediately, and I asked God to please not let me turn into a blithering idiot. I saw Groucho's face brighten when he saw my grandfather.

"Hey, Hesch!" he said.

Hesch. Only my grandfather's most intimate friends called him Hesch. I had no idea they were close. They hugged and then my grandfather said, "Groucho, I'd like you to meet my granddaughter, Melissa."

Groucho stuck out his hand and said, "It's nice to meet you. My daughter's name is Melinda."

"No, no, no," I said. "My name is Melissa."

He feigned bewilderment at my response.

"Well, what do you want me to do?" he said. "Change my daughter's name?"

His lightning-fast quip took me aback momentarily. I thought I'd said something that caused him to snap at me. Then I realized it was a joke and I relaxed. Later, in fact, we went back into the party and I danced with him for a little while.

That was the first time I understood my grandpa was kind of a big deal. Everyone knew him—well, everyone of a certain generation. And the power of this fact remained undiminished for decades. Many years later, I would go with my friend Katie Wagner to see Frank Sinatra perform in New York. Afterward, Katie took me backstage. She knew the great singer through her father, Robert Wagner, and she wanted to say hello. Normally I'm shy about introducing myself to people, but he went around the room saying hi and shaking hands, and when my turn came, I said, "It's nice to meet you. I think you know my grandfather."

Given all that statement conveyed, he sort of rolled his eyes and dutifully asked, "Who's your grandfather?"

"Harry Crane," I said.

He paused.

"Hesch? You're Hesch's grandkid?" He turned to some of his cronies. "Hey, everyone, this is Hesch's . . ."

Being Hesch's granddaughter provided entrée to Hollywood royalty, but my most special memories are from when I was younger and had Papa Harry all to myself. Like on Sundays when we went to Du-par's coffee shop, where I always ordered pancakes and afterward we made up our own games, using whatever was on the table as playing pieces, shouting moves, arguing strategy, and drawing crowds of onlookers who tried to figure out the rules. It was just as fun when we stayed home and I fixed him lunch. I remember one time asking if he wanted some fruit for dessert, and I rattled off the choices.

"I'll just take an orange," he said.

"Do you want me to peel it?" I asked.

"No thanks," he said, "I'll just step on it."

Laughter gives a household great resiliency, and I needed every ounce as I grew up. At eight, I made my first foray into prime-time TV, landing a part on the long-running CBS classic *Gunsmoke* as the child of dirt-poor farmers whose lives are made even worse when Marshal Dillon shows up at the house and arrests my father. It was an intensely emotional scene made memorable by the way my on-screen mother, Katherine Helmond, worked herself into a tearful state and then kept herself in the moment in between takes.

I've never forgotten how she put herself into a corner and squatted down in her big prairie skirt, with her elbows on her knees and head in her hands, closing herself off from the chatter and joking that went on as setups were changed. I watched her, trying to figure out what she was doing. Then, when we returned to work, she was back in the scene, tears streaming out of her eyes. I got it—and now I do something similar if I have a difficult scene. I go into "the Dungeon," my private vault of difficult memories and emotions.

My next job was playing the daughter of a heart attack victim on *Emergency,* NBC's popular hour-long drama about a team of paramedics. I was thrilled. I was a fan of the show (it was a toss-up between that and *S.W.A.T.* as my favorites), and I had huge crushes on both of the stars, Kevin Tighe and Randy Mantooth. In my scene, I ran after the guys as they carried my daddy out on a gurney and wailed, "Daddy! Daddy! Bring my daddy back!" As I reached out for him, Kevin caught me in his arms and I cried into his shoulder.

I thought I was incredibly good, and my mother raved about my brilliance and depth of emotion. I remember the whole family talking about my work as if I were an eight-year-old Colleen Dewhurst, and to be sure, it was a seminal moment that boosted my confidence and let me truly envision myself as an actor, not just a child getting work on TV.

I've gone back and watched that show, excited to see this moment that had proved to everyone around me that I was ready to join the pantheon of great child actors, like my idols Shirley Temple and Margaret O'Brien. My *God!* It was just awful. All whiny child actor horseshit. I was terrible. Seriously, rent it sometime. What dreck!

Then came a lull in the action when I did a few commercials but no episodic work. In hindsight, the dry spell may have been due to the whiny crap that I was dishing out. My mother was fine with that; she preferred commercials or the occasional guest spot because I didn't have to miss more than a day or two of school. I attended a good private school in Sherman Oaks and wore a uniform every day. I was expected to bring home good grades and was reminded that after-school dance lessons were a privilege.

Despite being a disciplinarian, my mom pulled out all the stops for holidays. On Easter, we hunted for eggs and paraded in our bonnets. Even though we were Jewish, friends and family came over every year to help us decorate our Christmas tree, and then on Christmas Day my mother hosted a gigantic dinner, complete with presents and singing amid the piles of endless food.

My mother was equally exuberant when it came to planning my birthday parties. She arranged pony rides, clowns, and performers. One year there was a revival of the movie *Gone with the Wind*, and she let me take all of my friends to the theater so I could see it on the big screen, which was amazing. My other favorite movies were *The Sound of Music, Mary Poppins, Cinderella,* and any film with Shirley Temple or Dracula.

My taste in TV ranged from kids shows like *Wonderama, Zoom,* and *The Electric Company* to *The Ed Sullivan Show* and *The Muppet Show.* I also liked *The Brady Bunch, The Partridge Family, Batman, I*

Love Lucy, and *Marcus Welby, M.D.* What I'm trying to get at is for all the natural ham in me, there was no cheese. I wasn't one of those show kids who always needed to be in the spotlight. As Michael Landon would later tell people, I was unspoiled and real, more interested in catching bugs than acting.

My mom, still a young woman after splitting from my dad, maintained an active social life, and though I don't remember her dating, my recollection is that at some point when I was around nine years old she went on a cruise to Mexico (my dad stayed with my brother and me) and shortly thereafter she married Harold Abeles, a prominent attorney. They had a reception at the Beverly Hills Hotel. Harold's daughter, Patrice, the older of his two children, who was my brother's age, and I wore matching powder blue dresses and bows in our hair. Harold's children—he also had a son, Joey—lived with his ex-wife.

Per my mother, it was all very much a done deal and not discussed beyond the formal rollout—*This is Harold, who is very special to me. He's going to be your new stepfather and he's going to live with us.* No questions were invited, no complaints were entertained. As with my parents' split, my mother assured us life wouldn't be any different than before.

But it was.

My mother and I were almost joined at the hip. Suddenly Harold came between us and I felt lost and displaced. It was hard for me to accept anyone, especially another man coming in and taking my father's place, no matter how many times Harold tried to allay my fears. The fact was Harold moved in with us, into the house that belonged to me and my brother and my mommy and, most of all, my *daddy.* Not only that, he brought with him his two German shepherds, Lady and Hank.

The dogs alone were more family than I bargained for. On day two, Hank attacked my beagle, Saulie, my best pal, and brutally ripped him up. Though Saulie was rushed to the vet and sewn back together, he was never the same.

Then Harold indulged an interest in archery. He was one of those people who develop passions, buy all the accessories, then move on. So he bought a target that was attached to a large bale of hay and put it in the backyard. Once everything was set up, he never used it. Saulie ate some of the straw that was leaking from the target's canvas covering. It blocked his intestines, and he died.

I blamed my stepdad, but I wasn't able to articulate it, to scream or rant at him or at anyone else, nothing beyond the normal grieving I was permitted after losing my dog: cry, get over it, and move on. I wasn't able to use Saulie's accidental death as a key to unlocking the anger and sadness I felt over my parents' split and Harold's arrival. No, I was expected and in fact told to accept my new instant family. My mother made it clear that everyone had to get along, that was the way it was going to be. I could cry over Saulie for a little while, but that was it.

As such, the porcelain doll stuffed her emotions away, which she was adept at doing, and quickly pulled herself together. Life continued. Thinking back, I didn't even know I was upset. If I so much as frowned, my mother would ask what reason I had to be sad or upset. *Why? Tell me!* God bless her and her fairy dust. According to her, there was never a reason—look how lucky I was! Look at all I had and did! I bought into that program hook, line, and sinker.

Talk about showtime. Things might have been awful, but we acted like they were great. When we went to a fancy event, my brother, stepsister, and I wore matching outfits (Joey was too young to attend). All of us looked fantastic together. When we ran into people we knew, we told them that we were wonderful and things couldn't be better. Back at home, though, Harold fought with his ex. They had a messy divorce and warred constantly in front of their kids. Joey was too little to be impacted, but Patrice, poor Tricie, was a mess.

Not that I was much better. I sucked my thumb in private for way too many years and wet my bed well into my twelfth year, though no one wanted to acknowledge I might be a little old for that sort of thing, or talked about why I desperately tried to hold things inside me till I finally lost control. Nope, things were perfect.

In any case, I preferred my drama on-screen, and soon enough I set my sights on something special: a remake of the movie *Miracle on 34th Street*. My audition went well. It was a job I really wanted, really cared about, talked and dreamed about. One of my other childhood idols, Natalie Wood, had been in it and I so wanted that part. When I didn't get it I was crestfallen. I wanted to talk about it with my dad, so I headed to the garage where he built furniture. It was filled with tools, wood, and various projects he had going; sawdust carpeted the floor, and it had a sweet smell that to this day I still associate with him. This hobby taught me that even though entertaining was his passion, there was more to his life. It gave me an appreciation for simple things, those that left one with a great sense of accomplishment and satisfaction. Maybe even greater than any standing ovation.

I spilled my guts and quite a few tears as he listened while he worked. My father probably realized I was crying about more than losing a part—there was the upheaval at home following Harold's arrival and also the painful loss of Saulie—because after I finished, he looked up and said, "You know, Missy-do"—that was his nickname for me—"this only means something better is going to come along."

I was much, much older when I realized that that advice, or at least the way I remembered him saying it, reminded me of something I'd read about a Buddhist monk who explained that bad things happen in order to open the door for something good to happen. In other words, bad things were kind of like the reverse side of the karmic tapestry, one half of the yin and yang of fate—where there's good, there's also going to be bad; where there's a kiss, there's also going to be a tear. My dad, as a former acrobat, one whose circus-performer parents died in an accident, knew about conflicting forces and balance.

But I was too young to understand anything like that, so I shook my head in disagreement.

"How could something better come along?" I asked. "This is the best thing ever. It's my favorite movie ever. What could be better?"

He shrugged and kissed the top of my head.

"I don't know," he said. "But something better will come along. I promise."

four

SOMETHING BETTER

I was nine years old when I went on a cattle call for a new series NBC was getting set to produce based on the classic *Little House on the Prairie* books by Laura Ingalls Wilder. I'd read a couple of the books, which my mom had introduced me to years earlier because they'd been among her favorites when she was a girl. I was trying out for the role of Laura. I didn't know much more than that about the project.

My mom drove me to NBC, knowing more than I did about the series, particularly that with Michael Landon attached it was a project the network was very much behind and thus an opportunity to be a part of something special.

I think my grandfather might've also gotten involved behind the scenes, calling executives he knew at the network and telling them to take extra good care of his grandkid. There were hundreds of girls waiting to be seen, and when my turn came I went into a room and read for the network's casting people. The casting director and I had a brief chat about nothing and then I was excused. But as I walked out the door, he had one more question.

"By the way," the casting director said, "how tall are you?"

I stopped, turned around, and looked at this person like he was crazy for having to ask such a silly question.

"I'm this tall," I said, wondering why he couldn't see something that obvious for himself.

I don't know whether it was rude or spunky. But it made a strong impression on the producers. They brought me back, along with a smaller group of girls, to read for Michael. I had no idea who he was, his level of stardom, or his clout with the network, but my entire family was beyond excited that I was going to be auditioning for Michael Landon.

I read for him in a room at Paramount Studios. I remember thinking, *Oh gosh, he's really handsome.* He gave off a different kind of energy than ordinary people. It was a higher wattage. I'd been around stars and thought nothing of it, but Michael was different, and that difference was tangible without him having to say or do anything. It was a power, a mix of charisma and confidence that affected other people.

In the hands of an actor, it was a powerful tool. It filled the room. Michael did more than that, though. He raised the temperature. And he wasn't just planning to star in the show. He was also the executive producer, writer, director, producer, cheerleader, boss, coach, and surrogate dad.

You're either intimidated by the kind of person who has that mojo or you're comfortable with it, and I was totally at ease as we chatted and he listened to me read. Midway through the reading, he poked his head out the door and gave the okay sign to my mother and grandmother, who were waiting anxiously for me to come out. Apparently my grandfather had also gotten word to him that I was Hesch's grandkid.

A week later I went back for a screen test. A couple other girls had also been called back. Each of us filmed a scene with Michael and another one with Melissa Sue Anderson, who had already been cast as older sister Mary Ingalls. We worked on a soundstage, which was always exciting. But the day ended and then I kind of forgot about it as I returned to my normal daily routine.

A couple weeks later I was at school when a girl came up to me at lunch and asked if my name was Melissa. I said yeah, and she introduced herself as Leslie Landon, Michael's daughter. I brightened as I remembered how much I'd liked him.

"Oh, hi," I said.

She smiled as if she knew a secret, which she did.

"My dad said you're going to be Half Pint," she said.

I didn't believe it.

"What?" I asked.

"My dad said you're going to be Half Pint."

I screamed and ran to the office where there was a phone available for students to use in an emergency. I called home and told my mom what had happened. She let out an excited shriek and made me repeat the story. As I did, I felt like booster rockets had ignited under me and I was about to blast off into some exciting, new, uncharted world. Meanwhile, as I finished the school day, my mom did some fact-checking and found out it was true, I'd gotten the role of Half Pint. Leslie had told me even before my agents knew—and boy, did she get grounded for that one.

Shortly before Michael died, I saw him at Leslie's wedding and he told me when it came time to show all the screen tests to the network executives, he only showed them mine. I looked at him, then said, "Really? You did?" He nodded.

"Oh yeah. I knew. I knew immediately that you were her and I didn't even want them to think about anybody else."

From there, we began the steps leading up to the pilot, starting with wardrobe fittings. That original fitting was the first time I grasped the importance of costume in creating a character. I was a little *pisher* and didn't have a formal process. Once I slipped on the dress, though, I felt different, transformed into someone else, as well as transported backward in time.

When I finally received the script, I went over my lines with my mother. I underlined them with a crayon. I memorized dialogue easily; I had a good memory, maybe a photographic memory. It came in handy, and I was prepared when the time came to shoot the pilot.

The story was straight out of the classic series of books, narrated and seen through the eyes of nine-year-old Laura. The Ingalls family—Charles, Caroline, and their three daughters—moves from their little house in the Wisconsin woods to a new home on the prairie about fifty miles west of Independence, Kansas. Leaving their family behind is hard, but the family's resilient spirit, as led by Charles's instant affection for the new land, despite its dangers, mirrored that of the rest of the country.

This slice of Americana, replete with chest-tightening dangers and a Christmas celebration guaranteed to open the tear ducts, was actually a two-hour movie, and if the network liked it, they would pick it up as a series, an arrangement known as a back-door pilot. Starting the second week of January 1974, we shot some scenes in L.A. and then went on location near the Sierras in Northern California. My mother and I treated it like a big adventure, which it was. We were far from home. It was cold. And there were numerous people to meet and get acquainted with, starting with Michael, who was quite clearly in charge and the center of the *Little House* universe.

Indeed, Michael pushed up his sleeves and rewrote the script on the fly after a surprise snowstorm before the first day of shooting. When one of the other executive producers wanted us kids to play the opening scenes without shoes, Michael lit into him with both a bark and a bite that made me pause and say to myself, *Whoa, I pray to God I'm never on the receiving end of that temper.*

But he couldn't have been warmer or more nurturing to me, and I could hardly take my eyes off him. I'd never seen a man in person who was built like him. He was an upside-down triangle, thick and muscular, and tough beyond my imagination. He chain-smoked cigarettes. On our first day of shooting, we were out in the snow and he was giving us direction when he took his cigarette and stubbed it out in the palm of his glove. I wanted to run over to my mom and say, "Did you see that?" He did that all the time. Then he took out the tobacco, sprinkled it on the ground, and put the filter in his jacket pocket, where over the course of the day he'd build up a fair collection, which he threw out later. I'd never seen such a macho man. He was like James Bond—or Batman.

His wife, Lynn, was one of the most glamorous women I'd ever seen. On location, she wore fur coats and wonderful boots. My mother was right next to her, dressed to the nines herself, in stunning, fashion-forward outfits that would've turned heads on Fifth Avenue. The two of them looked like movie stars. The thing was, though, we were in the middle of nowhere, knee-deep in mud and horse crap. Both ended up borrowing rubber boots from wardrobe. From the knees up, they were Hollywood glamour. From the knees down, they were all prairie.

My mom matched Lynn in the glamour department, but Lynn had a collection of jewelry that was unlike anything my little girl's eyes had seen. At some point each day I would stare at Auntie Lynn's fingers, wrists, and ears, hoping to see some new and remarkable piece, and usually I did. Michael showered her with every gemstone imaginable. It wasn't long before one of my favorite things to do when I visited New York City was to walk down Fifth Avenue and gape at the pieces in the windows of Tiffany, Van Cleef & Arpels, and every other major jewelry store there.

For different reasons, Karen Grassle, who played Michael's wife and my mother, Caroline Ingalls, also made a strong impression on me. Extremely beautiful, she was very different from the women in my life, especially my mother, who was dark and exotic, a gorgeous gypsy out of Beverly Hills via Brooklyn. Karen was blond and blue-eyed, cut from the Grace Kelly mold. She'd trained at the Royal Academy of Dramatic Art, one of the oldest acting schools in England and among the world's finest.

Karen did the same sort of actor exercises as Katherine Helmond, which had mesmerized me, except Karen went even further. For instance, she made strange sounds as she did her vocal warmups. At first, I giggled and had to hide my imprudence by turning away or making an excuse to leave the room momentarily. But over time my amusement turned into curiosity, and I watched her closely, the way she used her hands and the way she breathed. I watched her a lot, in fact, and I like to think there's some of her in me as an actor.

I'd met Melissa Sue Anderson at my screen test, but we got to know each other much better while on location. We played sisters and were only a couple years apart in age, but from the start, for whatever reason, we never had a real sisterly kinship. She was a strikingly pretty girl, and I wasn't, at least I didn't think so. As we got older, she was the girl everyone wanted to marry, and I was the plucky one they wanted to go fishing with.

There was a distance to her, a coldness, though sometimes I wonder if it was just that I never knew how to get her to let me in. She wasn't easy to get along with. I think her reserve came across on-screen and was certainly apparent offscreen, whereas I wore my emotions as if they were a neon green T-shirt that glowed in the dark.

My mother was the same way. Good or bad, our relationship was on full display whether we were behind the closed door of my dressing room or in front of the entire crew. Everyone experienced our affection and our arguments. Melissa and her mother were more contained, more controlled, more private, more connected. She was her mother's universe. The license plate on her mom's car was 3MISSY—it was her third car since Missy was born.

Right away we faced the dilemma of having two Melissas on the same set. Her nickname was Missy, and though my dad called me Missy-do or Wissy-do, almost no one else ever did because I made it clear I thought it was the stupidest nickname ever invented. Michael was the one who confronted the two-Melissas issue. He said, "Why don't we solve this problem before it even starts."

"Okay," I said, as others around the two of us nodded in agreement. None of us would've dared disagree with Michael.

"She's going to be Missy," he said, looking at Melissa Sue Anderson. And then turning to me, he said, "And we'll just call you Half Pint."

It worked for me. Half Pint was also my character's nickname, so it seemed like an obvious choice. Though at one point a short time later I walked up to Michael and said, "Or you can call me Moisha." He looked down at me with a scrunched-up face.

"What?"

"I don't know," I said, backpedaling slightly. "I said you could also call me Moisha if you wanted."

"Moisha?" he said.

"I heard it somewhere," I said. "It seemed cool."

Michael hadn't moved a muscle. He stared at me as if I was nuts. Finally, he shook his head and laughed.

"I think we'll stick with Half Pint."

Twins Lindsay and Sidney Greenbush played the Ingalls' youngest girl, Carrie. The girls were poised, pint-size showbiz veterans and impossibly adorable, with gorgeous, saucer-size blue eyes. I thought of them as toys, tiny living dolls that were there as much for my amusement between scenes as to actually work in front of the camera. I also gravitated toward Victor French, who played Isaiah Edwards, the kindhearted neighbor and Laura's special friend. He was hilarious and great with us kids.

Of course, Michael set the tone with all of the junior actors. There was a lot of tactile affection, hugging, embracing, and snuggling that made people feel good, close, and loved. I'd never been tossed into the air so much. It was all part of the bonding that took place as we became a family.

This coming together of various people was similar to what I'd been through when Harold and his family came into my life, only on a larger scale. There were people I liked very much, some I didn't, and a few I didn't connect with at all. For Michael, it was about creating a family. Many on the crew had worked with him on *Bonanza*, and some had even been with him before that on other shows. He inspired loyalty and expected it in return. You couldn't get a position on one of his crews unless your father was on the crew and left the job to you when he died. He treated his crews the same way he treated his friends and family: there was no special favoritism, no caste system. The only two people I remember getting their own trailer were Mariette Hartley and Patricia Neal. Mariette was breast-feeding a newborn, and Patricia was recovering from a stroke. Everyone else had the same kind of room on a honey wagon, including Michael.

Actually, he was always Mike. I was quickly corrected after the first time I called him Mr. Landon. "It's Mike," he said. Even though I'd never referred to an adult by his first name, it was Mike from then on. Everyone referred to him as Mike, never Mr. or sir or Michael. Just Mike. And Karen was Karen. Victor was Victor. Melissa Sue was Missy. And I was Half Pint.

Some of Mike's kids visited the set as we shot the pilot, including his daughter Cheryl, who was grown up (she was seventeen, but that was grown up to me) and beautiful, and Leslie and Michael Jr., all of whom added to the fun and sense of family. At night, the adults went out to dinner in various groups, leaving the kids at the motel to do our homework and study our lines. We were too young and well behaved to get into trouble.

The people who owned the small motel where we stayed had a puppy, a fluffy black poodle, which I played with every day after work. I ate breakfast and dinner at the diner there. It was such a different lifestyle than at home, and I was happy exploring this newfound freedom. I enjoyed the familiarity of seeing people I knew almost every place I went, whether roaming around the motel or sitting at the counter in the diner.

I still dream about that motel. I got to go down to the diner in the morning by myself, greeting the waitresses and manager through my sleep-filled eyes, carrying my mom's thermoses, which I filled with fresh, hot, black coffee (I can still remember the strong aroma) and left outside her door. Then I went back for my breakfast. People from the crew wandering in would say good morning and ask how I slept or if I felt good about the day ahead.

I sat at the counter, staring at the big machine from which the waitresses got hot cocoa. There was a sign on it that said "hot whipped cocoa supreme," and I spent most of every morning trying to figure out what the hell was so supreme about their hot cocoa.

It's funny to think about how much time I spent as a kid trying to figure things out.

Everyone grew close quickly, which was a new experience for me, and it explains why I became upset after shooting Victor French's last scene and saying good-bye to him before he returned to L.A. After developing family-like relationships, I didn't want to say good-bye to Victor or anyone else. I thought we were making a movie. I wasn't aware of the possibility that it might be turned into a series. My expectations were carefully managed.

I also had a real affinity for Victor's double, Jack Lilly. I liked everyone, really—they were all nice. Who wouldn't like being around people who showered you with affection and always had a kind word, a joke, or a funny face? Compared to the real world, it was like make-believe. A lot of the crew had their families with them, including their kids, which made it fun for me; it was also one of the reasons people wanted to work on Mike's shows. If you went on location, you got to bring your family.

Mike worked everyone hard. He was a perfectionist. But he did things first-class. We traveled by private jet, on big planes, and everyone piled in together. I can remember getting on board and hearing Mike playfully barking at makeup artist Whitey Snider to sit next to him because "if the plane goes down, I want to look good."

I was impressed when I was told Whitey had been Marilyn Monroe's personal makeup artist. That seemed incredible to me, to be that close to someone who had been that close to a legend, who'd touched her face and also touched mine. He carried a money clip she'd given him. The engraving said, "To Whitey, while I'm still warm. Love, Marilyn."

Sometimes he let me hold the clip. I'd clasp the metal in my hands and think, *God, she picked this out and had it engraved.* A few years later, when I was a teenager, Whitey told me that he did Marilyn's makeup after her autopsy, before she was placed in her casket.

I also counted hairstylist Larry Germaine as one of my instant pals. Considered among Hollywood's legendary hairstylists, he did my hair every day, and I treasured the time I spent with him. From the moment you sat in his chair, he transported you from reality into a private conversation that seemed more interesting than anything else going on around you. I was so pleased he seemed to want to talk to me; later, when I was older, he told me how he got his start in the business. He'd been an undertaker until one day they brought in a kid who'd been hit by a train and the parents wanted an open casket. He had to put that kid back together, doing the hair and makeup, everything, like a jigsaw puzzle, and it was too emotional for him. He quit and got into show business, where they faked the crashes and everyone looked pretty when they died.

The only trauma on the *Little House* set came at the end of January, almost four weeks after we began shooting, when it was time to pack up and say good-bye. I had a hard time returning home, but I soon fell easily into the same old routines. I went back to school and had sleepovers with my best friend, Tracy Nelson. Home life was the same as usual: cuddling with my mom and reading, torturing and being tortured by my nasty little brother. Still, I missed the work and the affirmation that came from it. I especially missed the attachments I'd made to people.

I was down in the dumps whenever I imagined not seeing them again, but my mood did a one-eighty at the end of February when Mike gathered everyone in a theater on the Paramount lot to watch the film on a large movie screen. My heart warmed upon hearing him call me Half Pint again. I cried and laughed through the movie, as did my family, who filled the seats on both sides of me. I was surprised by the music. I was even more surprised by my performance. Was that really me?

I can recall feeling calm as I sat in the theater. I wasn't nervous at all about what my family and others would think. All the self-doubt and pressure came years later. Back then, on that night, I was simply dazed and dazzled.

NBC aired the movie in March and it did extremely well. By then, we'd received word the network wanted to move ahead with a series. My mother was beside herself. I got a congratulatory call from Mike. My grandparents, on separate occasions, of course, since they couldn't be in the same room together, smothered me with kisses. Papa Harry gave me his own compliment, saved for truly special occasions. "What a girl this is!" My dad's reaction was the best. He gave me a hug, then stepped back and took in all forty-eight inches of me with a proud, satisfied grin.

"See, Missy-do," he said. "I told you something better would come along."

five

LITTLE HOUSE

In the late eighties, a friend of mine, Dean Cameron, was shooting a movie called *Summer School* on the Paramount lot. They were shooting a classroom scene, and between takes, he rummaged through the papers the prop guys had stuffed into the school desks and pulled out a paper that now hangs framed in my study. It was the call sheet for my original *Little House* screen test.

I don't recall the first day we began shooting the series or anyone talking to me about the impact doing a series would have on my life, especially if the ratings equaled or bested the TV movie, which would mean being on a hit series, which is an altogether different experience than just being on TV. At this stage of my life, *Little House on the Prairie* is simply part of my cellular makeup.

I remember life before getting the movie, and then the next thing I knew I was traipsing into Alison Arngrim's trailer to give her the lowdown on the cast and crew. Alison joined us on the second episode, which was titled "Country Girls." She played nasty Nellie Oleson and began referring to Laura and Mary as "country girls" almost as soon as we met her in school. My brother, Jonathan, played her younger brother, Willie.

Though she was my great rival on the show, Alison and I became instant friends from the moment I confided, "There's only one mean person on the show. Everyone else is great." At lunch, we constantly tried to gross each other out by mixing together the most disgusting combinations of food—and eating them! One of my more memorable creations was butterscotch pudding and radishes. It wasn't half bad.

It was great to have a friend on the set. We celebrated birthdays together, had sleepovers, and got into adventures on the lot.

I can't imagine any better playground for a kid than Paramount Studios' sprawl of soundstages, streets, and stars. We worked on stages 31 and 32, which were located at the back of the lot. Behind us, there was a cemetery on the other side of a large wall. Not any old cemetery, it was the final resting spot for Rudolph Valentino, Jayne Mansfield, Cecil B. DeMille, and other Hollywood luminaries. I thought being close to their and so many other grave sites was neat, in a creepy way, and I tried umpteen times to get a peek by climbing up the fence. I never made it, and I wouldn't have even if I could've pulled myself up. Coiled barbed wire was strung along the top of the fence, preventing any break-ins or breakouts.

I would arrive at work early in the morning, as the sun was starting its slow climb, and it would be dark on the soundstages—one held the interior and exterior of the little house and the inside and outside of the barn. The other held the interior of Oleson's Mercantile, the church/school, and Doc Baker's office—and it would be dark on the stage except for wherever we were shooting first. A white light bathed that corner of the *Little House* world and made it appear as if touched by a divine power.

Our dressing rooms were small mobile homes parked in an alley in back of the stages. I went to school in a little dressing room that looked like a house on wheels, which was located outside the soundstages. My teacher on the set was Mrs. Helen Minniear. She would instruct me in all subjects from fourth grade through my last year of high school.

At some point I would find my call sheet and look for my name, which was always third down from the top, following Mike and

Karen. It was a small affirmation that I was really there, really a part of this dreamlike experience that felt like the greatest game of dress-up ever.

Whenever possible I liked to wander into the writers' offices and try to get the scoop on what they were planning for future scripts and who was coming on the show next. I wanted to know everything ahead of time; they called me precocious, but I could just as easily have been called nosy or annoying.

I explored the lot whenever I was able to get away, which wasn't often; I was unable to resist the lure of checking out the places where scenery was stored, the other soundstages, and the commissary, which was a hub of activity and star-gazing. Everybody on the lot working on TV shows or movies broke for lunch at approximately the same time and headed for the commissary, where my eyes darted across the large dining room. Oblivious to my own profile as one of the stars on a hit show, I was always looking around. I got excited whenever I saw someone famous, like *Mork & Mindy* stars Robin Williams and Pam Dawber or the guys from *Happy Days*.

I used to meet up in line with Henry Winkler, one of the loveliest people in the business. As they'd say in *Prairie* speak, he and I took a shine to each other. We'd act out what we were having for lunch.

"What are you having today?" he asked.

"I'm having a hamburger," I said.

"Then I want to see you act a hamburger," he said with a note of challenge in his voice.

So I acted like a hamburger. I have to say, the first time he suggested that game I thought he was nuts. But lunch with the Fonz got to be something I looked forward to. It wasn't just a meal; it was a performance. He made me think as I ordered. How would I act a salad? What would I do to portray a grilled cheese? One day he cut in line behind me as I was taking my food.

"How are the French fries?" he asked.

I turned toward him.

"Zee fries, zey are v'reee French today," I said in a thick accent.

•　•　•

The frown I wore while making the fourth episode was extremely unusual, but easily understood: I was unhappy I wasn't in more of the episode. I was already starting to like work more than home. A week later, my smile was back and as bright as my mood. We were shooting the episode "Mr. Edwards's Homecoming." I had a scene at the end in which Dr. Baker softened the news I had to have my tonsils out by giving me a gigantic gumdrop. Since I wasn't allowed any sugar at home, getting a piece of candy was like being handed an Oscar, and I savored every bite of that magnificent candy.

We did five or six takes and I got a new gumdrop each time. Those were momentous occasions for me. I felt naughty as my mother watched disapprovingly. But what could she say? Eating the candy was part of my job.

Even sweeter, Victor French returned to the series in that episode. It hadn't been that long since I bid him a tearful good-bye both on and off camera during the pilot, but at the time I didn't think I'd ever see him again, so I was beyond excited to have him back. I didn't have to act in the scene when we were brought together again. I was genuinely happy.

I had no idea what I was doing in the episode called "The Love of Johnny Johnson," which had Laura falling for a boy who liked Mary. Till that time, I'd never expressed such feelings for a boy, but I'd seen the girls on *The Partridge Family* and *The Brady Bunch* get their first crushes, so I mimicked them. But not all the acting was pretend. The on-screen rivalry between Mary and Laura in that episode played off of the competitiveness that existed off camera between Melissa Sue Anderson and me. When we snapped at each other, it was fairly real.

The lines also blurred between Mike and me. Our special bond began on the pilot when we repeated the scene that I'd read in my audition, the one after we've lost the dog while crossing the river and Laura apologizes to him for thinking he didn't care about Jack being lost. It was a sweet father-daughter moment, one that was very real to me. It wasn't a stretch at all to think of Mike as my dad. I could easily imagine having such a conversation with him.

At the end of "The Love of Johnny Johnson," Laura cried about her broken heart to her father, one of those scenes that dealt perfectly with the necessary, cleansing pain of growing up. It was just one of the many times I would cry on that show. (I think I cried for some reason in every episode!) Sometimes it was hard for me to get to those emotions, and this episode was one of those times. Putting myself in Laura's shoes didn't work. Nor did dragging up some kind of horrible memory from the Dungeon. So Mike helped me.

He put his arm around me and walked us away from the set, off to the side where we could be alone. And in the time it took to walk fifteen to twenty feet, he got himself crying. Then he turned to me and with tears rolling down his face, he said, "Do you have any idea how much I love you?"

That did it. My heart swelled with similar feelings and a moment later tears poured from my eyes. Mike let me cry for a few seconds and then he said, "Are you ready?" I nodded and we shot our scene.

Mike employed that technique for many of the lovely father-daughter scenes that followed. Looking back, yes, it was a bizarre manipulation, a kind of twisted way to get a kid to perform. On the other hand, it worked. And I have no doubt that it was therapeutic; by crying, I was able to release some of my own emotions I kept bottled up.

A few weeks after "The Love of Johnny Johnson," we shot "Town Party, Country Party," an episode memorable for the friendship I struck up with Kim Richards, who played Olga, the little girl Laura befriends after hurting her ankle. Kim was a well-known child actor who'd been on *Nanny and the Professor*, and while I hit it off with her, I also enjoyed her older sister, Kathy, who served as her on-set guardian and was young and fun. Just eighteen when she was hanging around our set, Kathy later moved to New York and married Rick Hilton. We stayed in touch, and my mom and I were the first people to find out she was pregnant with her first child, Paris Hilton.

I was sure "The Raccoon" would be my favorite episode of the first season, since I was able to play with a real live baby raccoon between takes. That was pretty cool. The little critter played the role of the bad guy. In the story, Laura battled for her life after getting bit by a raccoon feared to be rabid. I played that part to the hilt, reveling in the attention I received from playing Laura sick in bed.

As it turned out, "The Lord Is My Shepherd," a two-parter we shot a few weeks later, became my favorite of that first year and still stands out as my favorite among the more than two hundred episodes we made over nearly ten full seasons. On-screen, this ultimate tearjerker was all about Laura's relationship with her father, but the lines we said about love and devotion applied off camera, too. After that episode, there was no question about the special bond between Mike and me. And now, more than ever, I cherish the opportunity he gave me to say such things to him.

Plus, we had a real newborn baby on that show. I played with it between takes. That was even better than playing with a baby raccoon.

Baby news wasn't confined to the show. Early in 1974, while *Little House* was in the midst of production, my mother announced she was pregnant. Our house filled with excitement, and I was the head cheerleader. No one could've been more thrilled. I was big into baby dolls and carried at least one from my plastic-headed brood around at all times, as well as diapers, bottles, a change of outfits, and sometimes even a stroller. I was beyond happy at the prospect of a real baby in the house.

Almost simultaneously Auntie Lynn revealed she also had a little bun in the oven. I remember it as a good, exciting time, though not everyone shared such enthusiasm. One night Harold's kids were over for dinner and we sat around the dining room table talking about the baby. One by one, we tossed out prospective names. From our various suggestions, it was apparent I was overjoyed about the forthcoming addition to our family and my brother, Jonathan, not so much; Joey was too young to care; finally, we turned to Patrice and asked what she thought. She scrunched up her face and said, "I think we should just call it Garbage." *Wow!* Even more amazing than Tricie's comment was the rest of the family's reaction to it. My mom and Harold sort of laughed it off and then we all just continued having dinner like nothing had happened.

The next few months were extremely busy. They included the end of the first season and the dreaded good-byes to everyone on the crew, a return to regular classes at school, and, in preparation for the baby, a move to a roomier home in Encino. Previously owned by actor Victor McLaglen, our new house had five bedrooms, a guesthouse, and a pool. My mother redecorated beautifully.

The move inadvertently uncovered one of my biggest secrets. My mother didn't permit candy, cookies, or anything else with sugar in the house. No Twinkies, none of the good stuff I found in my friend Collette's house. She lived up the street, and I'd go up to her house, grab a handful of candy, and sneak it back home and into my room. I'd eat the candy and then toss the wrappers on top of my canopy bed—the only place I knew my mom wouldn't find them.

That is, until the movers disassembled my bed.

I came home from camp one day and my mother was waiting for me. Before she uttered a word, I noticed her clenched jaw and fiery eyes, and I knew I was in trouble.

"I have something I want to talk to you about," she said.

I tried to think what I could've done to piss her off as she led me into my bedroom. Then I stopped in the doorway, aghast at what I saw in front of me. The movers had taken my bed apart. It was in pieces on the floor, including the gorgeous canopy. And on top of it were several years' worth of candy wrappers.

I took the Fifth when my mom asked for an explanation. What was there to say? My crime was evident. I'd eaten candy in violation of the household rules and lied about it. I was grounded.

But that was soon rendered insignificant by a more serious and dire turn of events involving my father. One day, after the move, my mom sat Jonathan and me down and in a shaky voice said, "Daddy is sick." It turned out my father had been on a cruise ship where he was doing his stand-up act and suffered a stroke. She said he'd been airlifted from the ship to a hospital, where he was recuperating.

"He's dying to talk to you," she said.

Of course, I never heard her say the words "to talk to you." All I heard was "He's dying," and I immediately fell apart. My mom quickly put me on the phone with him, and hearing my dad assure me that he wasn't about to die was probably the only thing that could've pulled me from utter panic and hysteria.

Though my father spent most of his time on the road, I knew he was proud of my work on *Little House*—he told me all the time—and I saw even more of him after his stroke, frequently spending weekends at his house. Early on, he was partially paralyzed on one side, and he had one of those metal triangle things hanging over his bed that he could use to help pull himself up. A couple times I hooked my leg onto it and swung upside down. He thought it was funny. My dad's girlfriend, Natalie, was not amused when I showed her.

My father's leniency on those weekend sleepovers accounts for some of my fondest memories. As he got stronger, we stayed up late, really late, past ten o'clock at any rate, which was the middle of the night to me, and watched my favorite horror movies on *Creature Feature* and *Chiller Theatre*. During commercials, we'd pal into the kitchen and make ridiculously thick, hard Italian salami sandwiches laden with spicy mustard and carry them, along with a frosty root beer float, back into bed, where we finished watching the movies. To this day, one of my favorite things to do is watch a scary movie with my boys while we eat salami sandwiches.

He seemed to have made a full recovery by the end of the summer when I returned for the second season of *Little House*. The relief I felt from witnessing his rebirth as he went back on the road was matched by my nearly out-of-control anticipation as my mom's expectant tummy got bigger and she sat farther from the table. As naive as I was about the birds and the bees—at that point all my knowledge of where babies came from and how they were born was gleaned from "The Lord Is My Shepherd" episode—I still knew she was about to pop.

At the end of January and already well into *Little House*'s second season, she went into labor. I was on the set when it happened. Harold called the production office to let them know, but they kept the news from me since there was no telling how long labor would take and they wanted as much work out of me as possible. I'm still a little steamed about that.

Finally, later in the afternoon, someone came up to me and said, "Half Pint, there's a telephone call for you." I hurried to the phone on our stage. It was Harold. As soon as I heard his voice, I asked, "Is it here?"

"Yes," he said. "You have a baby sister."

"What's her name?"

"Sara Rebecca." (They went with my choice for a middle name!)

I leaped into the air and let out a scream. Everyone within earshot knew of my excitement. When I turned around, the cast and crew, all of whom already knew about the good news, were gathered behind me, standing in a semicircle, and they cheered wildly. A few days later, my mom brought Sara home from the hospital and I was beside myself. With Jonathan's arrival, I'd felt intruded upon. Sara was different. She was my baby doll.

Just over nine pounds at birth, she was the most perfect, most gorgeous chunk of baby imaginable. I could barely keep my hands off her. I just stared at her and kissed her and smelled her little neck. At my insistence, Sara's bedroom was next to mine. I played with her in the morning and made a beeline for her when I got home from work, and often I got up in the middle of the night to watch her breathe, and if she was too still I would poke her gently and make her stir. Not only was she my mother's miracle, as far as I was concerned, she was mine, too. She still is.

My mother encouraged me to believe that I was blessed in every way. She would tell me my life was enchanted. What with Sara, a wonderful family, a job I adored, and, as my mother reminded me when I asked about my own entrance into this world, the genetic gifts of my prima ballerina and Rhodes Scholar birth parents, it was impossible to argue. Indeed, my life was full of moments of genuine happiness, laughter, and joy. My mother's whimsy rubbed off.

But there were troubling currents beneath the surface, complex emotions I would wrestle with later. I didn't know any better, but why were difficulties and heartaches denied, glossed over, shoved aside, or covered up? And why was I so determined to prove to my mother that I was perfect? I made sure things were exactly as she wanted them, happy and sparkly. I would've been nuts or a spoiled brat to complain about anything in my life at that time, so I didn't complain.

With a growing awareness of my notoriety, I moved gradually into adolescence, taking baby steps and feeling uncertain whether the coming events, whatever they might be, would be good or bad. My mom didn't permit me to think in terms of gray areas, as much of life is. No, it was one extreme or the other, good or bad, and with my mom it was all good. Maybe I sensed otherwise, and maybe that's why when I close my eyes and picture myself back then, I see my nose pressed against the window, looking for the comfort and security I'd left in the old house.

LOVE, LOSS, AND LOVE

six

GROWING PAINS

I had to be forgiven when it came to Hollywood stars. Unless it was Batman, Chuck Barris, one of the Bradys, or David or Shaun Cassidy, I was oblivious to who was who. And that's why the name Patricia Neal didn't register with me when she graced the *Little House* set a third of the way through the second season.

Patricia guest-starred on the two-part episode "Remember Me," playing a widow with a terminal illness. I wasn't aware she had won a Best Actress Oscar for the 1963 movie *Hud*, received another nomination five years later, and appeared in such memorable films as *The Fountainhead, A Face in the Crowd,* and *Breakfast at Tiffany's.* If someone told me, and someone probably did, the information didn't stick.

However, I knew she was important because all the adults on the show were beside themselves that she was there and because she had her own Winnebago, which was unheard of on our show.

I found out Mike had arranged the Winnebago for Patricia because she'd suffered a stroke a few years earlier and needed a private, comfortable place to rest. The crew also set up a teleprompter on the set for her dialogue. Though she had recovered, I learned her stroke had been much worse than my father's. We kids were told not to distract her, to be respectful, and keep our distance. That just made tenacious me more intrigued.

Early on the first day Patricia was on set, she and I had a fun exchange and she took me under her wing. I was allowed to go in her Winnebago and spent a lot of time with her. She made me feel comfortable, and as we chatted, she opened the door for me to ask her anything. So, being kind of guileless, I asked her why she needed a teleprompter and how come she couldn't remember her lines.

She explained what had happened to her, and more specifically what had happened to her brain.

"It's difficult for me because I only recently learned to walk again," she said. "I still have to think right-left-right-left. And when my brain is busy thinking right-left-right, it forgets everything else."

She gave me a lovely doll as a wrap gift, but more than the doll she gave me information and stuff to think about. In fact, I remember being profoundly moved and almost a little confused by her openness. We didn't discuss anything that openly at my house. My father's stroke wasn't mentioned. It had been bad, but he'd recovered, and now that he was back on the road we didn't have to think about it.

Or we weren't supposed to. But I still worried and wondered, and those thoughts rattled around my head until I spoke to Patricia. She told me more about having a stroke than anyone else did, including my own father. She let me see it was possible to recover, which enabled me in a sense to exhale. I didn't have to be scared all the time about my daddy.

I still think about the way Patricia's honesty cast a light on life, ridding it of some of my deeper and darker fears. I loved her for it. I'm one of those people who believe everything, good and bad, happens for a reason. You're always in the right place at the right time doing the right thing. And so I believe that the universe sent Patricia into my life when I needed her.

I also needed braces for my legendary buck teeth. Michael Landon once said I could eat an apple through a picket fence, and he was being kind. I could literally bite down and with my teeth clenched, stick my thumb between my bottom and top teeth. My father insisted on paying for my orthodontics even though I earned a nice paycheck; I'm pretty sure it was because my daddy was a proud man, and there was no way he'd let me pay for anything, and because he was staunchly against our family falling into the traps child stardom (and the money that goes along with it) can bring. I never got the chance to ask him. He kept himself booked on those cruise ships and worked hard when he probably should've taken it easier.

I missed my dad. I know that no one knew how much I missed him. I wouldn't dare say it out loud, as it might've hurt Harold's feelings and upset my mom. But I wished every day and prayed every night that I could spend more time with him. I do see now how lucky I was to have a wonderful daddy substitute in Mike. Our relationship continued to grow even tighter, though there were still the inevitable growing pains. For instance, one day, as we shot an emotional scene for the episode titled "The Gift," I sensed his famous temper was about to blow.

It was my fault. I couldn't remember my lines.

There was nothing I feared more than disappointing him. From the moment he chose me for the role of Half Pint on *Little House*, I felt a connection to him that transcended our TV relationship and made me want to please him. Plus, his anger was terrifying, and having witnessed it, I never wanted to be on the receiving end. But I thought I might be about to experience it after he called cut for the third time and turned to me with a look that sent a shiver up my spine. He was able to take it down a notch before leaning close to me.

"Half Pint, do you not know your lines?" he asked in a measured voice. "Did you not study the scene?"

I lost it. Tears gushed. I stammered while searching for an explanation, but all the words jammed on my tongue. Nothing came out but an apologetic wail.

"Okay, okay, okay," he said, switching gears. "Just calm down.

Take a breath—a big, deep breath." He leaned back and swiveled toward the crew. "Give me a script and then everybody go for a walk."

Then he went over the scene with me until I learned it.

"Better now?" he asked.

"Yes," I said.

"Good."

Feeling like the storm cloud had passed, I got up and began to walk away. Suddenly Mike grabbed my arm, spun me around, and stared daggers straight into my eyes.

"That's never happening again, is it?" he said.

I bit my lip, trying to hold off another downpour.

"No," I said.

Now, nearly three and a half decades later, I can say that I've never gone into a scene on any project unprepared. Mike would've expected as much from me. He taught me not to settle for anything less than my best, especially if I demanded it of others.

In the ensuing years, I've also realized his influence on me extended way beyond the set. As a kid, I didn't know he sipped vodka from his coffee mug every day almost as frequently as he pulled me into his sweat-soaked torso for a giant bear hug, but I'm sure he's one of the primary reasons why as a young woman, I almost always picked men who smelled like alcohol.

Likewise, I'm sure Mike was responsible for my preference for physical men with a sense of humor. Here's a perfect example: we shot exteriors on a Simi Valley ranch about ninety minutes north of Paramount, and if the sun was out, Mike would, by late morning, strip off his shirt and work in just his pants, boots, and suspenders. (In all fairness, it could be hellaciously hot in Simi Valley.) Well, women came out in droves to watch him work and to swoon, and he loved playing a certain prank on them.

He would send me to catch a frog from the pond (I can still hear his surreptitious whisper, "Half Pint, go find me a little one"), then pop whatever I brought back in his mouth, walk over to where the women stood, say hello, and let the poor freaked-out frog jump out at them. As they gasped and shrieked, he flashed a naughty, self-satisfied grin that made him even more lovable.

It would be years before I opened my eyes to Mike's shortcomings; and until then I thought he was perfect. His daughter Leslie was one of my best friends. I was also close to Mike Jr., who was a year younger than Leslie and me. I slept at their house and they at mine, often enough that they felt like my weekend family, and I thought Mike and Lynn were the most glamorous, loving couple.

As we went through the season, work seemed more like play. Various episodes required me to go fishing; fly a kite with a cute boy I kind of liked on- and offscreen (fellow child actor Eric Shea, who attended my school); do scenes with guest star Richard Basehart, a giant in my eyes for having starred as Admiral Nelson in *Voyage to the Bottom of the Sea*; and pretend to fight with Alison, who, though cast as my on-screen nemesis, was one of my best friends in real life.

When we had slumber parties at Alison's house, we got to stay up and watch *Saturday Night Live*. At my house, the lights went out much earlier and my TV intake was carefully monitored for age appropriateness. My mom had a long list of rules that were impossible to explain to my friends. Among others, she didn't believe girls should wear black or get their ears pierced until they were eighteen. I still haven't figured that one out, though I lived by it, and when I turned eighteen I did what any girl in my position would: I pierced my right ear once and my left three times.

I had no idea how she would've reacted to my first crush because I didn't tell her that my heart went pitter-pat whenever I thought about Craig Botkin. Nor, at the end of the school year, did I let her see my sixth-grade yearbook, where friends wrote they were sure I'd marry Craig and they'd see me at the wedding.

But that was the least of what went unspoken. In February, I was home from school with a bad cold when my mom came in with my brother and said she had to tell us something. The key words in that sentence were "had to," because my mom wouldn't have told us something if it wasn't imperative and inevitable that we know, which this was.

"Daddy died last night," she said.

For a brief second, I thought I'd misheard her, the way I had when she'd told us about his stroke. In fact, I almost ran to the phone to call him. Then it hit me. He wasn't dying to talk to me. He was actually dead. My brother was already crying when I let out a wail that sounded like the air was screaming out of me. I collapsed into uncontrollable, racking sobs. My daddy was gone.

For me, everything about my father's passing is still blank and mysterious. One day I had a daddy; the next day he was gone. After my mother broke the news, we didn't talk about it again. I don't remember ever going to his house again. I wasn't asked if I wanted any of his belongings. I wasn't allowed to go to his funeral, nor was my brother. I'm sure my mother thought it would be too painful for us. She wanted to shield us from that kind of sorrow, preferring our lives to be beautiful all the time. It was a long time before I found out that my father had died after suffering a second stroke. To this day, I don't know if he was at home or some other place. All I knew, all that mattered was that he was no longer alive and my life was never going to be the same again.

It was like there was a hole in my soul. No one came to sit with me. None of my friends knew. No one at work ever mentioned my father's death. No one put their arm around me, gave me a hug, or said they were sorry. I have a feeling people were told it would be too upsetting for me.

Not even Leslie Landon, my best friend, knew. Many years later, we were having lunch, now parents ourselves, and I mentioned something about losing my dad. Leslie was shocked. All those years she had thought my father died before she and I met. I had a hard time believing Michael never gathered his kids, who were my closest friends, and said, "Listen, Melissa is having a hard time." But he didn't. I assume my mother didn't want anyone to know lest they upset me by bringing it up.

A year or so after my father's death, my grandfather took Jonathan and me to the cemetery. We looked down at my father's headstone. I looked over at my grandfather crying and saw my mother put her arm around him. I wouldn't shed a tear that day. I wasn't supposed to be sad—ever. At least that's what I thought. So I just stood there. But I was very angry. I was angry that my mother would comfort her father, that she even had a father. That he could cry and I couldn't and I had to be a soldier as we stood over my father's grave.

More time would pass, decades, in fact, before I would find out the details of my father's funeral. According to my mother, hundreds of people turned out. Tony Curtis, who loved my father and tells me the most wonderful things about him whenever we cross paths, couldn't even go into the service. He sat on a hillside outside of the Old North Church at Forest Lawn Mortuary. Years later my mom told me that Red Buttons delivered one of the eulogies; she said the tributes were amazing and I should always know that many people truly loved my father. I of course had no way of knowing whether this was true or more fairy dust. I've since chosen it to be true.

My father's death was handled so differently than I would handle it today as a mother myself. I've made sure that my children were exposed to death and grief from very early ages. They were given the choice to come along when we had to put pets to sleep. We even had a funeral for a pet mouse. I've tried to give them an understanding of loss and a sense of grief as a necessary part of life. I wanted them to realize that without such sadness and pain, there can be none of the love and happiness, and loss doesn't mean you have to give up the good stuff in your heart. It means you cherish those memories that much more and think of the tears that may fall as smiles from the past. It's as Mike said in the beautiful poem "Remember Me," which he composed for the episode featuring Patricia Neal:

> *Remember me with smiles and laughter,*
> *For that's the way I'll remember you all.*
> *If you can only remember me with tears,*
> *Then don't remember me at all.*

seven

WHAT THE HELL HAPPENED?

We moved on in the same way we moved on after my parents' divorce, without acknowledgment that anything was different, or rather a tacit agreement that we'd believe everything would be the same even though it wasn't. Over spring break, we began a yearly tradition of going to Hawaii with the Landons. We stayed at the Kahala Hilton, where we bumped into other families we knew and all of us kids swam together, helped one another build sandcastles, and played epic games of kick the can, Frisbee football, and ding-dong ditch.

I was always the kid on the beach with cotton pajamas over my one-piece bathing suit and a thick slab of white zinc oxide on my nose because I burned easily and severely. In other words, I was a total dork.

To save a little money, my mother cleaned out the minibar in the room I shared with Jonathan or Patrice, depending on the year, and filled the fridge with milk, cold cuts, and bread. I can still picture myself at lunchtime, sitting in the sand in my pajamas, eating a bologna sandwich with mayonnaise dripping down my hand. Meanwhile, the other kids feasted on cheeseburgers and fruit salads served on a tray brought by the hotel staff directly to their rented poolside loungers. Dinner was more of the same while the adults went out. I was not a glamorous kid.

Right after school got out, my mom and I went to Roundup, Montana, where I shot the movie *The Christmas Coal Mine Miracle*. The cast included Kurt Russell, Andy Prine, and Mitch Ryan, who played my father—yet another daddy figure with whom I bonded. He was, incidentally, the one who many years later sucked me into the Screen Actors Guild politics, something for which I'll never forgive him.

They were a pretty wild bunch and apparently one night something really crazy happened, because the next day everyone on the set, cast and crew included, were laughing about it. But nobody would tell me no matter how much I begged, pleaded, and connived. It annoyed the heck out of me while we shot the film and lingered in my brain afterward as one of my life's great mysteries.

Ten years later, I'd gone on location for a movie, suffered an attack of appendicitis, went back to work too soon, and developed a horrible infection in my blood that landed me in a bed at Cedars-Sinai Medical Center. Every time I opened my eyes my bed seemed to be surrounded by concerned people with red-rimmed eyes and forced smiles, standing over me. (Just so you know, the forced-smile thing doesn't work. It just makes the patient sure he or she is going to die.)

In the midst of this, I overheard someone say Goldie Hawn and Kurt Russell were also at the hospital following the birth of their son, Wyatt. I scribbled a note to Kurt, congratulating them and asking him to come up and say hi. I gave it to a nurse, who got it to the hospital's PR department, and later on Kurt came into my room.

I gestured for him to sit next to my bed. He asked how I was doing. I could barely talk, but I managed to tell him that I was going to be fine. I used all my strength to prop myself up and say, "I have to ask you a question."

"Shoot," he said. "What is it?"

I gestured for him to come closer because I was too weak to speak above a whisper.

"What the hell happened in Roundup, Montana, when I was a kid?"

I had to know just in case I didn't pull through, and Kurt laughingly told me the story. It turned out there was a lot of drinking and sex going on, with the guys playing the role of Hollywood big shots in a small rural town and going through the local girls with élan, particularly Andy. Kurt secretly wired a van with a microphone and hid with the sound guy in the bushes outside the town's one bar one night while Andy was inside getting hammered.

Kurt had also arranged for a girl to come on to his costar. Soon the two of them walked out of the bar, got in the van, and began to fool around. At that point, Kurt had a local police unit quietly pull up behind the van. At the moment the girl told Andy she was only sixteen, as Kurt had instructed her to do, Kurt cued the police, who flashed their lights. All of a sudden, Andy burst out of the van wearing only his underwear and took off in the snow.

Though I wasn't able to eat or drink anything in my sickbed, I found the strength to laugh. I couldn't believe that story had been kept from me the whole time. Not that I would've understood it. I may have wanted in on the world of grown-ups, but I was still more comfortable in little-girl moments like the one on the first episode of our third season when guest star Johnny Cash beckoned me to where he and his wife, June, were sitting, put me on his lap, and said, "I watch your show all the time, and you just climb right into my heart."

I saw my classmates and peers start to go through puberty and wear bras, while my gingham dress hung on me as straight as it did on the hanger in my closet. Toward the end of my twelfth year, I had a double hernia operation and woke up only to be told that the three pubic hairs I'd grown had been shaved off by the nurses. That was how I heralded the onset of puberty . . . by being humiliated.

After I watched the movie *The Great Waldo Pepper*, I developed a crush on Robert Redford. He overtook *Batman*'s Adam West as the man I wanted to marry. I went through my *Tiger Beat* and *Teen Beat* magazines and papered my school locker with photos of him, John Travolta, David Cassidy, Shaun Cassidy, Parker Stevenson, and *How the West Was Won*'s Bruce Boxleitner, my future husband. Only in this industry can a girl grow up and marry the picture in her locker! I was also in those magazines, not that I gave a shit. I devoured the articles on those young men and believed every word, knowing full well the stuff written about me wasn't true.

Unlike some girls, I wasn't boy crazy. I was too reserved for such displays, which made me quietly selective. But I felt like my life might change the first time I saw Scott Baio on the Paramount lot. My friend and fellow Chachi devotee Tracy Nelson was even more excited. The two of us went to tapings of *Happy Days* whenever possible. Though she'll kill me for admitting this, we rewrote the lyrics to Linda Ronstadt's song "Blue Bayou" to "Scott Baio."

I started hanging around the commissary, waiting for him to show up so I could say hi to him, as if he might be remotely interested. He wasn't. In fact, he couldn't have been more disinterested.

I had no such delusions when I heard John Travolta was shooting *Grease* on the lot, but I put myself on red alert for any sightings. When it finally happened, I was eating lunch with Katherine MacGregor, who played Mrs. Oleson. Katherine's nickname was Scottie, and she was hilarious, one of my favorite lunch companions for her openness and sense of humor. But her lack of inhibition made her a less than perfect choice to be seated across from me when I literally went into shock.

"What is it?" Scottie asked, her back to whatever I'd seen that had caused such a reaction.

"That-that-that guy over there," I said.

She turned and looked over her shoulder.

"Him? With the greased hair?"

"Yeah," I said. "That's Vinnie Barbarino."

John was wearing the soon-to-be infamous Danny Zuko jeans and leather jacket. He was gorgeous.

As he walked toward the food counter, Scottie twisted around in her chair, leaned back, and signaled him over to our table with an animated wave that could've guided a 747 to the gate, even as I pleaded, "No, no, no, please don't do it." Just in case he didn't see her, she augmented her effort with a piercing warble: "Oh, young man!

Young man! Over here!" If you watched *Little House* you can imagine how she sounded . . . just like Harriet Oleson calling out to some young man in town. *Oy!*

I wanted to die. I literally slipped under the table. It wasn't like he wouldn't know who I was. I was on a highly rated TV program *and* I was in my *Little House* wardrobe.

John came right over. He was warm and gracious as I crawled out from under the table, and I was grateful he didn't laugh at me. Still, after he went to get his food, I turned to Scottie and said, "Please don't ever do that to me again."

A few years later, Tracy and I had the *Grease* album, and we'd stage it and sing along like devoted cult members. More often than not I let Tracy play Sandy. Our performances also included Holly Robinson (an amazing singer), who I befriended that summer when my mom and Harold began a short-lived tradition of renting a house in the Malibu Colony.

Joined by the Landons, I remember us girls—Leslie, Holly, Tracy, and me—decamped on the beach when we weren't singing, eyeing the chiseled bodies of surfers, studying the older surfer girls in their bikinis, and sharing whatever shreds of information we knew or thought we knew about womanhood. Leslie reported that she'd found a book on her parents' shelf that said yellow was the color to wear if you wanted to seduce a man.

"Yellow?" I asked.

"They find it sexy," she said.

"Crap," I sighed, "that's the one color that doesn't work on me."

It wasn't like I was ready to seduce anyone. I didn't know the first thing about sex—not what it was or how it worked. My mother never explained the facts of life. At ten, I'd found a box of tampons under the sink in her bathroom and when I asked what they were, she said they were for applying makeup. But now I was fourteen, and this other person inside my brain periodically clamored for details about how the different parts worked, not just generalities.

One day I was in the car with my mom when my need to know wrestled my usual reticence into submission. Flushed and over-heated by the breakthrough I was about to make, I asked her what it was like "to get Sara." She went into the whole story about giving birth to my sister. But that wasn't what I wanted to know, and I asked the question again. What was it like *to get* Sara?

My mother's expression revealed her sudden understanding of my question. I could almost see her brain go *Oh, shit, here it comes.*

"It was very lovely," she said.

And that was all she offered. As she turned her eyes back on the road, she left me with my mouth agape with disappointment, confu-sion, and questions. What did "lovely" mean? And, more important, could it still be lovely for me even if yellow wasn't my color?

I don't know when Melissa Sue got her period or began thinking about these same issues. But there was a certain point during the fourth season when all of a sudden she had really long fingernails (I bit mine ravenously), wore makeup, smoked cigarettes, and guzzled TaB. She was way beyond my league. Then when she began dating actor Lance Kerwin of *James at 15* fame, forget it. She wasn't just out of my league. She was in a different universe. It was like all of a sud-den she was grown up. After that, she dated Frank Sinatra Jr. But we never talked about any of that stuff. Alison was my great source of in-formation. She made sure I noticed her boobs on the day they popped out, and a short time later she came to work and whispered to me, "Guess what?"

"What?" I asked.

"I have a pillow between my legs," she said.

"Why would you do that?" I asked in complete ignorance. "Is it like some contest to see if you can walk that way?"

Alison looked at me dumbstruck.

"Helloooooo! I have a *pillow* between my legs."

I shrugged apologetically. "I'm sorry, I don't know what that means," I admitted.

She shook her head, mystified at my ignorance.

"I got my period," she said. "I had to use a maxipad."

In my defense, I knew what it meant to get your period; I'd just never heard of a maxipad. Luckily, Alison had provided a demo on tampons using a glass of water, given a lesson on hygiene, and demystified everything else by the time I got my period for the first time at fifteen. If she hadn't, imagine how surprised I would've been when I told my mom that I got my period and she handed me a box full of things she'd said were for putting on makeup.

I dealt with the confusion of those hormone-fueled changes, but hearing my girlfriends begin to giddily report about their make-out sessions with boys sent me into a near catastrophic panic that no one was ever going to want to date me. Forget the glam life of the young Hollywood star portrayed in teen magazines. (What turns Melissa on? How can you be her friend? Win a date with Melissa!) I spent my evenings lying on my bedroom floor, listening through my headphones to Janis Ian's terribly sad song "At 17." I played that song over and over again, crying as I sang the lyrics to myself, thinking they had been written specifically about me.

"Oh, honey, you weren't pathetic," my husband said after I described that scene to him. "Everybody loved you."

"Yeah," I said, "everybody but me."

I was melodramatic. I feared my grandfather's hugs and kisses on the weekend would be the only attention I'd ever get from a man. I envisioned spending my life alone, playing solitaire. No, it was worse than that. I pictured myself alone, pathetically *cheating* at solitaire.

Little did I know there was one guy who had his eye on me. In all likelihood, he had had his eye on numerous other girls, too. But one day I went to CBS to tape a guest appearance on *The Dinah Shore Show* and fourteen-year-old Rob Lowe made a point of standing in the hallway so he could meet me.

With a script under his arm so I would see he was an actor (he told me about his prop years later), he came over and introduced himself. I found out he'd recently moved to L.A. from Ohio to pursue a career, and he was already on the sitcom *A New Kind of Family*. I admitted having seen his picture in the teen magazines. After a quick chat, I left with the impression that he was cute (actually, he was almost pretty), sweet, and funny—just the kind of guy I could go for if he called me, which he didn't.

I wasn't ready to answer that kind of phone call anyway. I was still living in the midst of my dorkdom. However, with plenty of other business-related calls coming in, my mother, in a stroke of well-timed brilliance (which came naturally to her), decided to hire a manager to help build my career outside of *Little House*. She introduced me to Ray Katz, a very large, very round man with an equally large office in a high-rise on Sunset Boulevard. He'd helped the Osmonds establish their empire, managed Cher, Dolly Parton, and KC & the Sunshine Band, and seemed at one time or another to have repped everyone of consequence in the pop universe.

I'm sure the meeting was a fait accompli between my mother and Ray, with the only outstanding condition being my approval, which seemed a foregone conclusion when my mom introduced him to me as "Uncle Ray." And why shouldn't it have been a done deal? He had ridiculously successful clients.

I remember sitting in his office, quietly listening to my mother and Ray talk about the fortunate position I was in, namely a key ingredient on a hit TV series, embraced by mainstream America as one of its favorite teenage sweethearts. As both agreed, there had to be a way to parlay it into something more.

"I'd like her to show people her versatility as an actor," my mother said.

Granted, it was my mother talking, but that was the first time I heard anyone talk about my "versatility as an actor." Ray, of course, agreed.

"If you could hand-pick your dream roles for Melissa," he began, "what would they be?"

My mother rattled off Helen Keller, Anne Frank, and Joan of Arc. She said she'd love to see me in a remake of *The Song of Bernadette*. And that was how my movie career started. It was 1978, and I was about to turn fourteen. Suddenly my mother and I were sharing a production company, Half Pint Productions, and Ray set about producing *The Miracle Worker* for me.

I watched the 1962 original starring Patty Duke as Helen and Anne Bancroft as her indefatigable teacher, Annie Sullivan. I wanted to know what my mom and Uncle Ray were getting me into, and I was blown away after watching performances that earned both actresses Academy Awards. I remember thinking, *What if I can't do this?*

I didn't tell anyone, but the challenge of playing Helen scared me. It was beyond anything I'd done up till then. I couldn't envision where or how to begin. But there's this person in me who appears when my back is against the wall. She's part show-off, part Wonder Woman, and part too dumb to know any better. She says, "You don't think so? Well, watch this." And then she dives in.

And that's what I did. Then I was told that Patty Duke Astin, as she was known at the time—her real name is Anna—was going to play Annie Sullivan, which was both thrilling and intimidating. Our first meeting was a key moment in my life. It was in Ray's office, and it was the first time I sat down with someone who knew exactly what I was going through in my life. It was as if she could see into my brain.

She'd been one of the most successful child actors ever, the youngest to win an Oscar and the star of her own TV show. Behind her stardom, though, was a lifetime filled with abuse, drug problems, screwed-up relationships, and, as she courageously revealed in her 1987 memoir, *Call Me Anna,* a triumphant coming to terms with bipolar disorder that ultimately allowed her to reclaim her real name and identity, which had been taken from her at age seven "when tyrannical managers stripped her of nearly all that was familiar, beginning with her name."

Though my life wasn't anywhere near as troubled, at the very least she knew what it was like to be a porcelain doll. When I looked into her eyes, we had an instant connection beyond the normal exchange of fellow thespians meeting each other for the first time. I just knew she got me. Then she taught me how to sign the alphabet. I left thinking she was going to be great. She was more than great, and to this day remains one of my dearest friends and mentors.

Not only was *The Miracle Worker* my first project as a producer as well as my first test as an actor, it was also my first play. In a stroke of genius, which may have been Uncle Ray's doing, it was decided the best thing for us as a cast and a production in general would be to stage it as a play before we shot the movie. We'd get all the kinks out of the performances, all the nuances down, and then all we'd have to do is move it to a soundstage and shoot it.

Once the *Little House* season wrapped, Ray booked the production at the Royal Poinciana Playhouse, in Palm Beach, Florida, and we began rehearsals in Los Angeles. Despite our many conversations, Anna had, unbeknownst to me, been told not to coach or talk to me about playing Helen. It was extremely difficult for her because she realized I was skating across the surface of the part.

The problem was I didn't know any better. I thought I could take on the role the same way I had for four seasons of *Little House* and my one movie, *The Christmas Coal Mine Miracle*, which was essentially me being me. In reality, there wasn't much of a difference between Laura and Melissa. I didn't have to stretch to imagine myself as her. But playing Helen Keller was an entirely different situation.

At the core, I think all three of us—Laura, Helen Keller, and myself—shared a certain kind of tenacity. But I had no idea what I was getting myself into by playing this remarkable girl. Actors talk about their process of building a character, of climbing into a person's life and inhabiting him or her from head to toe, and I didn't have any of those skills, nothing that could've been described as a process.

With three weeks to go before we left for Florida, Ray and the director, Paul Aaron, met with my mother and told her that I wasn't delivering at the level they needed. In fact, they put it more bluntly than that. They said that while the cast, which included Anna, Diana Muldaur, and Charles Siebert, had gelled, as they'd expected from seasoned pros, it was obvious that I simply didn't have it.

My mother, the source of my tenaciousness, whisked me to her former acting coach, Jeff Corey. After being blacklisted for refusing to name names before the House Un-American Activities Committee in the 1950s, Jeff, a Shakespearean-trained actor with dozens of film and TV credits, turned to teaching and counted James Dean, Jane Fonda, and Jack Nicholson among his many students. He was an older, earthy type of hippie guy who lived and worked in Malibu. I adored him, and yet from the moment we met he scared the crap out of me.

I had a sore throat the first day my mother took me to his place, and Jeff made me drink milk with acidophilus in it. We went into his house and he talked to me about the role. He asked my ideas and thoughts. Then he said, "We're going to do something, and it's going to be scary. How are you with that?"

"Okay, I guess," I said.

"Don't worry," he said. "You'll make it through. I think it's going to help you."

He then blindfolded me, turned off the lights, and tossed me around the room for about forty-five minutes. He let me trip over furniture, and when I couldn't figure out where I was, he called to me from across the room, letting me stumble over furniture, fall, and cry through my frustration, until I found my way into his arms. He was Annie to my Helen. He also suggested I blindfold myself at home, have someone spin me around, and try to find my way around the house, which I did.

Despite the black-and-blue marks, I stepped deeper into Helen than I imagined I could. As he promised, Jeff helped give me a process that let me develop a layered performance. Some of the critics even mentioned the tentative way I walked and moved, very much afraid to leave where I'd just been because I wasn't sure where I was going.

There was also a quiet moment on the plane to Florida when Anna tapped me on the head and said, "Listen, would you like to talk about Helen Keller?" Grateful and eager, I swung around in my seat and got some vital information from her, including help with the one line of dialogue I had to deliver.

It was actually a single word, "water." That was the one word Helen knew before she went blind and deaf as a child. I was having trouble saying it correctly. I knew it was something she hadn't said for a long time, and it was also the crucial moment when she made the connection between the sign for water and water itself. I had to show the lightbulb of recognition going off in her head and also articulate the word much less clearly than normal but no less understandably.

No matter how I tried, it didn't sound like the voice of a person who hadn't spoken since she was a toddler speaking her first words. I confessed as much to Anna on the plane, and she understood exactly my frustration. She'd struggled with the same thing seventeen years earlier.

"Do you want to know the trick?" she asked.

"Please tell me," I said.

She grinned.

"Say it like you're sitting on the toilet and really, really constipated," she said.

"Really?"

She nodded. And lo and behold that most basic and embarrassing tip, along with the rest of her advice, unlocked a door to an acting dream. Each night during the play, I entered from the back of the stage and ran straight to the front, averting catastrophe by stopping just at the edge, and from opening night through the run, which was extended, the people in the front row stood to catch me, at which point I knew I had them. They really thought I was blind and deaf.

I felt like a conqueror. My eyes opened to the possibility that this thing I was doing as a hobby was something I could actually learn about and develop into a serious craft.

My eyes also opened to another reality about my life as an actor. On the flight to Florida, my darling sister Sara, who continued to be the most remarkable child, was absolutely wild. My whole family, including my grandmother, had come on the trip, and my mother, concerned about Sara's comfort on the plane, had given her a spoonful of Benadryl to make her a little sleepy.

Instead, it had the opposite effect and she ran up and down the aisle, this beautiful, three-year-old Botticelli child climbing under people's feet, taking their food, and yelling "kill, kill, kill" as everyone tried to rein her in. My turn to wrangle her came at the airport after we landed. I wasn't big; Sara was already half my size. As I tried to hold her in my arms, with our backs arching and my head dodging her flailing hands, a woman came up to me and asked if I was Melissa Gilbert.

"Yes, I am," I said above Sara's screams.

"Oh gosh, my daughter loves you," she said. "Can I get your autograph?"

I struggled to hold my sister, who was trying to wiggle out of my grasp.

"I'm sorry, I can't right now," I said, wincing.

"Oh, what a little brat you are," she hissed, her sweet, friendly tone evaporating faster than a drop of water in the Mojave.

She walked away, leaving me shattered by this, my first unprotected brush with my own celebrity. Later, I realized while everyone else in the airport had been able to behave in whatever way they felt like at the moment, including that woman who was insensitive, or just oblivious, and downright mean, I had to be perfect, smiley, kind, and polite, or else I was a little brat. That's a hell of a message to give someone who already stuffed her feelings away.

It wasn't fair, and I was bothered by that encounter for weeks. No one had ever told me how to handle such situations, and to be honest, although I was around famous people every day, I didn't have any understanding or awareness of celebrity, including my own. One day in Los Angeles, I was in the car with my mother when I asked her what it was like to be famous. She looked at me like I was out of my head.

"What do you mean?" she asked.

"What's it like to be famous?" I said again.

"Well, you are famous," she replied, kind of bewildered but trying to be matter-of-fact.

"No," I said. "I mean like really famous."

"Like who?" she asked.

"Like Farrah Fawcett."

"You are," she said.

I shook my head.

"No, Mom, you don't understand. I'm talking about—"

She put her hand up, signaling me to stop.

"No, Melissa, you don't understand," she said.

And you know what? She was right. I didn't understand. But I'd find out soon enough.

eight

OH SHIT,
THEY GOT A REAL MAN!

Immediately after the run in Florida, we returned to Los Angeles and filmed the movie. We used the same crew from *Little House*, the same exteriors in Simi Valley, and by then we'd moved to MGM from Paramount and we shot the interiors for *The Miracle Worker* there. I felt surrounded by family, comfortable, and safe. Mike even visited the set a couple of times. Sadly, about three-quarters of the way through the production, Fred Coe, one of our executive producers and a legend in the business, passed away. But we moved ahead knowing that Fred, like the rest of us, believed we were doing something awfully special.

There wasn't a dry eye in the theater when the movie was screened for the cast, crew, and network executives prior to its airdate. That was back in the day when certain TV movies were still considered special events. We had a private screening room on the studio lot, and my whole family was there, as was Mike. Back then I still didn't watch myself with any sort of critical detachment, certainly not the way I scrutinize every scene and every moment today. I was just a member of the audience watching the movie, and I was destroyed at the end of it. Everyone was.

The Miracle Worker is an emotional film, a total gut-wrencher, and as the music played over the credits everyone applauded and screamed bravo. Not me. Sitting with near paralytic stillness, I was dazed as the lights came on. I couldn't believe the little girl on the screen had been me. I couldn't comprehend that I'd turned in that performance. Rising slowly, I grabbed Anna, who was reaching out to me, and the two of us held on to each other and sobbed.

Then I turned around and saw Mike, who had tears pouring down his face. I jumped into his arms and let him squeeze me till it seemed like I melted into his chest. He said, "Oh my God. Oh my God. Oh my God." It was hard to render him speechless, but I'd done it.

At that point, I thought the sky was the limit. I didn't think acting could get any better, and I had reasons for believing I might have hit the apex of my career.

In the months that preceded the screening, *Little House* had started back up and I'd been having a difficult time with Laura's more grown-up interests and desires. The new, sixth season introduced a number of new characters, including Almanzo Wilder, the young man Laura would fall in love with, marry, and start a family with.

I knew this development was imminent. I'd read the books. Still, when on the first day I opened a script and saw the name Almanzo Wilder among the characters, I got a sick feeling in my stomach that didn't go away for the next two seasons. The nausea was all nerves. I knew I was going to have to show affection, kiss, and at some point go to bed with a guy when in real life I was a knock-kneed, flat-chested fifteen-year-old who looked thirteen, still wore rubber bands and a retainer in her mouth, and had never gone out with, kissed, or even held hands with a boy.

And suddenly I was supposed to get it on prairie style?

Uh, no thanks.

Well, that's not altogether true. I was somewhat excited about the idea of Laura growing up because I realized it was an easy way for me to gradually inch forward in my own life. And I was definitely excited to see who the producers chose for this all-important role of the person I was going to have to kiss. When I heard they cast an actor named Dean Butler, I freaked out a little from nerves, but in a good way.

But then came Dean's first day of work, and when we finally met I was hit by a perfect storm of disappointment, fear, anger, and nausea. I can imagine what my face looked like. No, I don't want to imagine. It couldn't have been nice. I'd expected the producers to cast a contemporary of mine, someone like Eric Shea, someone close to my age. Instead, they had cast a man!

That's right, Dean was a grown-up man. I looked at him as if he'd risen from Dr. Frankenstein's lab. He was in his twenties. He shaved, drove a car, and lived in his own apartment. He must have felt so bummed upon meeting this dorky, freaked-out fifteen-year-old with peach fuzz all over her legs (I hadn't even shaved them yet), and being told I was the one he had to fall in love with and marry. How inconvenient and disappointing for him.

I couldn't have cared less. We were supposed to fall in love, but all I knew was that I wanted to run away and hide. Thankfully, today we're great friends. He knows he scared the crap out of me and that as a result, I made a point of doing everything I could to make him as uncomfortable as possible.

I was also delighted when he messed up on his own. Take his first day on the job. Almanzo was supposed to drive a team of horses, and then stop and talk to me. For my part, it was supposed to be love at first sight. In real life, outside of rehearsal, Dean had no experience driving a team of horses. I could drive a team. I could drive a buckboard. I could drive a covered wagon. I could drive a six-up stagecoach. I probably could've driven an eighteen-wheeler. Anybody can with the right training.

The wranglers trained Dean and when he was ready, we began the scene. Almanzo drove his team down the road and came upon Laura. He was wearing this big hat I thought made him look like a doofus. Then his hat blew off. As he turned to grab it, he pulled the reins and steered the horses and buckboard into a tree. I collapsed in a spasm of giggles.

Mike was there, and he wasn't happy. He'd been driving teams of horses for decades and his first time on *Bonanza* was too long ago to remember. I remember he gave Dean a look that said, "What the fuck is wrong with this kid?" Nobody should've had to endure that look. Or my not-so-discreet snickers.

A week later, life took another inevitable turn. I was at home when I got my period for the first time. When I told my mother, she lightly smacked me across the face with no explanation. Later that afternoon, my grandmother and my aunt came over and we talked about the responsibilities of being a woman. It was a lovely, emotional moment and I found out the slap was a Jewish tradition; now that your daughter is a woman, this is the last time you can punish her physically. From here on in, the only punishment allowed from your mother is the verbal kind. Then my brother arrived home from school. He looked at the four of us, daubing our teary eyes, and asked what was going on.

"Melissa got her period," my grandmother said in a tone that seemed to convey he should've been proud or happy.

He was neither.

"That's disgusting!" he said before leaving the room.

That season of *Little House* opened with a two-part episode, and the very next day after I got my period we were shooting part two, which is best known as the cinnamon chicken episode. Nellie was cooking dinner for Almanzo—his favorite, cinnamon chicken—and I sabotaged her dish by giving her cayenne pepper instead of cinnamon. The two of us had a confrontation, a big wrestling match in a mud hole, which was essentially an old watering hole for cattle. As they reset cameras, I whispered to her, "I'm a woman now."

Alison, who had prepped me for everything I knew about getting my period, grinned.

"You're also covered in cow shit," she said. "How appropriate."

• • •

Early one morning a few weeks later, I was sound asleep when my mother burst into my bedroom and shook me awake. I opened my eyes as she exclaimed, "You were nominated! Oh my God, you were nominated!" I sat up in bed and asked what I was nominated for. She said, "An Emmy! Best Actress in a Motion Picture or Miniseries."

"Me?" I asked.

"Yes!" she said as she wrapped her arms around me.

"Wow," I said from inside her hug.

I was elated. The screaming and excitement was nonstop throughout the morning as my mom fielded phone calls and I thanked people for calling to congratulate me. Then Uncle Ray called with news that spun the excitement in another direction. My mother spoke to him, or rather she listened for a moment and then said, "Are you kidding me? You've got to be kidding. Oh my God, I can't believe it."

I stood next to her, begging to know what Uncle Ray was telling her. Finally she turned around and looked at me with disbelief and pride.

"Anna is nominated for the same award," she said, referring to Patty Duke. "So is Bette Davis and Lee Remick."

I smiled and threw up my hands in a mock surrender to the combination of age and greatness that had just stepped into the room. I had two immediate thoughts. First, there was no way I wanted to win. It would be beyond the valley of embarrassing to give an award to a child in lieu of any one of those three women. And second, there was no way I was going to win. But my God, just to have my performance considered on a par with the performances by those three women, well, it was monumental for me.

You hear actors say all the time that it was enough to be nominated. For me, it really was. In an interesting move, my "team" took out an ad in the trades thanking members of the television academy for such an unbelievable honor. It read:

"This is my acceptance speech, because for me this special nomination is an award. Whichever of these beautiful ladies wins the award, I am proud to have been allowed to share the moment, and the loudest applause and bravos you hear will be mine." Though that is exactly how I felt, the ad was not my idea. In retrospect, it was a pretty good play to get me the award. Thank the Lord it didn't work!

It turned out no one heard anything from me. In July, the Screen Actors Guild went on strike, along with her sister union, AFTRA, and though the Emmy Awards aired on television, SAG boycotted the ceremonies. Like every other nominee except Powers Booth, who in his acceptance speech said, "This is either the most courageous moment of my career or the stupidest," I honored the strike by not attending the awards, a show of my union stripes before I even knew what they meant.

I was sad I couldn't go, but Michael Landon Jr., with whom I had begun sort of a budding romance, took me to dinner at El Torito that night. Not a bad consolation prize. Afterward, we watched the show at my house and cheered wildly as Anna won the Best Actress award. Quite unexpectedly, I won as a producer when the movie was named Outstanding Drama. (I recently took the statue home and had it restored after finding it on a hallway floor when I was cleaning my mom's house before Warren's memorial service.)

As for my relationship with Michael Jr., it was a sure sign of change. It hadn't been contrived for PR purposes like so many teen romances in Hollywood. He was adorable; he had blond, curly hair and a great sense of humor. I would lie in bed at night and his face would flash before my eyes as I tried to fall asleep. It was the first time I experienced butterflies in my stomach when I thought about a boy.

It wasn't quite a romance, though there was plenty of hand holding and eye batting. We went to events together, talked excitedly about getting our learner's permits, and commiserated when our respective orthodontists gave both of us the same sad news that we had to keep wearing our neck gear at night.

One time he cooked dinner for me, spaghetti with, in lieu of marinara sauce, a can of Hormel chili poured all over it. It was actually quite delicious. My mother also sent a bunch of us kids on a ski trip to Sun Valley, where she had a condo. The gang included my brother and Mike Jr. Despite the fact I had multiple adult escorts, it was a big moment for me to be going away with a boy.

It was a little nerve-racking, and humor was my salvation in any tight situation. On that trip, I knew how to open the bathroom door when it was locked, and so Mike Jr. and I snuck in while my brother was in the shower and dumped a bucket of snow over him. Jonathan had never screamed as high or as loud in his life. I played similar pranks at work. My favorite was lifting the toilet seat and putting Saran Wrap over the bowl. As Alison Angrim once told *People* magazine, you didn't see it—until it was too late.

Without such antics allowing me to keep one foot firmly planted in childhood, I probably would've been more confused than I was as I dipped the toes of my other foot in the waters of adolescence. I got scared when I heard stories of peers smoking cigarettes, experimenting with drugs (that meant smoking pot), and doing more than just kissing boys. In my world, nice girls didn't let guys get to second base. For that matter, nice girls didn't complain. They didn't speak out of turn. They didn't wear black. They didn't dress provocatively. Nice girls took small bites, they sat up straight, they never called boys on the phone. Nice girls were nice girls. I didn't know any, but I was damn sure going to be one.

Apparently nice girls were also thin. One day Leslie Landon and I were roller skating on the paddle tennis court in my backyard, and when I went inside to get something to drink, my mom looked at me, looked out at Leslie, then back at me, and said, "Why can't you have a flat stomach like her?"

I was anything but chubby, yet because I was going through so many physical changes at the time, most of which I wasn't even aware of until they'd already happened, her comment turned out to be one of those moments that shoved me into a revolving door I couldn't escape.

Suddenly I was conscious of my body. I felt short and chubby. Whatever I was when I looked in the mirror, it was wrong—and the image I had of myself would only get worse. All of which made me covet my girlish ways even more. They were like a tortoiseshell I could pull my head into when I needed protection from maturity.

I marvel at how innocent I was able to stay for so long. By fifteen, Tatum O'Neal had been involved in a threesome, Mackenzie Phillips had used cocaine, Scott Baio was getting it on with his costar Erin Moran, and I was always worried about having extra rubber bands with me in case one snapped off my braces.

Part of me is grateful for my mom's overprotective ways. But it was getting harder, or rather impossible, to hide from the inevitability of change. A perfect example: my first on-camera kiss in the "Sweet 16" episode. I'd been kissed years earlier in another episode, but it had been an innocent little peck. This was Laura's first real kiss, one she desired, and it made me sick.

The episode came toward the end of season six, and I didn't want to do it. To those who came up to me and asked, "Hey, Half Pint, how do you feel about your big kiss?" I quipped that I would've preferred to kiss Scott Baio or Shaun Cassidy. I knew those teen-idol guys were unattainable and therefore safe to mention, though the truth was, I didn't want to kiss anyone. Especially Dean Butler. I didn't want to kiss a man. I didn't want to kiss anyone with stubble!

I was too scared to talk to anyone about it or ask questions. Nor did anyone offer information. For instance, how was I supposed to kiss this guy? How was I supposed to convey passion? Should I kiss him as if I was on *The Brady Bunch*? Or should I go for something closer to what I saw on *Dynasty*? How did they do it on the prairie? All I knew for sure was that the expectations were high. This was the real beginning of Laura and Almanzo's romance, which was one of the great romances of all time. When the time came to kiss Dean, I shut my eyes (inside, they were blank screens) and gently puckered up, letting him find the target.

I was never as relieved as when I heard Mike, who directed the episode, yell cut. I felt like I took my first real breath in a week. I turned and saw my mother, the woman who'd once told me tampons were for makeup, standing just off camera, smiling with tears in her eyes. She gave me a hug before I hurried off to the craft service table and popped some chips in my mouth to get rid of any cooties.

One bad taste lingered through the rest of the season, though it wasn't openly discussed by anyone until it was too late. Mike had become very friendly with a new stand-in on the show, a pretty young blond named Cindy Clerico. I first noticed her during production of *The Miracle Worker* when Mike visited the set one day and said hello to her before he did to me. I wondered who she was, then someone said, "Oh, she's a stand-in. I guess they know each other."

Though it didn't register with me then, I'm pretty sure that was the start of their romance. As the season progressed, I noticed they spent a lot of time together. It was nothing untoward; they weren't ever in a closed-off room, not that I saw. But Mike would walk around holding her puppy, and she was a pretty young thing who wore stylish tight jeans, leotards, and high-heel boots.

Their friendship hit my radar as something that might be wrong. I mentioned it one day to my mother and she snapped, "Oh, you're crazy." And so it seemed. Mike still bought Auntie Lynn gifts, thanked her when he picked up awards, told everyone how much he loved her, and fawned all over her when we went to Hawaii.

Things seemed perfectly normal during that year's vacation. Though that trip proved he wasn't the only one with a secret: I got drunk for the first time and didn't tell anyone. The event was the brainchild of Helen Reddy's daughter, Tracy Wald, whose family was also vacationing at the hotel. She came up with the idea of raiding the hotel room minibar while our parents were at dinner. Leslie pointed out mine was off-limits since it was full of cold cuts, sandwich spreads, and milk. But they figured out an alternative. Tracy was light-years ahead of Les and me in experience. They were both ahead of me physically; at seventeen and sixteen years old, they were girls who looked great on the beach in teeny bikinis, and knew it, while I was a year younger and still wearing a one-piece with pajamas over it. Anyway, the three of us parked ourselves in front of the minibar and drank everything in it. We had vodka, rum, wine, champagne, Crown Royal, and Baileys Irish Cream, which I liked.

We got rip-roaring drunk. Sick drunk. We were out of control and running through the hallways of the Kahala. Little did I or any of us know you weren't supposed to mix different types of alcohol or drink till you puked, passed out, or both. We did it all, and paid the price the next morning when Leslie and I decamped to the beach, feeling like we were an inch from death and wishing with each throb of our heads that we were dead.

We slumped in chairs on the sand and shielded ourselves from the world under layers of towels. We were probably groaning, too. At one point I peeked out from under my towel and saw a pair of legs— they looked like a man's legs—next to our chairs. I looked up and saw Mike, who stood next to us holding a tray with two glasses of what appeared to be tomato juice.

"I hear you two had a little adventure last night," he said.

Leslie looked out from under her towel. I could see her headache as she stared up at her father, then at me with a look that begged me to tell her when he had found us. I shrugged.

"Yes, we did," she said.

"Uh-huh," I agreed.

"Well, I'm assuming you don't feel very well today," he said.

"No, I don't," I said, and started to cry.

Leslie burst into tears, too, though I think both of us were crying from the pain we felt and the relief we hoped he could provide, rather than from fear or shame. Mike handed each of us a glass. They were Bloody Marys.

"This will make you feel better," he said.

'Thank you," I muttered.

"I trust neither of you are going to do this again," he said.

"No," Leslie replied.

"No way," I said.

Beyond that, there weren't any more repercussions. My mom never mentioned it to me. I'll bet she didn't have a clue. No further punishments were necessary, anyway, since we were already paying a steep price for our stupidity.

Back then, I was relieved. Now I'm not so sure I shouldn't have been given a talking-to. Put aside the potential benefits of a theoretical discussion about whether my biological parents might've had a drinking problem, something that would've been useful to know but was clearly beyond my mother, who still had not yet broken with the story that my birth mother was a prima ballerina and my father a brilliant scholar. It would've been good for me to hear that my actions, like anyone else's, had consequences for both me and those around me. Such a lesson can't be underestimated; none of us live in a bubble, even those among Hollywood's most privileged. I would have to learn this basic lesson myself, as did so many others around me, old and young.

nine

NOT SO SWEET SIXTEEN

After Hawaii, I went to work producing and starring in my second TV movie, *The Diary of Anne Frank*. As on the previous movie, I prepared with acting teacher Jeff Corey, who scared the crap out of me when he asked my thoughts on boys and tried to bring up issues of female sexuality. I understood the points he wanted to get at by alluding to Anne's relationship with Peter van Daan, the sixteen-year-old boy whose family hid out with the Franks until they were all given up by informants and taken to Nazi prison camps. But I didn't feel comfortable opening up to him or anyone else. Maybe it was his intention to make me uncomfortable.

Prior to filming, we rehearsed as if we were doing it as a play, and then we went through it scene by scene on a soundstage. As you'd expect from working on one of the most moving human tragedies of modern times, the daily expenditure of emotional energy took a toll on me. I would take a short nap as soon as I got home; it was a transition back to real life, which playing Anne made me appreciate so much more.

On the set, though, I would quake watching veteran TV director Boris Sagal, who was a screamer given to tantrums and dropping the F-bomb, including on days when we were visited by high-ranking dignitaries from the United Nations, Israel, and Great Britain. I'd never worked with anyone like him. Mike had a smoldering temper—he could kill you with a look—but he masked his intensity and perfectionism with a world-class sense of humor. Not Boris. One day a visitor made a noise and he whirled around and screamed, "What the fuck is this here, some sort of shit house?"

By contrast, the cast was a seamless group of talented, lovely actors led by Joan Plowright, Maximilian Schell, James Coco, Doris Roberts, and Scott Jacoby in the role of Peter. Scott was the first of my leading-man crushes, and it was my big secret. He was considerably older and beyond my reach. I was still listening to Barry Manilow. He was into Led Zeppelin.

With high ratings and three Emmy nominations, the movie turned out to be another respected achievement for my production company and me, but to tell you the truth, I was occupied by other, more personal milestones. Like turning sixteen. First, I celebrated the big occasion with a cake on the set of *Diary of Anne Frank*, and then I had a more fittingly girlish luncheon for all my friends at the Beverly Hills Hotel. The beautiful party made me realize I wasn't in any hurry to grow up, but I finally felt ready for this next baby step.

In one respect, I was like every other kid who turns sixteen. I couldn't wait to get my driver's license and then I wanted a car. A car meant freedom. A car meant escape. Of course, my mother set out strict rules before I even got one: No driving alone at night. No driving outside a five-mile radius. If I drove farther than that, I had to have a parent or my on-set guardian in the car with me. There were so many restrictions I might as well have bought a bicycle.

I'm sure my mother would've liked it if I had. But I was intent on having my own set of wheels. My mantra was simple: freedom and escape. I made enough money to afford any number of cars, including a cute BMW convertible, which, if I could live my life over again, would be my first choice. However, my mother talked me into getting a brand-new . . . station wagon.

For reasons that escape me, I went along with her plan. As I recall, our conversation was kind of rhetorical. My "uncle" Bud Barrish owned a Chrysler dealership, and Harold and I both got new cars at the same time. He got a LeBaron convertible and I got a cream-colored LeBaron station wagon, which was delivered to the driveway with a big red ribbon on it. It couldn't have been dorkier.

All my friends drove sporty cars like Mazda RX-7s. I pulled into school in a friggin' station wagon, singing Barry Manilow's "Mandy," which was cranked on my eight-track. Any chance I had to be remotely cool was again instantly squelched.

From across the set, the object of my horror looked to me like some sort of medieval torture chamber. In reality, I was staring at a bed—the bed Dean and I were supposed to get into for our first scene in our house after getting married. My head was full of vivid images of the vile things that could happen to me in there. Not that I had a clue what any of those things looked like; for me it was all imagination, and what I was imagining scared the shit out of me.

The seventh season of Little House had opened with Laura and Almanzo pledging their troth to each other for eternity. Their wedding, which aired in September 1980, was one of the major events of the fall TV season (from behind the cameraman, my mother sighed, "Oh, my baby's growing up"), and this scene in bed, like their wedding and their first kiss, was a highly anticipated moment that was supposed to convey their special love. But make no mistake, this was no love scene per se . . . this was prairie lovin'.

We were lying under the covers, reading the Bible and eating popcorn. Even Kermit and Miss Piggy had spicier scenes on Sesame Street. But just as we were getting ready Dean turned, put his mouth close to my ear, and like a slimy lounge lizard crooned "Strangers in the Night." He cracked up, thinking it was the funniest thing ever. Had I been a little older and more experienced, I probably would have laughed with him, but that was not the case. Singing that song in that place at that time was a fatal mistake. All my fears were confirmed. I thought I was in bed with Chester the Molester.

From that day on, any time I saw a script in which Almanzo was supposed to kiss Laura, I begged whoever was standing near me to find Mike and I'd ask him if we could change it to a hug. I was petrified by having to pretend to be in love when I'd never *been* in love. Obviously I wasn't experienced in everything I did as an actor, but love was different. Showing it required exposing more of myself and more places within myself than I was ready or able to do.

I was also questioning the concept of love itself. One morning my mother came into my room with a look on her face that clearly meant bad news. She prefaced her remarks by saying, "Something's happened," which made me sit up straighter, since that phrase was akin to an airline pilot coming on the PA and telling passengers to buckle up because the plane had hit serious turbulence. Whenever *something happened*, it was usually horrible. Something happened when my dog died and when my dad died, and so I looked at her, wondering, *What next?*

"Auntie Lynn and Mike are separating," she said.

"What?" I asked.

"Mike is seeing someone else," she said.

Everything about my mom—her voice, her expression, her gestures—was very dramatic and kind of defeated as she told me the news. She said he was seeing Cindy, whom she referred to alternately as the makeup artist and the girl who used to be a stand-in. I think she said Auntie Lynn had thrown a bottle of vodka at Mike's head. She also said we had to be supportive of Auntie Lynn, as well as Leslie, Mike Jr., and their little ones, Shawna and Christopher, because they were going through hard times and it was going to get even harder.

I was obviously concerned for my friends, who were like a second family. They did go through a tough time, too. Mike Jr. was hit hard, as was Leslie. I didn't know what to say to either of them. I had never been talked to about feelings, so how could I begin to discuss my friends' feelings with them? The split also rocked my world, which was dominated by Mike. At a certain point, I thought, *Hey, wait a minute. What about me? I have to work with Mike. I can't take sides, yet he's done something that's turned my world into angry, opposing sides.* I was put in a horribly uncomfortable position.

Worse, I'd seen it coming. I'd expressed my suspicion about Cindy to my mom. I'd told her something didn't seem right about the time Mike spent with her, but it had been like walking over a dead body in a room and no one commenting on it. My mom had said I was crazy. Not Mike and Auntie Lynn, they were the devoted, loving parents of children whom they adored.

In public Mike was seen as a pillar of morality and family values, a real-life incarnation of Charles Ingalls, not someone who would leave his wife for a younger woman. The public believed it. So did close friends like my mother. And to some extent so did I. Then, *bada bing*, the picture cracked. At home, the phone didn't stop ringing. My mother talked nonstop to Auntie Lynn. Hard as the news was to believe, it was really happening. It was like the *Titanic* hitting an iceberg.

Then the shit hit the fan in the tabloids and celebrity magazines. Mike lost lucrative commercial endorsements. He admitted he wasn't perfect and warned people not to confuse him with the character he played on TV. I watched it all unfold. Though it wasn't my family breaking apart, I still went to work every day with Mike and on weekends hung out as always with Leslie and Mike Jr., so I was more than peripherally involved. Yet no one said a word about it to me. I wasn't given any advice or direction.

It was so strange to watch this drama play out around me while being left on my own to figure it out. But that's the way it always was with me. After my mother and Harold married, they rushed Harold's daughter Patrice to therapists to help her through the difficulties she had with her parents' split and subsequent fighting. In the meantime, I wasn't asked if I needed help coping with this newly blended family situation. Nor did anyone ask how I felt about Harold.

No, there was an assumption that my life was perfectly fine—*Melissa's good. She's a trouper.* The same was true after my father died. I appeared to make it through that tragedy without consequences ("She's remarkable," my mother told people), though if anyone had asked they would've found out that getting up and going to work every day without complaint doesn't mean you're accepting and adjusted. It just means it's all stuffed away, ready to explode at any moment.

Likewise, it was assumed I could soldier on as always with Mike after he'd left his wife—and my mother's dearest friend—kind of date his son (who'd begun seeing other girls), and remain best friends with his daughter as their world crumbled and changed. Indeed, it was assumed I could manage all those relationships on my own without any guidance. I was given only two instructions: don't talk about Mike in front of Auntie Lynn, and don't mention Auntie Lynn or my mother in front of Mike.

I was caught in the middle as the people all around me chose sides. Everyone on the crew supported Mike and so did I. He was our boss *and* our pal. At home, though, we sided with Auntie Lynn. At the dinner table, my mom preached girl power and talked about what "a shit" Mike was being to Auntie Lynn.

Sometimes I would catch myself staring at Mike and wishing he would take me aside and say he knew it was awkward for me but things would turn out well. He didn't. I don't think he ever talked about it to his own kids either. He moved out of the family's home in Beverly Hills and got a house in the Malibu Colony. At work, his parts got smaller and he directed fewer episodes. He became less involved in the show. His name dropped down the call sheet from number one to . . . whatever.

He was creating a new life for himself—one that didn't include me. I get it now. My family's allegiance was with Auntie Lynn and the kids, so my relationship with Mike began to dissolve. No explanation. No discussion. No acknowledgment that I might be feeling confused, betrayed, and abandoned. To me, it was like a death but without the grief, since I'd never been allowed to experience that.

I wasn't supposed to feel anything because he wasn't my father, because it wasn't my family, because if you asked my mother, my life was charmed and perfect. I was on a hit TV show, met amazing people, and acted in movies during my time off. What complaints could I have?

Amid that upheaval, Harold suffered a brain hemorrhage. He collapsed one day in his bathroom and was rushed by paramedics to the hospital. My mother was a wreck. Brain trauma is very unpredictable, and Harold developed various issues that kept him hospitalized for quite a while. I resented being dragged to the hospital to see Harold when I knew it was mostly to impress the nurses who would give him better care if they knew he was related to a celebrity. But I didn't say a word. *Why start now?* I thought.

Look, I understood. My grandmother still lets people know her relationship to me and my sister if it means getting her air-conditioning unit fixed faster. But I didn't have any emotional investment in Harold other than he was my sister's father and I didn't want her to go through the same kind of pain I did when I lost my dad. At one point, Harold pulled out a shunt that doctors had implanted to drain fluid from his brain. He also went through a phase where he was combative and pulled out tubes from his arm.

Through all of this, he maintained the one thing about him that I did admire: his humor. One day a priest came in and asked if he wanted any counseling. Harold said no, but he introduced his doctor, who happened to be in the room, to the priest as "Dr. Antichrist." He was also delusional due to his condition, but we never knew when he was joking or when he was hallucinating. On his way to the operating room for a procedure, he told my mother not to worry because she owned the Rams. (This was back when L.A. still had a football team.) The ordeal, quite unexpectedly, inspired me to want to become a doctor. I felt comfortable in the hospital and fascinated by what went on there.

When Harold finally came home he seemed pretty much back to normal. He did, however, get hepatitis from a blood transfusion. All of us had to get a gamma globulin shot, which pissed me off because I wasn't fond of needles, and the fact that I had to get a shot because of him made me even madder.

That's awful to admit. Horrible, in fact. But it's true. This was around the time I told the press "I had my crying moments" over Harold, which was a lie. As I said, I didn't want Sara or my mom to suffer, but beyond that I really didn't care.

Did that make me cold? No, it made me brutally pragmatic, like a female Holden Caulfield, someone who woke up one morning and found that nothing in her life fit the way it used to. It was as if Mike's divorce and Harold's brush with death pushed me outside my old comfort zone and into a new place where I thought about myself a lot, if not all the time, which filled me with anxiety and confusion.

None of that showed on *Little House*, which was experiencing its own growing pains. As it moved toward the end of its seventh season, Ma was going through menopause, Laura announced she was pregnant (I jokingly thought of myself as the first pregnant virgin since the Virgin Mary), and we added two babies to the cast. Off camera, Mike was emotionally done and preparing to exit the show; at season's end, Melissa Sue also decided to leave and pursue a feature film career. At Sunday dinner the week of her announcement, my grandfather said, "What a moron this is! Who leaves a hit show?"

Not me, that's for sure. I had a career beyond *Little House*. In fact, Uncle Ray and my mother had already lined up a remake of *Splendor in the Grass* for my summer break. All I craved was to be cool and have a boyfriend. Despite my efforts, both seemed hopelessly out of reach—even when I took Scott Baio, by that time a good friend, to the homecoming dance my junior year. I thought he'd give me a modicum of cool; everyone would see Chachi and want to talk to us. But no one came near us. At my twentieth high school reunion, I found out that none of the boys asked me out because they figured I was dating movie stars, like Scott.

What was wrong with me? So much, as far as I was concerned. When I looked in the mirror, I saw a girl with squinty eyes, a chunky body, no boobs, thin lips, a big, fat nose, ugly yellow teeth, and unhip hair (I wasn't allowed to cut it, ever). I tried to improve the picture with makeup, but I wore too much and I looked like a drag queen.

Adolescence is torturous at best. For a repressed, dorky child star it is a living hell. I had no idea who I was, or what I was doing or feeling. I just knew that I was overwhelmed and ugly and unlovable. My mother described me as young for my age. "She's not what you'd call streetwise," she once told a reporter. Ya think? My days were fully scheduled. I was sheltered, overprotected, and rarely alone. In some ways, I was like the princess in the tower looking out the window and wondering what was going on out in the world. I craved information and wanted to be around people who were more open and honest, and spoke about things other than what "nice girls" would do.

I started to spend more time with my godparents, Mitzi and Charlie, and their daughter, Jennifer. Their house was funkier than mine, their friends were edgier, and things were looser, wackier, and louder there. Uncle Charlie drank and smoked grass, and he was open about it. Unlike the people in my house, they kept few things hidden. One time, Mitzi and Jenny got into a fistfight on the floor right in front of me. They would tell each other to fuck off, call each other names, and have screaming arguments. Five minutes later, they'd be kissing and hugging each other. They were like Eugene O'Neill rewritten by Neil Simon. I thought they were fantastic. I still do.

I also gravitated toward Uncle Ray's associate Alan David and his wife, Bunny. They were barely ten years older than me, very hip, and on the cutting edge of Hollywood, as typified by their modern-style, glass-and-steel home in the Encino hills. They actually lived near my house, but I may as well have been light-years away.

From their house to their lifestyle, they had a contemporary edge that drew me in. Alan was plugged into everything in town, and Bunny was effortlessly funky and elegant. Professional stylists got paid huge money to produce for magazines a look she was able to put together by herself. At their house, we listened to the Rolling Stones and the Who, as did Mitzi and Charlie (he liked Cream, too), but Alan and Bunny were also into the Cars, Elvis Costello, and other New Wave groups. I needed major help graduating from Barry Manilow, and they knew what was cool.

I didn't tell my mom or Uncle Ray about anything we did or said there, not that I did anything that had to be kept secret. But Alan and Bunny smoked and drank and talked about doing drugs and sex with even more openness than at my godparents' house. It was exciting and liberating to be around them and occasionally ask a question containing a word or words I wouldn't use at home.

At my house, no one talked about LSD. Bunny and Alan told me that when she got pregnant with their son Ari, Alan said, "What if what they say about acid is true? We might as well just go ahead and name this kid Bambi." Just that snippet of conversation blew me away. It referenced two of the biggest taboos in my world, sex and drugs—and not just drugs, which typically meant smoking pot, but acid. Through the combination of my mother and school, I'd been brainwashed into believing two things: (1) Charles Manson–like killers lurked in every canyon in L.A., and (2) doing acid or LSD would turn you into a vegetable. It was to your brain what salt is to a slug: instant fizzle.

Apparently, that wasn't true; at least the part about acid wasn't. According to what I picked up from Alan and Bunny, you could take LSD, not wake up with the IQ of a zucchini, have a pretty wild time in bed, and lead a normal life, too!

They realized I was a good girl struggling with normal issues. I think they saw that I felt things I couldn't articulate, that I was at that point in adolescence when a little voice inside me was about to whisper in my ear, "Get ready, we're going to go a little faster now. We're going to try a few new things. And, uh, your mother doesn't have to know." They used to tell me not to worry because I was going to turn into a whole different creature when I had my first serious relationship. Years later, in fact, they told me that one night they were having dinner when Alan made a bold but prescient prediction. He said, "Everything's going to change the first time that girl has sex." Bunny agreed.

They were right, too.

ten

ONCE, TWICE, THREE TIMES
A WOMAN

To prepare for *Splendor in the Grass*, I went back to Jeff Corey and had even more uncomfortable conversations about sexuality. If I had been older, wiser, and mouthier, I would have asked Uncle Ray and my mother why we were remaking a movie whose 1961 original starring Warren Beatty and Natalie Wood was nearly perfect. But there was a lot of excitement around the idea of letting Hollywood see me in a new light in this sexually charged story of two young people in pre–Depression era Kansas, whose attraction to each other was thwarted by the day's conservative mores and their small town's class divides.

So I had to talk to Jeff about falling in love and what sex was like, things I didn't know anything about and had no desire to discuss with an older man who looked like a skinny version of Santa Claus in Birkenstocks. When he asked if I knew what it was like to feel a strong attraction to a boy, I said no and tried not to openly cringe.

"Haven't you ever had any crushes?" he asked.

"Those, yeah," I said, shrugging uncomfortably.

"And you've felt butterflies in your stomach?"

"I guess."

"Well, just imagine what it's like to feel butterflies in your entire body," he said.

Then we talked—actually, he talked and I listened—about attraction, sexuality, and desire. I did my best not to freak out when he explained the difference between desire for another person and downright *hunger* for them. I feared he might ask me a question or that I would get way more information than I wanted, and I didn't know how I was going to manage if he took it any further.

I can appreciate the information Jeff was trying to convey. Relationships, and their sexual undercurrents, are at the heart of almost every performance a young adult and adult actor gives. I just wasn't ready to go there so openly.

Making it stranger was the process I went through simultaneously with wardrobe and makeup to get ready for the role. It wasn't enough for me to play Deanie; I also had to look like a ripe young woman, apparently riper than I was in real life. They literally rebuilt me for the movie, emphasis on *built*. In addition to new hair, makeup, and fingernails, they gave me visibly more pronounced curves with a girdle and a corset, and a sumptuously padded bra and painted-on cleavage.

I wore a padded bra on *Little House* because I didn't have any boobs to speak of, and once you were a woman on that show, you couldn't be smaller than a B cup. But the effect on *Splendor* was entirely different. I didn't know what to make of myself when I looked in the mirror. I wanted to say, "Good Lord, that's not me, it's like some creepy drag-queen version of me . . . help! Get me outta here!" However, as I began to assimilate the new exterior, my insides were beginning to change as well. Indeed, another side to the wholesome, tentative little girl began to emerge. Not coincidentally, Uncle Ray scheduled Douglas Kirkland to shoot my first true glamour photo session at this time. When my mother said, "Make the camera fall in love with you," my head was filled with a new set of thoughts. The shots came out great. Maybe a little oversexualized for a girl of seventeen, but pretty nonetheless; maybe I had to jump way beyond my-self in order to pull back to who I really was at that time.

Throughout this process, director Richard Sarafian and the net-work executives overseeing the production were casting for the young man to play Bud Stamper, the handsome object of my desire. Need-less to say, I was intrigued and, for the first time, involved in the deci-sion-making process.

The choice came down to two actors, and I had to do a screen test with both. I found out they were in their early twenties; one was blond and the other had dark hair. For the screen test, the director chose the "down on your knees before me, slave woman" scene, probably the most incendiary and sexually layered scene in the whole picture. I was convinced Richard picked it to test me as much as the guys.

In the scene, Bud grabs Deanie by the wrists and makes her kneel in front of him, her face to his crotch, and says, "Down on your knees before me, slave woman. Tell me you'd do anything for me."

She bursts out crying.

"I'd do anything for you," she says. "I don't want to hurt you. I'm sorry it has to be this way."

I was scared and uptight doing the scene with the blond actor, Michael, who went first. It was easy for me to break down and cry as he pushed me to the floor because the whole thing scared me. I knew what was being implied, but I didn't want to acknowledge it, and I didn't feel any chemistry with Michael. Then I did the scene again with dark-haired Cyril O'Reilly, and it was a completely different ex-perience.

I chalk it up to chemistry. From the moment I looked into Cyril's eyes, I was history. The wind was knocked out of the room. It was like the shot down the hallway in *Poltergeist*: dolly in/zoom out. I didn't feel threatened or intimidated by him at all. I felt completely safe. Maybe it was because he had my father's coloring. Maybe it was because he drank and smoked and the smell of alcohol and cigarettes had been programmed into my brain as good, familiar, and manly after seven years of being hugged by Mike. One thing I do know: it didn't hurt that he was absolutely gorgeous.

I was thrilled when Cyril got the job. Our first rehearsal was in an empty office in Uncle Ray's building. Richard Sarafian, Cyril, and I sat around a table and prepared to read through the script. It was a rare occasion when I was left alone with coworkers without a guardian, my mother, or Uncle Ray nearby. After a few minutes of friendly chitchat, Dick Sarafian said, "Okay, let's get down to business."

Cyril closed his script and looked at both of us.

"Before we do this," he said, "can we get something out of the way?"

"Huh?" I said.

"I've got to do this one thing so it's not hanging over us," he said. "Just so it's done."

"Sure," Dick said.

"I guess," I said.

Suddenly he leaned in and kissed me. I'm talking a real, mature, deep kiss. Then he sat back and stared into my eyes, looking for a reaction. Cyril seemed pleased. He said, "There. Now we don't have to do that for the first time again." Flushed and flustered, I said something like, "Well, then, there it is."

Had I been able to keep my wits about me, I might've asked him to try it again. But my head was spinning in a pleasurable daze the likes of which I'd never experienced. I felt that kiss somewhere deep in my abdomen and from there it spread warm and glowing out past the tips of my fingers and the ends of my toes and through and out each strand of my hair. It was like liquid electricity. That was it. Cyril had closed the sale before I even knew I was in the market for anything. All I knew was that I wanted more of whatever that was.

Shooting the movie was an extraordinary experience for me. There was the love story on-screen, and then there was the even better real-life romance that developed away from the camera. I fell in love for the first time. Cyril would come over to my house after work to rehearse and there was a lot of making out when my mother wasn't checking on us, and there was much more intense kissing in the trailer once we began production.

To replicate the look of 1920s Kansas, we shot in older neighborhoods in Altadena and Pasadena. We had fun learning to drive vintage cars. I was the youngest among the ridiculously talented cast that included Eva Marie Saint, Ned Beatty, and Michelle Pfeiffer, who was a new young actress generating incredible buzz within the industry. She had recently married actor Peter Horton and didn't want to work, but the producers wanted her to play Bud's older sister, which was such a terrific role that Michelle agreed to do it.

She came in and was mind-bogglingly beautiful and sexy sexy sexy in a really quiet, earthy way. We had one scene together, the New Year's Eve scene when she is gang-raped in a car and takes off. It's a pivotal moment for Deanie, who, in her desperation and pain, later tries to take on a bunch of dudes in a car and ends up trying to kill herself. I was entranced as I watched her work. She was grounded, centered, and focused. She clearly had a process, which fascinated me, as I didn't yet have one.

One day early in the production, my mother pointed to Ally Sheedy, who was making her film debut as one of Deanie's two close friends. She complimented her looks and predicted Ally would be a big star someday.

"I can just feel it," she said. "I can see something special in her."

I remember cocking my head toward her, feeling slightly jealous that she would say that about someone other than me. She was right, of course.

I was just glad she wasn't peppering me with questions about my relationship with Cyril. I spent all my private time after rehearsals and before I was needed in front of the camera with him, talking, sharing secrets, and of course, making out. The movie's crew was for the most part from *Little House*, so it must have freaked them out to see me, their little Half Pint, following this guy around the set like a puppy. Making out with him on camera, though, was awkward for me.

He would whisper in my ear, "Relax. Relax. It's okay." And I'd say, "They know that we do this in private."

"No, they don't," he insisted. "They really don't."

But they must have.

Bizarrely, much of the time I was with Cyril, talking or making out, I was dressed in the Deanie garb. My butt was girdled and my boobs were padded. My face was made up and my fingernails were acrylic and I was wearing a hair piece. On the outside, I was totally artificial. I was the best Hollywood could create, painted-on cleavage and all. Yet none of that stuff mattered to Cyril. What was underneath was exactly what he wanted—the real me.

Though he never commented directly, Cyril looked past the shading, highlighting, and padding; he got past all of that figuratively and literally. By my seventeenth birthday, which I celebrated on the set, we were on the edge of going all the way. We would get right up to it and then one of us would go "no, no, no." It was usually Cyril who would stop and say, "You're not ready. You don't have to do this."

He read me correctly. He really was a hell of a guy. After growing up slowly, I felt like the pedal was suddenly pressed against the metal and I was hanging on tightly to prevent myself from crashing. I wanted to go all the way, but then I would get scared and convince myself I wasn't ready to add that milestone to my life. My brain and body were at war. I would push Cyril, then back off, and then push again. It was like a dance, a very frustrating dance, one we did in my trailer, in his trailer, or at my house.

Since he lived in Hollywood and I wasn't allowed to drive that far by myself or alone at night, he would usually come to my house. He would show up on the doorstep smoking a cigarette and my mother would turn to me with a disapproving look and say, "It's just gross to walk up to someone's house with a cigarette."

Oh, and he would usually have a beer, which was something else my mother would comment on. Don't get me wrong, it wasn't that she didn't like him. It was more her way of talking around actual concerns. Cyril and I would sit outside and talk while he drank his beer and smoked his cigarette, and then at opportune moments when no one was looking we would make out wildly and go through our yes-no-maybe-not-yet dance.

We spent the last week of production shooting at High Falls State Park in Forsyth, Georgia. My mother accompanied me to this small southern town that was no more than five miles from the "Welcome" sign to the next town. The film's cast and crew took over the local Best Western, where my mother and I had adjoining rooms. A wrap party was scheduled for the last day of production, and after shooting the last scene, everybody went back to the hotel to shower and change.

Somehow I managed to get Cyril into my room without my mother's knowledge. I was determined that this was going to be the moment when it all happened, when I changed. I knew this was a monumental time in any girl's life. It really is a moment when we first try on our woman shoes, which is especially challenging and scary when the whole world wants you to stay a child! Once again I relied on that voice inside me, the one that pushes me to move forward even if I'm terrified. Particularly if I'm terrified.

I knew it was a momentous occasion. Not an ounce of magnitude was lost on me. I was scared it was going to hurt. I was scared of not knowing how to do it. I was scared of all the things that could be horribly wrong with doing it, including the possibility I could end up pregnant. I was scared that if I did go all the way, Cyril wouldn't want to see me anymore because nice girls didn't do it. I was scared I couldn't be Half Pint anymore. I was scared my mother would disown me if she found out. I was scared I'd be thought of as a skank.

I was scared of so many things, and yet when push came to

shove, the voice in my head took over and said, *Look, at some point you're going to do it. You love this man, he clearly loves you. Sooner or later it's got to happen.*

Well, it turned out to be sooner. Cyril couldn't have been sweeter, nicer, kinder, or gentler. It wasn't scary, and it wasn't awful. In fact, it was actually very sweet and very tender, exactly the kind of experience I would highly recommend to any young woman. God bless Cyril O'Reilly and his dear, gentle heart.

Afterward Cyril snuck out and went to his room. We arrived separately at the wrap party, where we had an even more exciting time stealing glances at each other from across the room as we talked to people, knowing we had done this incredible thing and nobody else knew. It was the sweetest secret, and just a wee bit dangerous.

We flew home the next day, sitting next to each other on the plane. As we snuggled up against each other, I started to sing a Lionel Richie song, which was very uncharacteristic of me. But the words just floated out: *Thanks for the times that you've given me. The memories are all in my mind.* (It's "Three Times a Lady," but the verses were more important than the chorus here!) I sang it into Cyril's ear from beginning to end. It was a whisper sort of singing. Soft, warm, and just for him. It made him cry. I wiped tears from my eyes, too.

I think both of us felt strongly for each other. We had shared a great deal of intimacy but we also knew we weren't going to stay together. (Someone else knew, too. Years later, Cyril told me that my mother had made it clear to him that he was not going to get anywhere near me once the film was completed.) It was a beginning and an end all at the same time.

After returning to L.A., Cyril and I saw each other a few times and we talked regularly on the phone. But I could feel us drifting into our separate lives. I was a high school senior, and he was already a man. That was real life.

I had sent for applications to Harvard, Northwestern, and USC. I couldn't decide between a career as a brain surgeon or an obstetrician, though whenever I thought seriously about heading off to college the next year, I heard my grandfather's voice chime, "Who leaves a hit show? You have to be a moron to leave a hit show."

I didn't know for sure what I was going to do until early June, when I was scheduled to take the SAT. On the morning of the four-hour test, I grabbed my No. 2 pencils, said good-bye to my mother, and drove to Cyril's apartment. We made love until the afternoon. Then I drove home, looked my mother right in the eye, and said, "The test went great."

That sealed a new kind of deal. Such deceit and rebellion were brand-new to my repertoire. Sitting here as a parent now, I'm cringing! So many things could've happened on my way to Cyril's. I could've had a flat tire or gotten in an accident. I could've lost my way. I could've been murdered; after all, I was terrified of driving through Laurel Canyon, since for years my mother had drummed into my head that its twisty streets were filled with monsters like Charles Manson and the Hillside Strangler.

But the lure of a booty call proved stronger than all those potential mishaps and fears. And that's just what it was, a booty call. Both Cyril and I knew it, and knew we were at the end of the line for no reason other than we were living two completely different lives. The veneer of our romance had worn off and it was simply time for us to move on. The decision was a mature one, but that didn't make it painless. In fact it hurt like hell. I had a burning sensation in the middle of my chest. (About a year later, well into my relationship with Rob, we would name that feeling. We called it "the Sharp.")

That itself was a lesson. I learned love could be as painful, hard, or perplexing as it was wonderful and intoxicating. As with everything, the rewards didn't come without risks. For me, talking about it with friends helped get me through the weirdness and withdrawal of no longer receiving the love and adoration that had been pouring over me the last few months. I told my ice skating friend Beth that I'd lost my virginity, and after that went well, I told my *Little House* set guardian Julie and her sister Katie (I think their mother knew, too), and I told Bunny, who passed the news along to Alan.

I also told Brooke Shields. We weren't exactly close friends, but our paths did cross pretty regularly. (There's an unspoken bond among former child actors. Even if the experience of being a working kid wasn't hellacious, there's still a sense of having been in the trenches together.) So, there we were at a celebrity ski event in Sun Valley, Idaho, a few months after Cyril and I had ended things, talking about boys, when I dropped the bomb. I said, "I've done it." Brooke put the brakes on whatever she had been about to say and her whole face seemed to shape itself into a big, shocked oval. She pulled me closer to find out what I knew that she didn't.

"What was it like?" she asked.

"Not a big deal," I said, though my nonchalance didn't ring true with me and I corrected myself a moment later. "To tell you the truth, it was very romantic."

"Really?"

"Yes," I said. "It was."

We were silent for a little bit.

"Where'd you do it?" she asked.

"In my motel room. In Forsyth, Georgia."

"Are you still together?"

I shook my head no.

"Really?" she asked.

I smiled, thinking back on those few months, which had already assumed a dreamlike status in my brain.

"I think in my heart of hearts I saw Cyril and it was kind of a Romeo and Juliet thing," I said. "You know, raised by the Capulets and the Montagues and never the twain shall meet." I thought of how romantic that sounded, and then added, "It was doomed from the start. But it was so good for me." Ah, ever the little drama queen, wasn't I?

Though I didn't intend it to be public knowledge on the *Little House* set, the effect on me was noticeable when the show regrouped for production of its eighth season. In an interview, Dean, who had to have heard gossip from someone on the crew, said something along the lines of "I don't know what happened to Melissa over the hiatus, but she sure is different."

I didn't think so, but maybe it was true. At any rate, my life would shortly become *very* different.

eleven ───────────────────────────────

MEET CUTE

Given L.A.'s immense size, you would think the odds of falling in love with the person in the car stopped next to you at a red light would be next to impossible. Except that drivers in L.A., when not talking on their cell phones, drinking coffee, putting on makeup, reading, or doing all of the above, are also checking one another out, as if the freeways are a singles bar, which raises the odds slightly.

I should know. It happened to me.

It was a beautiful day late in the summer of 1981, and I was on my way to pick out a dress to wear to an upcoming black-tie gala. I'd left MGM after work and my friend Katie Daley was with me in my car. I turned up La Cienega Boulevard, one of the city's main north-south arteries. I was complaining to Katie about my makeup, which I hadn't had time to wash off. Because Mike was always tanned, the makeup artists made the rest of us a few shades darker. My makeup was called Natural Tan, but it looked orange, and I used to call myself Pumpkin Face. I hated it. In truth I looked more like an Oompa-Loompa.

Katie cracked a joke about my sunglasses. I didn't do much reading those days, since reading was my job and I found nothing about it relaxing, but I read *Lolita*. Several times. Mercy me, did Mr. Nabokov churn my imagination. My shades were large, red, and heart-shaped. I called them my Lolita sunglasses. There we were, laughing about that and my clashing orange skin, as I came to a red light. After stopping, I looked over at the car next to me and saw this absolutely gorgeous guy. Ordinarily I would have turned away after a quick glance. After all, I'd been trained by my mother not to make eye contact with anyone lest he turn out to be a serial killer.

But I thought I knew this guy, so I continued to stare at his profile, trying to come up with his name and how I knew him. My synapses were crackling as I tried to place him when he turned and looked at me straight on. It was Rob Lowe. I immediately blurted out his name—"Rob!"—and said hi. Except that he couldn't hear me. He motioned for me to roll down my window.

"What are you doing?" he asked.

"I'm on my way to buy a dress for whatever the hell thing I'm supposed to go to next week," I said. "I just finished work. What are you doing?"

"I'm going to an audition," he said.

"Well, I'm going to be at Holly's Harp looking at dresses," I said. "Meet me there when you finish your audition."

He said okay, and I told him where the boutique was located on Sunset Plaza. I went directly there and tried on dresses, purposely taking longer than was necessary in the hope that Rob would show up. I kept telling Katie how gorgeous I thought he was, and when I wasn't telling her, I was asking her to validate my opinion.

"Don't you think he's so good-looking he's almost beautiful?"

Of course she did. Who wouldn't?

When Rob didn't show after nearly two hours, I was disappointed. I wrote down my phone number and asked the women helping me to be on the lookout for a very handsome young man who might come in and ask for me.

"Please tell him to call me," I said.

I waited anxiously the rest of that day and night for him to call. He didn't. Nor did he call the next day or the next. I had given up. Then, several days later, the phone in my room rang and it was Rob.

We had a fun, easy conversation and he asked me out on a date. I said yes, and I don't remember a thing after that. Not where we went or what we did. All I remember is that I felt like I got hit on the head with a brick. I fell instantly, hopelessly, and stupidly in love.

I wasn't expecting it. Between Cyril and Rob, I had dated a few boys, including Tom Cruise, who I met at an event he'd attended with Emilio Estevez. We went on a couple of dates and made out in my mom's living room. He was nice, funny, and sweet. But it wasn't like being hit with an arrow.

From the moment Rob and I went out, I never wanted to be away from his side. We went from first date to instant couple—just add water. Almost overnight everything was suddenly all Rob or all Rob and Melissa. I thought my feelings for Cyril had been intense, but this was crazy. I remembered my acting teacher Jeff Corey describing love as a hunger throughout your entire body. He was right. I felt like I was starving for Rob. I wanted to bite him. He felt the same way about me. He wrote me poetry. He left notes. He cooed the sweetest messages into my answering machine.

Rob lived with his family north of Malibu on Point Dume and still attended Santa Monica High School. Since I was out of school and not that busy on *Little House,* I would meet him there for lunch and hang out with his friends. At night, he came to my house and we ate dinner, watched TV, and talked for hours.

In November, by now a couple months into our relationship, Rob and I were still having intensely personal conversations and quivering inside with excitement and desire as we showed each other parts of ourselves that no one had ever seen before. One day I told him that I wasn't a virgin. I wanted him to know everything about me. I didn't want there to be any secrets. I also wanted him to know that while I was no expert in the ways of lovemaking, I was game.

The following weekend he came over for dinner. After my mother, now separated from Harold (there's no story; one day she simply said, "Harold and I are getting a divorce"), and my brother and sister were safely asleep, Rob and I moved into the family room to watch *Saturday Night Live*. Bernadette Peters was the host and Billy Joel and the Go-Go's were the musical guests. As Billy Joel finished his song "She's Got a Way," Rob looked at me and said, "That's how I feel about you. That song. That's exactly it."

I melted, and with *Saturday Night Live* playing in the background, we made love for the first time on the sofa in my mother's family room. It was sublime. We connected on a level that I'd never experienced before. He was sweet and intense. He wouldn't let me close my eyes. He made me look right into his eyes the whole time. It was profound. Beyond sex, it was free and honest and vulnerable and it was ours.

We were like that in every way. We had our own special words, our own signals, and our own secrets, especially after that night. Above all else, the physical attraction between us was palpable, almost intrusive. People would get between us, see the way we looked at each other, like two sides of a vise closing in on them, and you could see them think, *Uh-oh, watching the two of you hurts the back of my head. It's painful. I have to get away from this.*

At seventeen, we were still babies and learning how to handle that highly combustible combination of serious feelings, unbridled passion, and raging hormones. I started to climb out of my bedroom window at night and drive up to Point Dume. After several trips, we decided it was too dangerous for me to make that trip by myself at night. Too many things could go wrong.

Rob worried about my safety on the roads. I worried about my mother catching me. Having experienced her anger and the punishment that sometimes ensued, I didn't want to risk it. My biggest fear was that she would catch me doing something and forbid me to see Rob. I didn't know what I would do in that case.

So we devised a system where Rob would come for dinner pretty much every night. Then he would say good night, I'd walk him to the front door, and he would back out of the driveway and park down the street, where he would sit in his car for thirty or forty minutes. I would excuse myself to go to my room and watch TV in bed. In the meantime, I would be listening for a rustling outside my window.

It would be Rob climbing up the ivy-covered wall outside the house. He would hop our fence, come around to my side of the house, shimmy up the wall, and finally climb through the window into my room. It was sneaky and forbidden and delicious. No one ever really came to my room after I said good night, but the few times my mom did knock on my door, Rob scrambled into the bathroom or the closet. Otherwise he spent the night without anyone ever knowing he was in my bed.

Or so we thought.

About six months into this routine, my mother went out of town with friends and left my grandmother in charge of Jonathan, Sara, and me. That first night Rob—or Robbie, as my grandma called him—came over for dinner. Following dessert and some TV, he got up to leave. I walked him to the front door. My grandmother trailed behind us. At the door, Rob turned around and said, "Well, I guess I'll see you soon."

"Bye," I said. "Talk to you tomorrow."

Suddenly my grandmother took hold of Robbie's shirt, stopping him from going any farther.

"Robbie, don't be silly," she said. "I know you're just going to drive down the driveway, park your car, and climb in Melissa's window. You should stay here."

"Really?" I said, shocked.

My grandmother nodded.

"I like the idea of having a man in the house," she said. Looking at me, she added, "And so do you."

Rob stepped back inside, shut the door, and put his arm around me. I put my arm around my incredibly cool grandma.

"Just none of you tell Barbara," she said. I thought, *How cool is this?* My grandmother had basically just given me *permission* to have sex.

• • •

On the *Little House* set at MGM, it was easy for me to feel like things on the show were no different than they had been when we began. But there were changes. The beloved Walnut Grove of the Ingalls and Wilders, which had survived floods and tornados and other disasters, was facing its biggest challenge ever from NBC executives, who were mulling the previously unimaginable: cancellation.

Although melodrama was still the core element, story lines in the eighth season strayed from the biblical struggles of Charles Ingalls and his family, causing ratings to slip. They brought in new kids because the rest of us had grown up, and they tried to create a new family around Ma and Pa with James, Cassandra, and Albert. They also brought in a new Nellie—Nancy—to create tension with the kids. But people had always tuned in to see Laura, Mary, and the original Nellie, and we just weren't there like before.

Most of that was unavoidable. While some, like Melissa Sue, had left the show, the rest of us had grown up, especially me.

Rob entered the prairie picture. He visited frequently, and Mike and others let me know they approved of him. He came to the Simi Valley set (which he dubbed Screaming Valley) often, and was there when we shot the epic two-parter "Days of Sunshine, Days of Shadow." In terms of ratings, it was that season's savior. Viewers were riveted as Laura and Almanzo faced a tidal wave of disasters, maladies, and mishaps, a juggernaut of doom and gloom not seen since Noah said "We're gonna need a bigger boat." Consider: Almanzo had diphtheria, our first crop was destroyed by hail, and Almanzo had a stroke and suffered partial paralysis; then Laura gave birth, a tornado destroyed the house, and Almanzo got terribly depressed until Pa arrived and slapped him back to reality, when he realized he had to be a man and rebuild our house and our lives. As we shot those episodes, Rob joked they should be retitled "Get Doc Baker!"

I contended that episode was when the show jumped the shark, but I have since learned that all those things did actually happen to

Laura and Almanzo. Except we made it seem like it all happened in a matter of two weeks. Mike, who was finalizing the financial part of his divorce with Auntie Lynn and was about to find out his new wife, Cindy, was pregnant, wrote a season finale befitting a man who often appeared not only like he carried the world on his shoulders but like he could save it. Another two-parter, it began with James, Pa's adopted son, played by thirteen-year-old Jason Bateman, getting shot during a robbery and Pa, Mr. Edwards, and Albert tracking down the criminals.

In part two, James was in a coma and everyone thought he was going to die—everyone except for Charles. Refusing to give up hope, he took his adopted son to the top of a mountain, built a temple, and prayed for a miracle. At the end, there was a huge explosion as a bolt of lightning struck nearby, waking James and returning him to life. By this time, Mike had made up his mind he wasn't going to be back the following season. He literally left *Little House* with a bang . . . a really bad computer-generated bang.

For the first time in three years, I didn't have a movie lined up during the show's hiatus. But I was still just as busy. Somehow, through my mother, I got hooked up in early 1982 with First Lady Nancy Reagan, who was launching her Just Say No drug awareness campaign. I was named the youth spokesperson for her ACTION Drug Prevention Program and I traveled across the country with Mrs. Reagan, speaking to groups about the evils of drug use.

Prior to our first appearance, her people gave me an intensive tutorial on the subject, which scared the shit out of me, and then invited me to meet the first lady at the White House in February. On the way to Washington, D.C., my mother and I stopped in New York, where I participated in Night of 100 Stars, a benefit for the Actors Fund of America. The gala took place at Carnegie Hall and assembled a once-in-a-lifetime group of famous actors, athletes, and artists.

At one point during the taping of the show, my mother and I stepped into an elevator with Grace Kelly and Gregory Peck. My mom was paralyzed. Gregory Peck was her example of the perfect man: gorgeous, dashing, tall. And Princess Grace, well, she was the woman my mother, and consequently I, wanted to be. After a moment, Princess Grace turned to me and said, "Hi, Melissa. Remember me? I'm Stephanie's mother." My mother nearly passed out. She'd forgotten that on one of our Hawaiian vacations a few years earlier, I had spotted Princess Stephanie sitting on the beach amid her security and looking bored. I approached her as I would have any kid ("Hi, I'm Melissa") and asked if she wanted to play ding-dong ditch with us. She did, and we had a fun time. (Princess Stephanie would come to play a role in my life later on. What is that famous line? "All past is prologue.")

"Hi," I replied to Princess Grace.

"Isn't this fun?" she asked.

"It is," I said.

And it truly was. In addition to star-studded elevator rides, there were dressing rooms overflowing with celebrities, including Bette Davis, Olivia de Havilland, Sidney Poitier, Dustin Hoffman, Laurence Olivier, Whoopi Goldberg, Dinah Shore, Joe DiMaggio, Hank Aaron, Donnie Osmond, Raquel Welch, Barbara Walters, Rosa Parks, Dr. Christiaan Barnard, Rock Hudson, Jim Henson, Orson Welles, Cher, and Dr. Seuss.

At one point during rehearsals, all hundred stars were directed to particular spots on bleachers for the big finale, and in a rare moment of silence, Bette Davis cracked, "If a bomb goes off in this building, Charlene Tilton is going to be the biggest star in Hollywood."

Brooke Shields collected autographs. On the day we shot the show, I ran around with her. We met Lena Horne, and Brooke dragged me along as she asked Diane Keaton and Warren Beatty for their signatures. As a result, Warren sort of locked onto me and we talked for a bit as Brooke bopped around getting more autographs.

Then she caught up with me and gasped, "Oh my God! You aren't going to believe it."

"What?" I asked.

"Can't tell you here," she said, motioning for me to keep walking.

"What?" I asked again a few steps later.

"Warren Beatty was looking at your butt," she said.

"No way," I said.

"Yes, I swear," she said. "I saw him."

My mother had me dressed in a skin-colored, ruched column Halston gown. My hair was huge. My makeup was crazy. I had a gold-snake arm bracelet. It was a pretty progressive look for a seventeen-year-old. I remembered Warren asking how old I was. After I said seventeen, he asked when I was turning eighteen. "Hmmmmmmm . . ." And that was the end of the conversation. I walked away, and a few moments later, Brooke told me the backstory.

The next day, as my mom and I got ready to leave the hotel and catch our train to D.C., the phone rang. I heard my mother in the other room say, "Hello, yes, it is," and then ask, "Who's calling, please?" There was a pause, and then I heard her say, "Yeah, right, and I'm the queen of England. Who is this?" After another pause, she said, "No, really, who is this?"

I listened from the other room. I was both fascinated and intrigued. Then she called me into the room. She put her hand over the receiver and said, "Warren Beatty is on the phone for you."

"Really?" I said.

"No," she said, shaking her head.

"He's not?" I asked.

"He is," she said. "But I want you to say no. Whatever he asks you, no matter what it is, you're going to say no."

I knew damn well who Warren Beatty was. I'd watched him in *Splendor in the Grass*, obviously. I'd marveled at him in *Reds*, which I considered a masterpiece. I'd drooled over him in *Shampoo* and *Heaven Can Wait*; hell, I'd spoken to him the night before. He was gorgeous, brilliant, and iconic. What was this business with no? I gave her a puzzled look.

Well, over the years, various people and members of the press had described my mother as determined, purposeful, strict, protective, and overprotective. And it was true. Every syllable was accurate. Suddenly, though, she took all of those qualities to a new level as she said, "You. Will. Say. No."

"What is it he's going to ask?"

"It doesn't matter," she said. "Whatever it is, it's no. No, no, no, no."

"Okay," I said, and took the receiver from my mother. "Hello?"

"Hi, it's Warren," he said. "What are you doing?"

"I'm getting ready to go to the White House," I said.

"Would you like to have lunch?" he asked.

"No, thank you," I said. "I can't. I'm going to the White House. I have a meeting with Mrs. Reagan."

"All right," he said. "Let me ask you one more question."

"Okay."

"When's your birthday?"

"May eighth."

With that, the conversation ended and I relayed everything to my mother, who asked, "Why did you tell him your birthday?"

"Because he asked," I said.

My mom sort of shook her head, and we headed to Washington. (Three months later, I would get a phone call from Warren, who sang "Happy Birthday," and we began a friendship that continues to this day.)

At the White House, we were escorted through an entrance off-limits to the public and taken to the private quarters into a room done in a yellow floral theme, where Mrs. Reagan soon joined us. Over tea and cookies, my mother and I talked with her about the program. We also talked about Hollywood and Los Angeles, where she and the president had lived.

I felt the mood in the room change as we talked. I wouldn't call it intimate, but it was less formal and more personal. Mrs. Reagan started to talk about her life at the White House and how she thought people had misjudged her, and she said it was not just unfair but hurtful.

My mother sympathized with her, noting Mrs. Reagan had been through so much since her husband had taken office, in the last eleven months in particular, since the assassination attempt on the president. Prompted by that comment, Mrs. Reagan started talking about the day her Ronnie was shot. As she shared details, she began to cry, which made me uncomfortable. Then her tears turned into a full-on sob and my mom scooted over on the couch and put her arms around her.

My head was spinning. A few hours earlier, Warren Beatty had asked me out to lunch, and now the first lady of the United States was weeping in my mother's arms. But it would get even weirder.

The official reception for ACTION was the next day. My mother and I stood in the reception line to meet Mrs. Reagan. I grew more excited the closer we got because of the special bond we now had with her. I watched people ahead of us shake her hand and get their picture taken with her.

Then I stepped up in my way-too-grannylike St. John knit suit, wearing way too much makeup—not quite drag queen level but close—and with my big hair. Mrs. Reagan said hello, and, while looking me in the eye, asked, "And you are?"

It stopped me halfway through my own hello. Just fourteen hours earlier, she had been crying in my mother's arms. Now she had no idea who we were. What was the deal? Had she been acting the previous day? But who would do that? And why? I'll never know.

Later, I assumed she was so overwhelmed by the number of people she met every day that she went on auto pilot, turning off everything but her smile, her handshake, and a scripted greeting. By the end of the tour, though, she no longer looked at me like a stranger. Able to recognize me through her thicket of handlers and Secret Service agents, she knew my name and complimented my increasingly strong and emphatic delivery to large groups of teenagers and their parents about the dangers of drug use.

Indeed, I got into the part of America's antidrug cheerleader. It was truly heartfelt. I had been tutored and taught about the evils of drug use virtually my entire life. The training I got from the White House was intense and I practiced what I preached. Never, ever, ever, ever would I do illicit drugs.

What is it they say about good intentions?

twelve

I'm Eighteen, and I Like It

Around the time Rob turned eighteen (for the next two months until my eighteenth birthday, we joked that having sex with me could get him twenty years in jail), word was circulating through Hollywood that Francis Ford Coppola's next project was a big-screen adaptation of S. E. Hinton's classic coming-of-age novel *The Outsiders*. Everybody, and I mean every young actor in town, all the young lap maidens and princes, auditioned for the movie. Some of us went on to screen-test, including my brother and me.

The buzz and chatter surrounding the project guaranteed it was going to start a new chapter in Hollywood's history, usher in a new generation. It was palpable. For many involved, it was the last time they themselves would ever be outsiders looking in on the star-making process. Afterward, they would be the stars, full-fledged insiders, and way too involved to ever look back with detachment.

Rob tested and was among those cast early; I was cut from the first group. While the cast was put together, Francis's costly musical *One from the Heart* came out. It starred Frederic Forrest, Teri Garr, Raul Julia, and Nastassja Kinski. Rob and I went to see it. As I recall, he was barely interested in the neon-lit sets of Las Vegas that bankrupted Francis or the marvelous soundtrack from Tom Waits and

Crystal Gayle that I still listen to today. He focused instead on Kinski. Several times, he remarked, "She's really something."

Call it a woman's instinct, but I was unable to find anything kind or desirable about her, and said so: "She's not *that* great. She has kind of a weird nose." If that wasn't the pot calling the kettle black! After the movie, he brought her up again. I let it slide. Later, I would regret not having paid closer attention.

In the meantime, the cast for *The Outsiders* was put together. It included Rob; Emilio Estevez, a friend from Santa Monica High School; Tom Cruise, whom we knew; Matt Dillon; C. Thomas Howell; Patrick Swayze; and Ralph Macchio. I bid Rob a tearful good-bye as he and the others embarked on a four-month shoot in Tulsa. He was excited; as far as I knew, all of them were. They had no idea what they were getting themselves into.

I was on the receiving end of Rob's many phone calls and letters, which started out mostly as complaints about the hardships on and off the set, though over time they changed into a sort of litany of triumphs, both personal and for the movie in general. *The Outsiders* told of the tensions and clashes between two groups of boys from different parts of a small town, the poor greasers and the rich kids known as the South Side Socs. Rob's account of behind-the-scenes drama was often as gripping as the movie.

From the time they arrived, Francis created tension among the actors playing the Socs and the greasers. The Socs were put up in a nice hotel and provided trailers with dressing rooms, while the others stayed in a place that was significantly more downscale and were made to change clothes in whatever public restroom was available. (Eventually, Gray Frederickson, one of the executive producers, put his foot down and screamed, "Francis, you fat-fuck pasta chef, these kids need dressing rooms!")

With this group, though, the hardships didn't preclude hijinks. There were many phone calls where Rob, Emilio, and Tom, as well as other cast configurations, shouted into the phone all at once or passed it back and forth, letting me know they had been drinking and carousing, as if I couldn't hear for myself. I also heard about the time they put bubble bath in the town's fountain, about what Leif Garrett did when he was wasted, and how Diane Lane desperately tried to keep her head above water as the sole female among all these lunatic guys.

It sounded like a blast, but I wasn't allowed to visit. As my mother explained, nice girls didn't travel alone.

In May, I celebrated my eighteenth birthday on the roof of Uncle Ray's building on the Sunset Strip. The party included a DJ, all my friends, and Rob's younger brother, Chad, who was like my own little brother. From location, Rob sent a couple dozen roses with a card that said, "To my legal baby."

I spread my wings by moving fourteen feet from the house into the guesthouse. That seemed like a big jump. I didn't realize the implications of turning eighteen for a child actor who had been earning a couple million dollars or more for at least the past four or five years. I didn't know I was responsible for my union membership or that I would receive my Coogan account, a percentage of the money I'd earned, which was considerable, that had been put away until I became an adult.

I had some inkling that I was financially well-off, that I could handle some stuff on my own. Magazines reported my salary at thirty thousand dollars per episode. Despite my ignorance of the business side of my career, I knew that over twenty-two episodes (a full season), that added up to a pretty good sum of money.

I'd only discussed money once with my mother. A few years earlier, I went to her and Harold as we were getting ready to go on our annual Easter trip to the Kahala, and I said, "Listen, I want to fly in first class with you guys." Even though I was one of the most recognizable actors on TV, I still flew in coach with the kids when we traveled. My mother and Harold flew in first class. I also said that I wanted my own room—and room service, like the other kids in the other families we'd be with.

"I'll pay for it myself," I said.

My mom gave me a bewildered look and said, "Of course. Whatever you want."

Occasionally Rob referred to me as "Franchise." It was one of the many pet names he had for me. I earned this one because I came with a complete package of people, everything a star needed: the manager, the business manager, the publicist, the mother, the manicurist, and the hairstylist. And they could be intrusive.

But they were an extension of me, part of the way I did business. The deal was simple: love me, love my team. Though Rob had never seen anything like it, he understood. My mother was team captain and coach. The two of us had our difficult moments, disagreements, and communication problems, but we were impossibly close. A clinician would have called us codependent. Someone else would have defined our relationship as unconditional love.

We had laughed our way through the Just Say No tour, and we would have won a gold medal if there'd been a competition for mother-daughter power shoppers. It had always been that way with us. I told her almost everything, certainly as much as she needed to know, and in turn I received a front-row seat to her one-woman effort to get the most out of life, whether she was guiding my career, Jonathan's, or Sara's, or chasing down another potential husband after she split from Harold.

Over the years, we had numerous discussions about the myriad rules she imposed or made up under the guise of my well-being. But until I turned eighteen, I never questioned her role in my career. Then one day, shortly after my birthday, she sat me down and said we needed to take care of some stuff. She was very matter-of-fact about it. She said, "We've always been partners in your career, and I think we should continue to be partners."

"Absolutely," I said without hesitation.

I was surprised by the statement. I had never considered any other arrangement. I took the yin and yang of our relationship in my professional life for granted.

"Absolutely," I said again. "Of course."

"Good, and now that you're eighteen, we need to make sure this is okay," she said. "I think it would be a good idea if we drew up papers and, you know, shared everything like partners, fifty-fifty."

Turning eighteen didn't mean I was more mature or smarter. It simply meant I was legally an adult. I could vote. And I had to take responsibility for my life. As for business, my mom was still my mom. She was still in charge, the oracle who guided me and who I turned to with questions. Beyond that, she was single, and she deserved to be taken care of. She had sacrificed a lot for me. As a result, we signed a contract, giving her half of everything I earned, including my Coogan account, till I turned twenty-five.

Though I didn't see anything wrong with it, Rob asked, "Are you sure you want to agree to that? I mean, are you really sure?"

"Yeah," I said. "I owe my mother everything."

I signed the papers and we were good. My mom and I were partners and I was in love and nothing else really mattered.

Actually, one thing was bugging me.

My nose.

Lord almighty, I hated my nose. When I was little, it was cute. But as I grew up, it grew wider and flatter and it had a little bump in it. And the fact is your nose keeps growing after the rest of you stops. I feared I would stop at five feet four inches but have the nose of a six-five NFL lineman. Every time someone did my makeup, they shaded the sides of my nose. The first time that happened I asked what they were doing. Then I made sure every makeup artist I worked with contoured it to look narrower.

A couple of months after my birthday, I said, "Let's make it permanently narrower." The decision wasn't a big deal. In my family, a nose job was a fairly common and accepted procedure. My mother and I began consulting with doctors.

One day, shortly after we began the search process, my mom was at a luncheon in Beverly Hills when she saw a girl with an adorable nose. She stared as if she'd just seen a sweater at Nieman Marcus that she thought would look good on me. She approached the girl and said, "Excuse me, this is going to sound like a really rude question, but I'm going to ask anyway. Were you born with that nose or did you have it done?" The girl laughed, gave my mother the name of her plastic surgeon, and we made an appointment.

Even though elective surgery, or luxury surgery as I call it, is much different than necessary surgery, I still came out of the procedure with my face hurting like hell. The doctor broke the bones beside my nose, drew them in to make my nose narrower, shaved down the cartilage and the bump, and rebuilt the tip. To stop the bleeding, I'm told they packed my nose with large strips of gauze that had been soaked in liquid cocaine. I was also sent home with a heavy dose of painkillers. As I found out later, those pills didn't actually stop the pain. They just made it so I didn't care. And I liked not caring.

It was the first time I was ever really high on drugs, and though I was the girl who had crossed the country telling others to "just say no," I enjoyed the sensation of my insides turning milky and calm. There was a real sense of belonging. All the edges in my life dulled. I loved everyone and everything. Though I didn't abuse the painkillers, my reaction to them was more than typical.

Despite the discomfort, I was chatty through my recovery. After I spent a few quiet days at home, the doctor pulled out the packing, slapped a bandage across my nose, and, after warning I would be a little bruised, said I could resume my normal life. I stepped back into the flow without giving a moment's thought to hiding the fact I'd had my nose done. It wasn't a secret.

Oddly, it wasn't even an issue when *Little House* started up again at the end of the summer. Though I returned with a completely different nose, not a single person asked me about it. Nobody said, "What did you do, Half Pint?" I assume it was because the change wasn't drastic. I wasn't like Jennifer Grey, who got her nose done and looked like a completely different person. My nose simply fit my face better.

But there would be complications. As it healed, the tip became very puggy, making me look like everybody else who'd had a nose job, and about a year after the original operation I would go in again to have it fixed. After, it still wouldn't be right. When I was about twenty, I would go in a third time and meet with a specialist who did nothing but fix botched nose jobs and other highly specialized prosthetic procedures. Because he had to redo the entire nose, as well as take cartilage from behind my ear, it would be the most painful of my recoveries.

Again, I would hide it from no one. It wasn't a big deal. Back then there weren't any paparazzi stalking celebrities. Nobody gave a shit. (I certainly didn't.) If they had, I would have wondered why.

After Rob came back from four months in Tulsa, there was a little decompression, but we were really happy to see each other and be back together again. I didn't know what he did or who he did while he was gone, but it didn't have any bearing because he was home and he was mine. We knew there was a buzz around *The Outsiders*, but we were still somewhat oblivious to the way it would change our lives.

Soon after his return, Rob wanted to buy a new car. He drove a beat-up Mazda 626 and traded it in for a spiffy new Mustang GT. It was the first big thing he bought for himself. A short time later, I bought a souped-up convertible Toyota Celica at a charity auction. Rob and I couldn't have been happier. We thought those silly cars had changed our lives. We *did* drive many miles to see each other between Encino and Point Dume, but those cars were symbolic of a change that was taking place whether or not we knew it or liked it. We were moving into the fast lane.

We were nervous. We were giddy, too. Having money, freedom, and fame was new to both of us. It was like a fast, powerful car itself, and we had to learn how to handle it.

I spent weeks watching Rob loop his lines in a studio. The post-production was long and hard. One day a couple girls showed up at the studio to see Rob, and he was uncomfortable. He stammered a surprised hello, until they got the message he didn't want to see them. My antennae went up, and I made catty comments. I didn't directly ask if he had slept with either or both of them; I didn't want to know. It was still easy to ignore. But that would change pretty quickly.

As press for *The Outsiders* began, Rob and the other guys in the movie bid good-bye to their last days of anonymity. The pendulum of fame had shifted. They were put on an elevator that began to take them to levels of fame few people ever experienced. We would walk into a room and practically hear the *whoosh-whoosh-whoosh* of heads turning. People pointed and whispered.

And there were the women. No matter where we went, they stuffed their phone numbers into Rob's pockets. These were not girls my age with a crush on him. Grown women, including major celebrities, hit on him. They were very direct and frequently very graphic about what they wanted and were willing to do for him. At restaurants, I would go to the bathroom and when I came back there would be two or three women in my chair. I'd stand there and clear my throat and they wouldn't move. And this was just the beginning.

By this time, I was well into the ninth season of *Little House*. It would turn out to be the last full season. Did I know it was the end? No, none of us did. With Mike continuing as writer, director, and executive producer but essentially off as an actor, I was being rewarded for my loyalty. I was making a lot of money and a small percentage of the show itself had been negotiated into my contract. So I was in for the duration.

The changes at Walnut Grove were ushered in immediately in a two-part opening episode aptly titled "Times Are Changing." They included Ma and Pa's bittersweet departure for Iowa, the introduction of Etta Plum (played by Leslie Landon) as the town's new teacher, and the arrival of Almanzo's dying brother and his ten-year-old daughter, played by Shannen Doherty.

Shannen, then twelve, was an adorable little girl and very sweet. In her pigtails and dress, she would literally walk in my footsteps, following me closer than my shadow. She wanted to know what makeup I wore, what jewelry I liked, and did I prefer my Jordache jeans or my Calvin's? ("Both, thank you very much . . .") She looked up to me even though I was in many ways still a kid myself. In fact, she used to say she wanted to be just like me when she grew up. I would think to myself, *Hey, I'm not a grown-up!* But I understood: she had the stage mom, the pigtails, the dress, the show . . . she wanted to be like me.

Nearly ten years later, as I was getting back together with my first husband, Bo Brinkman, after a trial separation, we attended therapy sessions. During our time apart, he'd moved into the Oakwood apartment complex in Burbank. Shannen, then a young adult, was living there, too. When Bo and I reconciled in therapy, he confessed everything that he'd done during our separation, and his laundry list of dirty deeds included a one-night stand with Shannen. That story in particular irked me.

Then a few more years passed, and in 1991, the year Michael died, I was narrating a tribute to him at the Emmy Awards. As I came offstage, Shannen and Luke Perry were in the wings, getting ready to present an award. She looked at me and attempted to give me a hug. I pushed her away and said, "I don't think so."

She looked surprised.

"I know," I said. "I know what you did with my husband."

She looked me square in the eye. I thought I saw a barely perceptible smirk. Then she said, "I told you that when I grew up I wanted to be just like you."

After that, I hurried away. It was too *Single White Female* for my taste.

As originally established, Pa was the show's patriarch, the one who made decisions and passed on advice, while season after season Ma did a lot of coffee pouring. They were not equal partners. With both of them gone, I watched to see how much coffee pouring I was going to do as Laura.

Interestingly, in the ninth season, the writers made Laura a hybrid of the male and female protagonist. She wore a dress and poured the coffee, but she also worked, dispensed wisdom, and stepped into the middle of situations and defused problems the way Pa had when he was on the show. Her evolution both pleased and fascinated me. I felt like that wouldn't have happened if I hadn't been able to pull it off. I wish the show as a whole had been able to step up in the same way.

Toward the end, Mike returned for the emotional two-parter "Home Again." Stepping back into the humble yet heroic shoes of Charles Ingalls, he brought his troubled son Albert back to Walnut Grove, thinking the good values of small-town life would turn him around. Then he discovered Albert's real problem, a terrible drug addiction, and suddenly he had the fight of both their lives.

Ironically, on the day we shot the scene where he came back and saw me for the first time, I felt guilty because I'd stayed up way too late partying. I hadn't gotten much sleep, and I was hungover. Half Pint was half out of it.

And so, it seemed, was the show. The ploy for ratings, so successful in the previous year's "Get Doc Baker" episodes, didn't work a second time. Nor did gimmicky guest stars from Billy Barty to an orangutan. And other blatant grabs for the viewers' heartstrings, like the episode "A Child with No Name," in which Laura gave birth to a son who died before she and Almanzo could name him, also failed;

though it happened in real life, the episode had a been there, done that feel.

After the season wrapped, I breathed a sigh of relief and returned to the splendid irresponsibility of my romance with Rob. He was the center of my universe. I wanted to hang out with him and goof around with our friends. In those days, before they were labeled the Brat Pack, they were a raucous, carefree boys' club. Rob was the troublemaker; Emilio was the cruise director; and Tom was the one who'd say, "Guys, I don't know if this is such a great idea."

The mischief we got into was harmless. We stayed up too late, watched TV, and on one particularly fun night, someone made pot brownies. I was not a pot smoker by any means. I had tried it a couple of times but either barfed or fell asleep. I ate one of the pot brownies with great trepidation and soon, I wasn't asleep or barfing, I was laughing my ass off. We watched tapes of *Monty Python's Flying Circus* and laughed hysterically until we fell asleep on top of one another, piled up like little puppies. It was innocent, just a bunch of kids having fun, nothing weird or sexual at all. I woke up with sore abs from laughing so hard. I'd never had many friends my own age, and now I was suddenly part of a fraternity, this group that hung out together as if we were a bunch of friends at college. In a way, this was our college. We did the same things as our friends who were in school. Emilio dated a new girl every week, and Tom fell into a serious relationship with his *Risky Business* costar Rebecca De Mornay, who was a very serious actress herself.

We made silly home videos, including a hybrid of Leonard Nimoy's *In Search Of* and *Scooby-Doo*. We shot it in the Sheens' backyard, and it was about a mysterious monster called "La Pelou," a name improvised by Charlie Sheen.

One night at the Sheens', the boys were telling stories about working with Coppola on *The Outsiders*. Sure, it was grueling, but their hardships paled in comparison to the stories Marty then told about working with Francis on *Apocalypse Now*.

"You think you had it hard changing clothes in a gas station bathroom?" he said. "Let me tell you what it was like working with the same megalomaniac director in the jungle."

He recounted the now infamous stories about how he had been wasted while shooting the movie's opening scenes, how he had lacerated his hand on the mirror and actually bled, and how production was shut down after he suffered a heart attack. But he also told a story that no one else knew. A couple months after his heart attack, he said, they were shooting scenes on the river in God knows where, and out of the blue Francis turned to him and said, "You know, I could cut that opening footage and make you look like Mickey Mouse."

Without missing a beat, Marty replied, "Well, that would make you Walt Disney, wouldn't it, Francis?"

There was a take-away to Marty's story, of course, one he reiterated in a more direct manner another time. We were all together one night, all of us just hammered (Marty was still drinking then), when he turned to me and said very seriously, "Don't be an actress. Quit now. Just get the fuck out of the business."

Don't be an actress? Quit? Get out? I was baffled.

"What are you saying?" I asked.

"You don't want to be a fucking actress," he said with a pleading intensity that grew and grew as he focused his eyes on me. "It's the worst job in the world. It will break your heart, and then it will break your heart again, and then just because it doesn't give a fuck it will break your heart yet again."

I understood what Marty was saying, and why. Few businesses are crueler than show business. But as things turned out, acting wouldn't break my heart. An actor would.

thirteen ———————————————

CHOICES OF THE HEART

Shortly after my nineteenth birthday, Uncle Ray brought me the TV movie *Choices of the Heart*, the true story of young American lay missionary Jean Donovan, who was killed along with three nuns by a military death squad while working in El Salvador in 1980. Until then, I was a wholly apolitical creature. I didn't pay attention to the news, including the headlines about Jean's murder. However, after reading the script, I was fascinated by this young woman from upper-class Connecticut who answered an inner calling to do relief work with poor, starving people in a war-ravaged country.

To say the least, I had a very comfortable, insular, and safe existence. I wondered why this girl was willing to risk everything, and ultimately her life. I later found out Jean wondered the same thing, having once said, "I sit here and talk to God and say, 'Why are you doing this to me? Why can't I just be your little suburban housewife?' "

Along with Rob, I was moving in some pretty rarefied air, and I wondered if I could ever give it all up to work with the Peace Corps. What would it take? Part of me wanted to be that person, which was interesting to acknowledge. Who wouldn't want to be that pure and brave and giving of her heart?

Doing it was another matter. I was the first to admit it required a leap of faith beyond what I was capable of. But I hoped to memorialize her courageous life and work in the movie. The project had a good pedigree: John Houseman was one of the executive producers, Joseph Sargent had signed on to direct, and there was a brilliant script by John Pielmeier, who had also written *Agnes of God.* We also signed Mike Farrell, Marty Sheen, Peter Horton, who had just married Michelle Pfeiffer when we shot *Splendor in the Grass,* Pamela Bellwood from *Dynasty,* and Helen Hunt, who I knew from a dance class I took.

We set up production in Mexico City and a small town just outside of it that doubled as El Salvador. I'm convinced that if God ever gives the world an enema, he's going to put the tube in Mexico City. I'd never been to a filthier place in my life. At our hotel, I was warned not to leave the windows open because the room would get dirty from the air.

Don't think for a minute, though, that that stopped me from having the time of my life there. I deeply liked and respected my director, Joe Sargent; as a former actor, he spoke my language. I wasn't anybody's kid on the set. There were no pats on the head. I was there by myself, and I felt the pressure to step up. During the shoot, I grew close to Peter. In fact, after he and Michelle divorced, she asked him if we'd had an affair. We didn't, but we were probably closer than we should have been considering one of us was married and the other was, for all intents and purposes, living with a boyfriend.

Once we got to Mexico, it was like a whole other world. It was my first experience traveling to what I now refer to as Pretendia. In Pretendia, everything is possible. In Pretendia, you're always pretty. In Pretendia, you can make out with your costars and not get in trouble. In Pretendia, everyone works very hard and parties even harder.

Pretendia is a very dangerous place for an addictive personality, though my addict self wasn't yet at its self-destructive height. I was happy. Peter and I had fun exploring the nooks and crannies of that dirty, horrible city. Mike opened my eyes to politics, though to be honest, he was way too wonky and most of it sailed over my head. We saw *Gandhi* with Spanish subtitles, and it was still a moving film.

I was miserable when I couldn't be with Rob for the premiere of *The Outsiders.* Hearing about the fun over a terrible long-distance connection made me miss him even more. He flew to my side in Mexico as soon as he could break free from promoting the movie, and we had a wonderful time. All of us hung out together. I snuck Rob into a scene; he played a photographer at a press conference.

At one point, a group that Mike and Marty were involved with, and I think Peter, too, tried to arrange for a bunch of us to travel to El Salvador. Because I was playing Jean, I was looked at, albeit briefly, as a symbol of what she was trying to achieve. It was all a little bit over my head, but I was game. Then word came that the Salvadoran government wouldn't guarantee our safety, specifically mine. That jarred me. I'd grown up with some safety concerns, mostly as a result of crazies obsessed with *Little House* who wanted to take me away to some cave because they thought I was the second coming. But I had the hardest time understanding that someone might want to shoot me because a film I did was political in nature. I was naive.

After we wrapped and were back in L.A., Jane Fonda decided it was time to mobilize young Hollywood. She had a function at her house that Rob and I attended. Melanie Griffith and Ed Begley Jr. were among the others there. Ed convinced all of us to cut up our gasoline credit cards to protest something. Pairs of scissors were passed around the room, and I blithely snipped my Chevron card in half. The next morning I called my business manager and asked him to get me a new one.

"Why the hell did you cut it if you want another one?" he asked.

"I don't really know why," I said. "Everybody in the room was doing it, so I felt like I should. But I need a new one, please." I can be such a Gidget!

Back in L.A., Peter and I went to see *Scarface,* which was Michelle's movie. She was phenomenal, and the film blew both of us away. As the end credits rolled Peter said, "Oh my God, my wife is a huge movie star. My life is going to change."

I held his hand and nodded knowingly and sympathetically.

"It is," I said. "Just you wait."

What changed with me and Rob was our privacy. Although I was very recognizable when Rob and I fell in love, we were able to go about our lives, see movies, and have dinner in a restaurant without being stopped or interrupted for more than the occasional autograph. But after *The Outsiders* was released, Rob and I saw what privacy we had left get absolutely obliterated.

Daily life went from ordinary to extraordinary. Restaurants comped meals, invitations to premieres, parties, and events arrived for every night of the week, the phone rang constantly, and women continued stuffing their numbers into Rob's pocket with unnerving frequency. It was the first time I felt strong pangs of jealousy. The pretty surfer-girl blonds, beautiful, sexy, Farrah-like blonds, and supergorgeous, Catherine Deneuve–like blonds seemed to materialize wherever we went. I could never be that blond no matter how hard I tried.

I felt threatened and I couldn't possibly compete. In Eddie Murphy's first standup movie, *Delirious*, he describes what it was like when he first became famous and all of a sudden women were coming at him from every direction. It was, he said, pussy, pussy, pussy. There was pussy falling out of his pockets. And that's what it was like for Rob.

I don't know for sure, but I think he fooled around whenever possible. Now I'm a forty-four-year-old woman with a nineteen-year-old son, and I don't know how any guy that age would say no. Boys that age are walking erections. Chicks are the whole reason they live. In addition, Rob was funny, charming, and gorgeous. He was irresistible. These stunning girls who looked great on the beach and didn't have to wear pajamas over their bikinis pursued him. It was free candy. Of course he was going to sample them.

The only way I could preserve what we had was to put blinders on. I didn't want to know what he was doing. It scared the hell out of me.

Even without the crazy female fans, I was uncomfortable being in this new world that was opening to us. Instead of bowling or hanging out at someone's home, we found ourselves at much groovier social events, where, as we walked in, I prayed I wouldn't blow it by saying something stupid, revealing my true self as a complete geek.

To relax, I would have a glass of beer or a shot of tequila and a beer ... or two ... or three. ... Cocaine helped, too. We were at a party in Malibu the first time I was offered coke. I said no thanks—and not because I'd been the youth spokesperson for the White House's Just Say No campaign. I was afraid I'd do it wrong. I pictured myself sneezing over the mirror, like Woody Allen in *Annie Hall*. But our friend said, "Just try it. You might like it." So I summoned the courage and did a couple lines. I didn't feel anything at first. About twenty minutes later, I did another little bump and took off. It was like walking through a door and stepping into a new, more confident, more gregarious skin.

I immediately set out to find the best, most discreet dealers I could, and from then on, when Rob and I went to a party or a premiere, I'd do a bump, grab a drink, light a cigarette, bid good-bye to the image I had of myself as the dorky girl with the zinc oxide on her nose, and feel absolutely comfortable having a conversation about anything with anyone. I probably sounded like an idiot, but I was high enough that I didn't give a shit.

Nobody did. The talk was smarter, the music was better, everyone was more beautiful, and the sex was fantastic. The party-time atmosphere extended to the East Coast, too. In New York, Rob and I walked straight into the VIP areas at Limelight and Area. Studio 54 owner Steve Rubell gave me my first quaalude.

In the spring of 1983, Victor French called and asked if I wanted to go on a talk show he was doing; it was either *The Dinah Shore Show* or *The Tonight Show*. He said, "You ought to do this thing to protest." I heard the word "protest" and immediately said, "I'm down for a protest. What are we protesting?"

"The cancellation," he said.

"The cancellation of what?" I asked.

"The show," he said. "*Little House.*"

I had no idea.

"What do you mean the show is canceled?" I asked.

We spoke for a few minutes. Then I said I'd call him back after I talked with Mike. I got Mike on the phone and asked if we were canceled. He said he hadn't received an official call from the network, but had heard *Little House* wasn't listed among the shows on NBC's fall lineup. I called Uncle Ray for more information and he confirmed we weren't on the schedule.

By the time I called Mike back, he had done his own reconnaissance work and he was furious that he had never received an official phone call from NBC president Brandon Tartikoff or anyone else at the network, letting him know the fate of the show. He had been on the network since 1959. Perceiving disrespect, Mike's temper redlined. He wanted to destroy all the sets—Walnut Grove, everything in Simi Valley.

"I'm going to blow the whole fucking thing up," he threatened.

Uncle Ray called and asked him to put those thoughts on hold. He suggested they milk the situation for a couple of *Little House* movies.

"Then do whatever you want," he said.

We got the go-ahead from NBC and then life took on a semblance of routine as we made three *Little House* movies, *Look Back to Yester-*

day, *Bless All the Dear Children*, and *The Last Farewell*. The Christmas-themed *Bless All the Dear Children*, which was horrible, actually ran last. But we shot them out of order, and Mike saved his best for what the cast and crew knew as the show's final curtain.

For *The Last Farewell*, he devised a script where Charles and Caroline return for a nostalgic visit to Walnut Grove. But their reunion with Laura and friends sours when a coldhearted developer comes forward and reveals he owns the land on which the town is built. He offers to let them stay under his conditions, but the townspeople reject his proposal. Laura finds it so untenable she throws something through the kitchen window, prompting Mr. Carter, who's there, to say, "You want to do something more than break windows? I got a wagon loaded to the gills with dynamite."

The whole town gathers in church the next day, and they devise a plan. Rather than surrender everything they worked to build, they decide to blow it up.

That was Mike's fuck-you to the network. He didn't want to leave anything behind. TV and movie sets tend to get recycled over time, and none of us wanted to see Oleson's Mercantile being used in some other production and have other people tromping through places where many of us had grown up.

Certainly I had grown up there. I could look around and see memories everywhere: the first place I held a boy's hand, my first kiss, the schoolhouse where I'd gone to school. Those were my places. They were all of our places.

Mike shot everything except a few interiors and the final scene where the town residents say good-bye to their beloved Walnut Grove, which they'd blown up. On the day before we shot the good-bye scene, Mike and the crew went in with the special-effects guys for the demolition. Multiple cameras captured each building exploding in flames. None of us were allowed on the set that day. It was too dangerous.

The rest of us arrived the following morning for our last day of work. Normally, at the ranch in Simi Valley, there was a spot on a hill away from the town where all the honey wagons and makeup and wardrobe trailers parked. We would get dressed and trickle into town, walking down either a path that led directly into town or a longer road that went to the lower portion of town by the mill and the footbridge.

On this last day, though, no one wandered down. Without it being planned, all of us got dressed and waited until everyone was ready. We would make the final walk together. We knew it wasn't going to be easy.

The situation was ironic. I had spent the previous season forcing myself to go to work. I didn't want to do it. Many days it was like pulling teeth and I had to tell myself, "Paycheck, paycheck, paycheck. You have to do this. You made a commitment. You're a team player." Once it was being taken away from me, I couldn't fathom not doing the show every week. The implications of no longer being around all these people was unfathomable to me. It was like Joni Mitchell's line in the song "Big Yellow Taxi": *Don't it always seem to go / that you don't know what you've got / till it's gone.*

Finally, after the last one of us was ready, the entire *Little House* cast made their final trip to Walnut Grove. We walked in silence. I had no idea what to expect when we rounded the corner, but I didn't expect what I saw. There was nothing there. All the businesses were gone. Only one structure was left: the church. I guess Mike didn't have the balls to blow up a church. But chunks of its wall were missing as a result of shrapnel from the nearby Oleson's Mercantile and Nellie's Restaurant.

I stopped and gazed in shock at the area where the town had stood. It was small. Just piles of rubble. There was something profound that struck all of us dumb. Seeing this town, albeit a made-for-TV town, reduced to dust made us feel like we had all lost a favorite relative. We were like a family that had gathered at a funeral. Everyone was in shock.

They shot our reactions to the buildings being blown up. In between takes, we would tell stories, and every conversation triggered a flood of tears. One person would tell a story or bring up a memory, start to tear up, and within moments all two hundred of us were crying. Anytime one person cried, all of us cried. And I mean everyone—actors, makeup artists, wardrobe, grips, electricians, wranglers. It was like that all day.

It was the longest good-bye, and it wasn't nearly long enough as far as I was concerned, even though it was drawn out by a sumptuous steak and lobster lunch. The last shot of the day was all of us walking out of town from the church as we sang "Onward Christian Soldiers." I would have chosen "The Long and Winding Road," but John Lennon and Paul McCartney hadn't written it in the 1800s.

We finished shooting and the cast wound our way back to the trailers to change out of our wardrobe for the last time. I finished changing and came out of my room on the honey wagon. I hugged and kissed people, and cried with them, as they climbed into the shuttle that took people to their cars.

But I wasn't ready to go yet. I wanted one more look at the place where Walnut Grove had stood. I walked back to town, savoring this last time by myself. I felt as if I was retracing steps of my life. Everybody had taken mementos from the town. An idiot, I didn't take anything. Instead, I wanted one last chance to gather memories, as if they could be scooped up and carried home in a basket like apples that had just fallen from the tree.

When I rounded the corner, I saw Mike standing in the middle of the town. He was by himself, bathed in the orange glow of twilight. He had his back to me. I walked up to him without his knowing until he sensed me there. He turned around and he was crying. I immediately lost it, too. Standing by ourselves, we held on to each other and sobbed unabashedly until we ran out of tears.

It was the healthiest grieving I'd ever done. I felt like I cried for everything in my life, including my father.

"Thank you," I said finally. After a deep breath, I added a drained and plaintive "I don't know. I just don't know."

"You don't know?" he asked.

"I don't," I said. "I don't know. For all practical purposes, this has been my whole life. It's weird."

"Well, don't be scared," he said. "Don't be afraid. It's not the end for you." He enveloped me in his arms like a proud daddy, like someone who had genuinely watched me grow up. "For you, this is just the beginning."

I didn't believe him. But he was right.

Hollywood Is the DEVIL'S TOILET

fourteen ———————————————————

THE WORLD ACCORDING
TO . . .

Aware I was feeling blue following the *Little House* sobfest, Rob invited me to visit him in Montreal, where he was shooting *The Hotel New Hampshire*. I flew up, excited for the change of scenery and to hang out.

I was a huge fan of the earlier film made from John Irving's sensational novel *The World According to Garp*. I identified with Garp, who didn't know who his father was and was raised by a freewheeling, strong-willed woman. I don't know if Rob knew it, but I had also read his *Hotel New Hampshire* script, as I did all his other scripts. I wanted to see what I was in for with the love scenes. Those were red flags.

I liked *New Hampshire*. So did Rob. He was excited about working with director Tony Richardson, who virtually guaranteed the film would have the author's oddball sensibility, and the talented cast led by Jodie Foster, Beau Bridges, Seth Green, who was a baby, and Nastassja Kinski. When I learned she was involved, I thought, *Uh-oh*. I remembered Rob had drooled over her when we saw *One from the Heart*, and I had seen the guys go cuckoo over her exotic, overtly sexual, and very popular snake poster.

My radar was on high alert when I got to Montreal. Everyone was in the same hotel, and I thought they were a madcap, loony group of people. Everybody was sleeping with everybody else, except for Rob, who I deluded myself into believing was an angel. I was able to visit him on the set until it was time for him to do his scenes with Nastassja. Then he didn't want me there.

At first, I stayed in our hotel room, stewing in worry and anxiety. Having never traveled by myself to a foreign country where I wasn't involved in a project, I was scared to go out alone. I also have a notoriously horrible sense of direction (as in no inner GPS). Bored out of my head, I decided a good thing to do would be to teach myself how to smoke. After all, everybody smoked. So I buckled down and made a concentrated effort to smoke in a way that looked practiced and cool. I was such an asshole.

At night, Rob would come back to the hotel for dinner, and on the weekend we would party like crazy with everyone else. We had such a good time that the four days I had planned to stay turned into two weeks. But he still wasn't allowing me on the set. I began to sense something missing between us. All signs pointed to one reason, and I started to freak out about Nastassja. In person, she was gorgeous. I could only imagine her effect on Rob.

One night I got really ripped and as the sun came up, I poured my heart out to one of Rob's castmates. I said, "I don't want to go home." She asked why, and I opened my heart up to her.

"It's Rob and Nastassja," I said. "It's freaking me out."

"Don't let it," she said.

"I can't help it," I said. "It's going to happen."

"No, it's not," she said again.

"How do you know?" I asked.

"Because," she said, "she's mine."

Relieved, I went back to the suite and wrapped up my visit on a good note. Despite my suspicions, Rob and I got along well that trip.

Once I was back in L.A., though, I began to have a hard time getting ahold of Rob. He wouldn't be in the room when I would call.

Nor could the production office find him when I tried there. He would call me at his convenience, but then he skipped calling for a day or two. I knew what was going on.

One night I called Rob's room. After numerous rings, the hotel operator came on the line and asked if I would like to leave a message. Frustrated, I asked her to ring his room again. Instead of saying "of course," she paused. She must have thought long and hard about what to do because a moment later she sighed and said, "Miss Gilbert, shall I ring Miss Kinski's room?"

"Excuse me?" I said.

"Mr. Lowe," she said hesitantly, "just asked for a wake-up call from Miss Kinski's room."

"Oh."

"Would you still like me to put you through?"

I declined her offer and instead booked a flight to Montreal the next day so I could see for myself what was going on. I didn't tell Rob. I was going to walk into a catastrophe or . . . something else. I had no idea.

I let the hotel know in advance that I was coming and asked them to not mention it to Rob. I arrived before he finished work. The hotel let me put my stuff in his room and I went downstairs to surprise him in the lobby. I was by the entrance when I heard raucous laughter and saw Paul McCrane come through the door. Others from the film followed him in, including Jodie and her Yale roommate John Hutman, who was working on the movie.

Then Rob and Nastassja walked in, talking to each other. Though it looked innocent enough, I knew it wasn't. Shaking like a nervous Chihuahua, I called to him. Rob turned toward me, shocked by the sound of my voice. I saw the blood drain from his face, then his arms, and then his hands as he turned white.

A moment later, though, his expression changed. It was as if he flipped a switch inside himself. Brightening, he yelled one of his pet names for me—Mouse, Bunny, Franchise, Baby Girl, I don't remember which—and ran toward me, enveloping me in his arms and pushing me into a corner where he smothered me with affection, and at the same time hid me from the view of his castmates.

His power of self-control was impressive, but his act didn't work on me. We went up to his room and I confronted him.

"I know you've been sleeping with Nastassja." I said.

Rob denied it. I said it again: "I know you have been sleeping with her." Again he denied it. Finally, I said, "Look, last night I called your room and there was no answer. The hotel operator took pity on me and told me that you had just called down from Miss Kinski's room asking for a wake-up call."

Rob was frozen; he stammered and stuttered, like a tire spinning in the snow. Finally, he said, "What? What the fuck? No way. I don't get it. The hotel operator sold me out? Why the hell would she do that?"

I walked up to Rob, put my finger in his face, and said very calmly and slowly, "You don't fuck with America's sweetheart."

With that, I walked out of the room and went to the airport, where I sat for the next twelve hours, waiting for my flight home.

If I had felt beaten and humiliated before I left, I was in agony by the time I landed in L.A. My friend Kate Franklin picked me up from the airport and drove me straight to Jack in the Box. I bought a Chicken Supreme sandwich, took it back to my house, and gnawed at it while sitting cross-legged on the floor. Mayonnaise and snot ran down both sides of my face as I wailed, "Why? Why did he do it? What's wrong with me? Why doesn't he love me?"

For days I called Rob incessantly and hung up as soon as I heard his voice. I called her room, too. It became even more painful once the tabloids got wind of the affair. A broken heart is such a wonderful thing to share with the world. I loved going to the grocery store and seeing my face on the cover of tabloids just above a bright yellow banner that said DUMPED!

I called Warren Beatty and asked what I should do. It was more like a plea. *Tell me, what the hell am I going to do?*

He just said, "Oh, she"—meaning Nastassja—"is such a silly girl."

"What? This is not helpful," I said. "What am I going to do? You don't understand. My whole world is completely falling apart and all you can tell me is she's a silly girl."

He was silent.

"So apparently she's a silly girl," I continued. "Now what?"

"It will pass," he said. "It will pass."

"But he said he loved her."

"That, too, will pass."

"You're not helping," I said.

Unfortunately, oracles typically communicate in riddles packaged as mysteries, and Mr. Beatty was among them.

"What can I physically do right now to make this change?" I asked.

"Nothing," he said. "There's nothing you can do to change it. You're going to have to ride it out and wait till he comes home. And he will come home."

"If he doesn't?"

"You move on."

My friends who were my age and relationship morons like me had said pretty much the same thing. But it seemed different coming from Warren. I managed to stuff away the Stalky Stalkerson side of my personality and try to maintain some dignity in a very painful situation.

I was more upset after speaking to Rob, who said he wanted to think things over by himself in Paris and then Munich when he was done shooting, which, I assumed, meant he was going to follow her and continue their love affair. But he changed his mind and came back to L.A. By the time he arrived, I was mad. I had gone from crushed to perplexed to fucking pissed. He'd call and say he wanted to see me and talk, I'd tell him to go fuck himself. He called and pleaded.

I said I didn't want to see him. I told him that I hated him. I described how he had ruined my life, explaining if this was the way it was going to be between us, I wasn't up to it. I didn't want to be that person who every time Rob went on location sat at home wondering who he was screwing.

Eventually he convinced me to let him come see me. Once we were face-to-face, we talked and yelled and cried. He let me get everything out of my system, and then like two comets colliding, we kind of exploded in each other's arms. When all was said and done, after something like fourteen or fifteen hours of crying, screaming, talking, making love, carrying on, and laughing, we got very quiet. I looked at him as if he had turned into a puzzle I couldn't figure out.

"Can you just tell me why?" I asked. "I get that she's beautiful, but you've got to explain it to me."

Rob thought about it. I saw he wanted to provide real insight.

"It's like when you walk down the beach and you see a beautiful shell in the sand," he said. "You either pick it up and listen to it. Or you walk by. I had to listen to the shell."

My eyed widened.

"That is the stupidest analogy ever!" I said. We laughed our little asses off. Humor was our savior. With that, we were back together.

I sometimes felt self-conscious about not landing feature films, especially as our circle of friends widened to include Sean and Chris Penn, Tim Hutton, and Matt Dillon, among others, all of whom were rocketing to movie-star status. Even Michael J. Fox, who Rob dubbed Money J. Fox, was making the transition onto the big screen. But my life was no less busy. I starred in the made-for-TV movie *Family Secrets*, a drama about three generations of women helping one another through problems. The cast featured Stephanie Powers and Maureen Stapleton. Again, I snuck Rob into a scene, this one where Stephanie and I are in the grocery store. As we walk past a cute guy in the produce section, I turn to check him out. It was Rob.

The movie was uneventful except for getting to know Maureen. More than one of the most amazing actresses of our time, Mo was an amazing woman. She was a ballsy broad, and she was just the tonic my soul needed. A real dame, she had a tremendous appetite for life. She liked to drink and eat, and she didn't mince words.

I would sit down with her before work as she sipped a Bloody Mary and listen to her tell stories about herself that were legendary even then. My eyes bulged as she recounted the ribald speech she gave at the wrap party for *Bye Bye Birdie*, and we laughed together as she recalled seeing a critic she didn't like at a restaurant and setting the back of his blazer on fire with a cigarette lighter. My favorite was the night Alan David took her out to dinner. After cutting into her steak and seeing it was medium instead of well done, as she'd requested, she summoned the waiter.

"Take this back and tell the chef I said to piss on it," she said.

"Excuse me?" the waiter replied.

"Well, that's what they do when you send food back," she said. "I just want him to know that I know he's going to piss on it. So tell him to piss on it."

I discovered my own ballsy side when the production moved briefly to Chicago, where we shot a couple scenes. Rob had made *Class* in Chicago and he called ahead to his buddy John Cusack, who lived there, and asked him to show me around while I was there. He did, and we ended up having a little fling, which I kept from Rob. It was my own private "screw you."

Only John and I ever knew about it. He was very sweet—and funny. Funny was a problem for me. Rob's sense of humor kept me going back to him as much as our physical attraction did. He was brilliantly funny. I think the public finally caught a glimpse of his sense of humor in *Wayne's World*, the *Austin Powers* movies, and *Thank You for Smoking*. But I knew how funny he was. He is also a gifted mimic. Lots of actors do Christopher Walken, but Rob's Walken was dead-on.

We were very tight when he left for London to shoot *Oxford Blues*. Letters from him arrived by the bundle, and I joined him there for a couple of blissfully fun weeks. He had become close to Cassian Elwes, one of the movie's producers, as well as Cassian's brother, Cary, who was acting in the movie. It also featured Julian Sands and Amanda Pays, who freaked me out when I first saw her because of how similar she looked to Nastassja Kinski.

"Did you notice?" I asked Rob.

He nodded.

"Well, it's freaking me out," I said.

"Don't," he said. "There's absolutely no reason. Believe me."

"You're right," I said. "You've already picked up that seashell, haven't you?"

London was a nonstop party. We drank and caroused our way through the city. I may have seen the sun rise too many times for my own good, but I felt secure and loved and in a really comfortable place. It seemed like Rob and I had been through a fire and come out much better for the pain.

Back in L.A., young Hollywood entered its golden age, a time when everyone made movies that seemed to define our generation. With his laserlike focus, Cruise was already in a league of his own, and Sean Penn, Tim Hutton, and Matt Dillon were very serious actors. Though he pursued his career with more levity, Rob was thrilled when he landed one of the leads in *St. Elmo's Fire*, a coming-of-age film about a group of friends just out of college who are trying to figure out the rest of their lives.

There was good buzz around the project, whose cast included Emilio, Demi Moore, Ally Sheedy, Andrew McCarthy, Mare Winningham, and Judd Nelson. We'd met Judd a couple of years before in New York, and I was sure he was going to be the next huge movie star. He was scary smart, brutally honest, and hilariously funny.

However, my favorite person on the picture was its brilliant director, Joel Schumacher, a wonderfully talented and entertaining man who was beginning an ascent that would make him one of Hollywood's most successful and beloved filmmakers. He adored and, more than that, understood Rob, who would preen in his movie wardrobe (the school jacket, the hoodie sweatshirt, and the ribbed Henley T-shirt, as well as the high-top tennis shoes and mushed-down socks) and check himself out like Dorian Gray as he practiced the saxophone.

Joel referred to Rob affectionately as "the shameless creature." I loved him for that brazenly honest and funny insight—because it was absolutely true. Rob was a shameless creature, whether he was admiring the highlights in his longish hair or listening to seashells.

He was a horny young man, as Tony Richardson once said, and he enjoyed the attention he got from girls who hounded him on the set at all hours. One day he was changing clothes in his dressing room with Emilio when, on a lark, he threw open the door and gave a full frontal flash to a crowd of delirious female admirers as he asked his wardrobe guy if he knew where his clothes were. Joel said they had to call the police to get the guys out of the trailer.

Nevertheless, we were going through one of the best times in our relationship. Joel welcomed me onto the set, and Rob had no qualms about having me there no matter what they were shooting. I watched the scene where Demi drives Rob home and he makes a move for her by dropping his keys in his sweatpants. They were shooting in an alley deep in Hollywood. Rob's trailer was parked next to a church and above it was a neon sign that said, "Hollywood Is the Devil's Toilet." I thought that was brilliant. It reminded me of the scene in *Scarface* when Tony Montana sees the sign on the side of the blimp that says, "The World Is Yours." At that moment, I felt the universe wink at me.

• • •

After those set visits, I went off and did *Sylvester,* a coming-of-age story about a young Texas wrangler who tries to make a quick windfall on the back of her best bronco at a three-day eventing competition. It was considered a hot project. The director, Tim Hunter, had launched Matt Dillon's career in *Tex,* and the writer, Carol Sobieski, had done *The Toy, Annie,* and *Honeysuckle Rose.* Before getting the role, I auditioned numerous times during a nationwide search for the quintessential teen actress to play this scrappy, horse-breaking Texan.

I was thrilled when I got the part. It was my first feature film, and it finally put me in the same club as some of the guys in our crowd who occasionally thumbed their noses at me for being on TV.

They weren't the only ones. From what I understand now, the producers, Ray Stark and Marty Jurow, wanted me, but Tim Hunter was against hiring me in the lead role of his movie. I represented everything he didn't want. I got that message at our first meeting when he sat me down and said, "So we have to change everything about you."

"What does that mean?" I asked.

"It means you have to change everything about you," he reiterated. "Your mannerisms. Your look. Everything . . ."

As he explained it, everything included cutting off all my hair, which I'd anticipated. I wanted to get as deeply under the skin of this character, Charlene—Charlie—Railsback, as I could. Then he laid a big bomb on me. He said he wanted me to do as much of my own riding as possible.

"Meaning?" I asked.

"I don't want the majority of your stunts to be done by a double," he said. "We will have doubles on standby, but I don't want to use them if I can use you."

I knew this director didn't like me. His opinion came through clearly. But I had grown up around wranglers and tough guys, Michael Landon being the toughest. I didn't let Tim get to me. I knew that pros sucked it up. I thought, *Pal, you're going to like me by the time this fucking thing is over.* As it turned out, I don't think he did.

For months, I trained six hours a day, five days a week, with Benita (Bunny) Allen, a riding expert who worked the crap out of me. My arms quivered as I lifted the saddle over my head twenty-five times, but I needed to be in incredible shape. The horse Tim picked as Sylvester was over seventeen hands high and towered over my five-foot-three frame. I looked like a pea on top of him—but a determined pea.

By the time I left for the shoot, I had boy hair, a flat chest, and big biceps. My thighs were black-and-blue from that damn horse, and I had calluses on the insides of my knees and all over my hands. There wasn't an ounce of femininity left in me. I cried to Rob, "I'm a boy!" He was sweet about it, though. "It's okay, Bunny-Mouse," he said. "I think you look cute. I still love you."

I lost whatever vanity was left once I got to Marfa, where I spent the next few months shooting *Sylvester.* Actually, we stayed in Alpine, Texas, where there was one streetlight and one motel. I got to stay in the motel owner's swanky apartment behind the front desk. I called it the Norman Bates Suite. I'd wanted Rob to come with and help settle me in because I knew it was going to be a rough shoot. I was right, too. Unfortunately, he was learning to play hockey for his next movie, *Youngblood,* and then was off to Toronto.

As soon as I arrived in Marfa, I started to butt heads with Tim Hunter. Though I was playing a Texan, he didn't want me to sound like a Texan. There are five dialects in the giant state of Texas, and he wouldn't let me have a hint of any of them. My sanity was saved by my leading guy, Michael Schoeffling from *16 Candles,* and my leading man, Richard Farnsworth, who was unflappable. He'd been around. Nothing ruffled him, which was a good lesson for me.

It seemed to me that I could never do enough to please Tim, and on top of that, my horse hated me. As much as the director didn't want me in the movie, my horse wanted to be in it less. There were eight different horses, one for bucking, one for jumping, one for falling, and so on. But the main one, which I rode most often, was a monster. He nearly killed me one day. I was supposed to ride him straight away from the camera, into a field. Suddenly he took the bit in his mouth, stretched his neck out, and bolted for the trees at a full run with me on his back.

There was nothing I could do. Behind me, I could hear the head wrangler, Corky Randall, screaming, "Motherfucker! Someone get a horse!"

But the catch horse wasn't able to catch up. From some remote corner of my brain, I remembered a safety talk that Benita had given me. I dropped one rein, grabbed the other with both hands, and pulled the horse's nose into my knees. Suddenly he crow-hopped around and around. I stayed on him until he stopped, then jumped off and walked in a daze back to the crew. Grown men, seasoned cowboys, stared at me with their mouths agape.

Farnsworth was the only one sort of grinning, as if to say, "'Atta girl, you can handle anything." In reality, he said, "That's bullshit! It's bullshit they made you ride that dumb animal. Everyone knows that horse is a dink."

I walked into my trailer, sat on the sofa, and sobbed. My whole body was trembling. I remember watching my hands shake uncontrollably as I tried to drink water. Then there was a knock on the door. I opened it and saw Bunny holding Sylvester by the bridle. The horse was covered in sweat. She told me she punched him in the face a couple times. "Sylvester says he's sorry," she said.

I looked that horse straight in his big, seemingly remorseful eyes and said, "You better be sorry, you bastard, because I'm not going through that again."

•   •   •

I got back on him and he tried his funny business two more times over the rest of the shoot, once when I was riding with Farnsworth and another time when we were doing dressage moves in an arena. Every day was hard and scary. We worked terribly long hours, but on the weekends, we partied our brains out. Our caterer had access to a private jet, and he would fly in the best food from L.A., as well as the best cocaine.

Still, the nights were extremely lonely. I rescued a kitten and named him Sylvester. He became my constant companion and I'd have him for the next fifteen years. He would ride to work on Richard's shoulder, curled up in a little ball. It was such a cute sight: this big, old, rough cowboy with a little kitten sleeping next to his ear.

But the kitten wasn't enough company for me. With Rob in Toronto, I began an on-set romance with the third AD, Frank Capra III (FC3). Though it wasn't intentional, I got a taste of what Rob went through on *The Hotel New Hampshire,* and he got a taste of what I experienced on the other end. He would call and I wouldn't be in my room. Marfa is famous as the place where *Giant* was filmed, and for the Marfa lights, these unexplained bursts of light that can be spotted off Route 67. They appear to bounce through the nighttime sky like giant glowing basketballs. A lot of our weekend parties were based around going to watch the ghost lights and getting obliterated. Rob sensed the distance I was putting between us as I spent time with Frank. He wrote me a letter from Toronto, saying he didn't believe I was out all night looking at some stupid Marfa lights, and he warned that what I was doing was dangerous to us.

Even rereading his heartfelt words—"I hope you'll give me a chance"—as I did often, didn't deter me. I was lonely, scared, and by myself, which was, I discovered, not a good place for me. I didn't do *alone* well. Performing the stunts, risking my safety, knowing the director disliked me, and just living every day on the edge got to me, and I spiraled downward quickly. I had no clue how needy I was, how

I needed a man to fill me up. I still hadn't acknowledged in an emotional sense that my father was actually dead. As a result, if I found myself in a needy place, as I did in Marfa, I would climb into someone else's lap, like a kitten craving affection.

Then we moved locations to Lexington and Rob was able to visit, which ended my fling with FC3. I left as soon as filming ended and joined Rob in Toronto, where we argued and nitpicked at each other until he confronted me about my behavior in Marfa. Sobbing, I confessed, apologized, and begged his forgiveness. He also apologized for not having been available to me when I needed him.

With the Sturm und Drang behind us, we fell into the cozy lock-step of lovers. I'd planned to stay for a week and ended up there a month before I returned to L.A. for postproduction. The PR campaign kicked off when I became the youngest actor to be honored with a star on the Hollywood Walk of Fame. Afterward, I celebrated with my family and Rob at the old Brown Derby restaurant, where we devoured their famous cobb salad and grapefruit cake.

Sylvester's opening coincided with the release of Rebecca De Mornay's picture *The Slugger's Wife*, so I crossed paths with her and Tom Cruise in different cities as we did a press junket across the country. To help with PR, my mother and Uncle Ray hired top Hollywood publicist Warren Cowan, who soon thereafter became the great love of my mother's life and, years later, my stepdad.

Ironically, I missed walking the red carpet for my own premiere at the Equestrian Center because I was on the road doing PR. My mother dressed my sister Sara in a full equestrian outfit for the event, including jodhpurs, boots, vest, and helmet, and later showed me photos of her and Warren with various stars who'd attended.

Openings in other cities were planned, but they were canceled one by one as the reviews came in. Despite all the publicity efforts, I started to realize the movie was going to be a disaster, or, as Rob and I used to say, a whistling, screaming bomb. Indeed, you could hear *Sylvester* dropping from the sky.

And so it was. I wasn't particularly shattered. I didn't feel like my career was pinned on that one project. Aside from all the hard work that had gone into it, I was disappointed because I wanted to be able to say to Rob and the other guys whose movies were big hits that I was also in the club. I wanted to go, me too!

But I was realistic about my work. I had much more ego invested in my actual life.

ANDY WANTS TO KNOW IF
ANY FAMOUS PEOPLE ARE HERE

The tabloids only focused on breakups and bad news, so they were nowhere to be found when I took my mother on her first trip to Europe. It was their loss. They missed a good story—and a mostly good time.

We went with friends of my mother's who were on a buying trip for their clothing store, with stops in London, Paris, Milan, Rome, Florence, and Venice. Even though she wasn't paying the bill, my mom insisted on sharing a room with me to save money. She also prohibited me from calling home (again, it was the cost). As a result, I spent a lot of time talking to Rob from house phones in hotel lobbies.

In Paris, my mother and I were walking up the Champs-Elysées when I spied Jodie Foster on a movie set. I said hello, and she invited me to hang out with her that night at her flat. "We'll do something," she said. After a week of nonstop togetherness with my mother and her friends, whom we nicknamed Stinko and Poo Poo Foot (at every restaurant, he ordered a veal dish called Stinko, and she kept stepping in dog poop), I accepted immediately, and with a sense of relief bordering on desperation that could have easily scared Jodie into reconsidering her offer. Fortunately, she didn't.

Jodie and I had a delicious dinner at a neighborhood café and then hung out at her place. I spent the night there after we realized it had gotten very late. When I went back to the hotel the next morning I saw my mother waiting for me with a concerned expression on her face.

"What is it?" I asked.

"Melissa, I have to ask you something," she said.

"Yes?"

"Are you a lesbian?"

I scrunched up my face, puzzled by her query.

"No," I said. "Why do you suddenly think I'm a lesbian?"

"Well, you know what they say about Jodie."

"Ma, she's a friend of mine," I said. "And I don't care what she is. That's really immaterial. She's a wonderful person."

"I just wondered," she said.

"I spent the night at her house. Big deal. That doesn't make me a lesbian. I'm a very heterosexual woman. In fact, maybe too hetero-sexual."

Our laughter was short-lived. Not to sound like a spoiled brat, but I was nearly out of my mind by the time we got to Venice. Aside from craving my own space and conversation with friends my own age, I couldn't smoke around my mother and it was driving me crazy. (I was forty-one when I finally gave up cigarettes, and in all that time I never once lit up around her.)

At any rate, Little Miss Can't Do Anything on Her Own decided to leave a few days early. I schlepped my luggage and all the crap I'd bought across Europe and found my way from our hotel, through the canals, and to the airport and caught a flight to New York, where I fell into Rob's arms and spent the next three weeks as a raving hetero-sexual.

When I got home, my mom told me about a cute girl she had met at Warren's PR firm, Rogers & Cowan. She was Robert Wagner's daughter, Katie. My mom thought we would make great friends. Knowing I didn't have many close girlfriends, she suggested I give her a call. I sloughed off her recommendation just because it came from her. At almost twenty-one years old, I didn't want my mother picking my friends or making play dates for me.

A few days later, though, I found myself with tickets to a Genesis concert and no one to go with me. Rob was out of town, Emilio didn't want to go because Peter Gabriel had left the band and Emilio insisted that Genesis wasn't Genesis without Peter. Rob's brother, Chad, my backup date, was busy. I thought what the hell, and I called Rogers & Cowan and got Katie on the phone.

"I don't know you and you don't know me," I said. "But I have great seats for a Genesis concert tonight. I also have a limo. Want to go?"

She said yes and from that moment forward we were joined at the hip. We were the same astrological sign, Taurus, born just three days apart. She shopped the way I did, with gusto and power. We favored Fred Segal and the boutiques on Sunset Plaza, where her mom had a store. We would go to New York for three-day shopping sprees at the B stores—Barney's, Bendel's, and Bergdorf's. Best of all, she didn't go gaga over Rob, as had some previous girlfriends. She was unfazed by him.

I adored her father, an amazing man who was exactly the way you would think he would be. At her house, we would come in late from a night of partying, find her dad in the kitchen, and sit with him till four in the morning as he told the most mesmerizing stories about everyone in Hollywood. This was twenty years before he had published his own memoir, and the stories about his affair with Barbara Stanwyck and his life with Natalie Wood, as well as Katie's mom were still private and precious.

By the time I met Katie, I had figured out L.A.'s late-night scene and knew the hot restaurants, clubs, and exclusive haunts. Celebrity was the best ticket in town. Whether I was with Rob or Katie or the three of us were out together, the door at the private back entrance of any club would open and we would be ushered directly into the VIP area, or the VVIP area if they had one. Air kisses and drinks followed.

On Friday nights, we went to Helena's, a dinner club in an indus-trial part of Silverlake that stood out only for the Rolls-Royces, Fer-raris, and Mercedes parked in front. There wasn't any sign. You had to know where it was, and then to get in you had to know its owner, Helena Kallianiotes, a former belly dancer turned actress who opened the place as a hangout for her famous friends.

On opening night, Jack Nicholson gave Anjelica Huston a baby elephant. Goldie Hawn turned forty there. Sean Penn and Madonna used it as a haven from paparazzi. Beatty held court at a favorite table. So did Michael Douglas. It was quite a pickup joint. Then Hel-ena started poetry night, which was hilarious. Ally and Judd got up and read poems they had written. I never had the balls to try.

One night, I was at Spago for dinner with Rob, Andrew McCarthy, and Rob's agent, Michael Black (one of the most viciously funny men in Hollywood, and one of my favorite people). At the time, Wolfgang Puck's gourmet pizzeria on the Sunset Strip was Hollywood's night-time commissary. Being there was like an A-list party with surprise guests. Indeed, as Wolfgang brought over special appetizer pizzas, I heard someone scream, "Michael!"

It was kind of amazing how the familiar voice pierced the dense hum of conversation from all the way across the restaurant. I turned and saw Liza Minnelli flying over to our table. She kissed Michael, sat down between Andrew and me, ordered a greyhound, and stepped into our little party as if she'd been there from the start.

Then Michael Jackson walked in. He came straight to our table and sat down just as dinner was served. Wolfgang kept sending over food, and everyone talked—except for Michael Jackson. Other than his kiss-kiss with Liza, he didn't say a word. Nothing.

We finished dinner and were nearly through dessert when we began talking about what to do next and where we should go. Ideas were tossed around. All the options were nixed and everyone ran out of ideas at the same time. The table fell silent. And that's when Mi-chael finally spoke the only words he would say the entire evening.

"You can come to my house," he said. "I got a llama."

The already strange evening got stranger when Liza suggested going to Sammy's. I thought she was talking about a club I'd never heard of. She laughed at me ("You're so silly," she said) and explained she meant Sammy Davis Jr.'s house. Andrew, Michael Black, Rob, Liza, and I bid good-bye to Michael Jackson, who didn't want to go, and caravanned to Sammy's house in Beverly Hills, where I'd learn Sammy was friends with my grandfather (surprise, surprise) and see a wigless Liza (the woman had six hairs on her head!). Eventually we ended the night at Michael Black's apartment, where suddenly Andrew and Liza started making out. That was it for me. I said to Rob, "What is Android (our nickname for him) doing?" Rob said he didn't have a clue, but agreed with me that it was definitely time for us to get the heck out of there. So we said our good-byes and drove home laughing uncontrollably as we recounted the crazy events of the evening.

Life was terribly fun. It was still basically pre-AIDS, back when it was only just whispered about as that gay cancer, and things were still fairly wild and permissive. We were in the midst of the Reagan era, and those of us earning good paychecks were not being overly taxed in any way, shape, or form, so people had oodles of money to toss around. There was the sense that all of us were at one of the great parties in human history.

It is important to note that around this time my brother, Jonathan, completely cut himself off from the family. He turned eighteen and simply disappeared. Though he would turn up a couple of times over several years, I have only seen him three times in the last two decades. Surprisingly, I am at peace with it. Though my heart does ache for my mother: I would learn later on what it means to let go of a son.

Rob and I wanted to work together. After years of looking for a project, we thought we found it when, in September 1985, he was cast in

About Last Night and I was asked to do a screen test with him. Ed Zwick, who was directing this dark-humored relationship story based on the David Mamet play *Sexual Perversity in Chicago*, set up the test in New York. Though I heard the test was strong, Demi Moore got the job. Ed was honest and straightforward with me about his decision.

"Casting is casting," he said, "and the studio wants what the studio wants, and beyond all that, just look at the two of them. Even you have to admit they look good together." I gotta admit, they did.

Rob soothed my sore feelings by taking me to see Bruce Springsteen, who was on the last leg of his monumental Born in the U.S.A. tour, and then he went off to Chicago to make *About Last Night*. I visited a couple times before starting my next project, the TV movie *Choices*, which explored the issues surrounding abortion. The picture shot in Montreal with Jacqueline Bisset and George C. Scott, who was every bit the intimidating, ferocious, opinionated, unbelievably talented George C. of legend. For whatever reason, though, we took a shine to each other instantly. Somehow he would know when I was walking by his trailer. He would lean out the door and say, "Kid, come here."

The first time that happened, I entered tentatively.

"Hi. What's up?"

"Have a drink with me," he said.

"George, it's the middle of the day," I said. "You're working. So am I."

"Oh, what's wrong with you, you pussy," he said. "Have a drink with me."

I hesitated for a minute and then thought to myself, *How many times in my life is the opportunity gonna present itself?* He poured a couple of Bloody Marys, and from then on, that became our thing. He was hilarious—and apparently very thirsty.

George was a completely no-nonsense guy. He didn't like all the petty bullshit that was often part of the acting scene, and I think we hit it off because he saw the same no-BS attitude in me. One day we were covering a scene with Jackie, who was a lovely woman and ungodly beautiful. As much as I struggled with my own looks, it dawned on me that being so beautiful must be a huge mind-fuck. You know that inevitably it will go away. And if that's all you're known for, you're screwed.

Jackie didn't fall into that one-dimensional category, but she took extraspecial care when it came to her looks. As she got ready for this scene, she had someone behind her with a mirror and someone in front of her with a mirror so she could check her hair from all angles. She had her own stylist, too. George and I were off camera, watching and waiting as she brushed her hair. Suddenly he put his face next to my ear and, in a gravelly voice I can still hear today, he said, "If I ever hear that you're standing on some film set with a bunch of mirrors around your head, I will come there and I will fuck you up."

"Really, Mr. Scott?" I asked.

"Yes, I will," he replied. "I promise."

"Then I guarantee I will never, ever do that," I said.

"Good." He laughed. "We'll drink to that later."

George played my father, a retired judge, who objected when my character got pregnant and wanted an abortion. Then, in an unexpected twist, he had to decide whether he wanted to be a father again at his age when his wife (Jackie) announced she, too, was carrying a child. The movie was actually pretty controversial for its time. Our most dramatic scene was when I told him that I wanted to terminate my pregnancy. He was supposed to roar, "No abortion," and then we were to have a heated father-daughter argument.

We rehearsed it several times, trying to keep something in reserve for the close-ups. Then we shot the master, and after I delivered the big news, George turned to me, crossed his arms, and stepped forward so that he was looking down his nose at me. His gaze was an intense fire ready to explode in my face. But rather than yell, as I expected him to do, he harnessed that rage and passion and instead calmly and slowly said, "No. Abortion."

It was like getting bitch-slapped across the face by George S. Patton. Startled, I totally went up. I forgot everything I was supposed to say. After a long pause, he asked, "Are you going to say your line?" I shook my head no.

"I can't do it, you Pattoned me!" I said in a meek, embarrassed voice.

I was relieved when he laughed. I assumed I wasn't the first actor who'd been handcuffed by his prodigious talent.

Looking back, I realize there was often someone on a project who was a sort of father figure to me, whether it was Mike, Dick Farnsworth, or George, and I loved hearing George call me kid. Later, whenever our paths would cross or if he saw my mom, he'd ask, "How's the kid? What's going on with the kid?"

In turn, I was able to boast to Rob and the guys that you haven't lived until you've gotten absolutely plowed with George C. Scott—something none of them, despite their movie-star stature, could say. I also told another story that wouldn't have happened to any of them. At the end of *Choices*, we went to New York City to shoot some exterior scenes. One night I took a few people from the crew out to a club, either Limelight or Area, and I was in the VVIP area when Andy Warhol sidled up to me.

He looked straight at me. I'd been in close proximity to him at various clubs over the years. He knew full well who I was. As soon as I smiled at him, though, he took a few steps back and whispered in the ear of a pretty man who was part of his little entourage. The guy stepped forward and whispered in my ear, "Andy wants to know if there are any famous people here tonight."

I turned toward this well-dressed little homunculus, aghast at the insult he had just delivered with a blithe ignorance.

"Tell Andy to eat my shorts," I said.

The guy seemed stunned.

"Okay," I said. "You don't have to tell him to eat my shorts."

He smiled, relieved.

"Just tell him to fuck off," I said.

My identity suffered another kind of crisis when I got back home

only to find Rob wanted to break up. It was a new year, and after finishing *About Last Night*, he wanted to see other people. It was awful,
heartbreaking, and inevitable. Despite getting along, our separate
projects had caused us to spend too much time apart. I cried and
wondered how I was going to get through it. At nearly twenty-two, I
resigned myself to life with my cats and my beagle, Sidney, the only
living creatures who understood me.

But I had people around who pulled me out of bed, picked me
up, got me dressed, and dragged me out. Especially Katie. She was
the one who kept me on life support when I wanted to pull the plug.
She responded with pithy answers when I cried, "What am I going to
do now?" She ignored me when I wailed that I was never going to get
through the heartache. She kept me out of the house and social when
I argued with her and everyone else that my life was over and I was
better off spending the rest of my life under the covers in sweats and
a T-shirt. And she was right when she promised that if I got my ass
out of bed and got dressed, a new door would open.

sixteen

WAIT A MINUTE, WHO'S THE PRINCESS IN THIS LOVE STORY?

In May 1986, NBC celebrated its sixty-fifth anniversary with a black-tie photo session, for which they gathered together the stars of its biggest shows from past and present. I took my sister, who enjoyed seeing all the stars. Numerous people said they couldn't believe that I'd finally grown up, but Don Johnson wasn't among them. The *Miami Vice* star hit on me the whole afternoon.

Not that I minded being the object of his attention when the room was practically overflowing with beautiful women in gowns cut much lower than mine. It was exciting, but I also knew nothing was going to come of it because if anyone in the world was dangerous to women, he was. Even with very little knowledge about Don and even less experience, I knew guys like him were unhealthy for women wanting to preserve their wits and sanity.

I was in my dressing room with Sara after the shoot when Don banged through the door, pushed me against the wall, and planted a kiss on my mouth. Not a polite good-bye, nice-to-meet-you kiss, it was the kind of kiss you felt in your toes. It lasted long enough that I had time to look at Sara with one eye and see her mouth hanging open. Don finally stepped back and looked me directly in the eye with a puckish half smile on his face.

"I'm going to call you," he said.

Then he left.

I exhaled as if I had been holding my breath for two days. The whole thing freaked me out. At the same time, I had to admit that more than my curiosity was aroused. Then he called and invited me to dinner with a group of his friends. I put myself together for the evening and arrived at Sonny Bono's restaurant on Melrose, not sure what to expect, but promising myself I would do nothing more daring than order dessert. Don seated me next to him at a large, round table, and things were fine until Patty D'Arbanville walked in amid a trail of spinning heads.

They had been in a long relationship and had a son together, though I didn't know if they were still together, married, or what. All I knew was that she was one of those unattainably glamorous women. A total knockout way beyond my league and one tough dame. Once she sat down, I felt like I was intruding on something and the rest of the night seemed awkward. It didn't help that I felt like I was a child who'd mistakenly gotten seated at the grown-ups' table.

For a couple weeks afterward, I fielded calls from Don, who wanted me to visit him in Miami. He showed tremendous persistence. I considered going but ultimately, I chose to preserve my own well-being.

Instead, I hooked up with a different Hollywood bad boy, Billy Idol, who I met one night at Tramps when Katie and I were seated at the far end of his table in the VIP section. My first thought was wow, he is gorgeous. We started out shouting at each other over the loud music pulsing through the club. Then I moved to his end of the table. As I settled in, I thought if Don Johnson was a bad idea, this was beyond crazy.

However, as we talked, he impressed me as a sweet, gentle, and soft-spoken charmer. He wanted to know all about Michael Landon and he asked what it was like to grow up on television. At the end of the night, we exchanged numbers and a few days later he called and asked me out. We went on several dates, and of course the second we showed up anyplace, we were met by paparazzi. The tabloids had a field day trying to figure us out. In the public eye, we were the ultimate odd couple (though not to my mom, who liked Billy a lot—then again, she really had no idea what I was up to at the time). He even called me Priscilla, likening us to the pairing of bad-boy Elvis and his oh-so-sweet wife.

I never had any doubt it was more of an adventure than a long-term arrangement. When he returned to town after a brief trip abroad, he threw a party in his suite at the Bel Age Hotel and I saw serious drug use and people out of control. I stayed until the following afternoon, but afterward I was bothered by the glimpse of darkness I saw that night. The turning point was when Billy took me to Rick James's house, which was the scariest place I'd ever been. I felt a bad vibe as soon as I walked in. Twenty minutes later, I made him take me home.

After that, I began to pull back from Billy. That I was even with him shocked the hell out of people, including myself. But I didn't want to get involved any further and then have to disentangle myself from something I sensed could turn ugly fast.

I also grew wary of living too fast and loose. AIDS was making headlines as a fierce and mysterious killer mostly of gay men, but no one really knew anything about the disease except there wasn't a cure.

I came of age right before AIDS, when people were obsessed with California cuisine, parachute pants, and partying all night at clubs. Everyone shared coke straws and glasses. People still hopped from bed to bed. No one talked about condoms or protected sex. The only time I heard anyone talk about losing their life from sex was when some guy half-jokingly expressed concern about the possibility of picking up a psycho stalker who might slit his throat.

At the time, Hollywood was indulgent and decadent, a nonstop bacchanal where everyone was doing everything and everyone all at once. But AIDS changed that sense of wanton freedom and promiscuity. It reshaped the geography of our lives. Some needed more time before they realized this. For me, it was almost immediate. But then I was never one who went on the prowl for casual sex to fill empty hours. Despite my few flings, my search was for a genuine relationship, a love that would last.

It was at this time I left the William Morris Agency and signed with Michael Black at ICM. Ordinarily, when an actor signs with a new agency, there's a meeting in the conference room where agents from all the various departments say that you are brilliant, explain that your previous agents have done everything wrong, and promise to do everything different.

Uncle Ray tried something different by hosting a cocktail party at his apartment. But it was the same old thing, different location. I stood next to my mother and made small talk with the guys from the different departments, like the film guy who introduced himself and said he'd be sending scripts, and the theatrical guy who wondered if I had ever pictured myself doing Broadway, and the TV people who wanted to know how I felt about sitcoms, and so on.

It was just a lot of yada yada yada and listening to how fantastic I was, all of which put me on the verge of exploding from boredom and bullshit. My mother scolded me for rolling my eyes. I couldn't help it. I wanted to be out with my friends, and I was trying to think of an excuse to leave when the door opened and in walked the best-looking man I had ever seen in my life.

Rob was handsome. Michael Landon was good-looking. My father was a good-looking man, too. But this guy was phenomenal. At first glance, he struck me as a more chiseled and more handsome, blue-eyed version of the Doors' lead singer, Jim Morrison. He wore a suit, as all the agents did, but I also noticed a braided rope bracelet around his wrist that revealed something more.

I didn't know what more that could be, but it didn't stop me from feeling like his arrival had changed the entire room. He turned to say something to an agent he knew and about forty-five degrees into that turn he saw me. Our eyes locked and I swear it was as if time stopped and the entire room disappeared so that it was just the two of us there. I pulled myself away from his gaze long enough to lean close to my mother and say, "I'm in deep shit."

"What do you mean?" she asked.

"Look," I said.

She turned and gasped.

"Oh my God," she said.

"I know. Have you ever in your life?"

"Never," she said.

"Neither have I. What do I do?"

"You'll figure it out."

I didn't have time to figure out anything. He walked straight across the room, shook my hand, and introduced himself. I'm pretty sure I heard him say his name was Alan Greenspan. He could've said Jack the Ripper. I was done. Gone. We chatted briefly, then visited with people around the room for a few minutes, until we met each other again on the other side of the room.

"I'm really bored," I said. "How about you?"

"Yeah, it's kind of silly, isn't it?" he said. "Where are you going after this?"

"No plans," I said.

"I'm going to meet friends at the Hard Rock," he said. "Want to come?"

"Can we leave right now?" I said.

I found out more about him over burgers that night. Born in upstate New York, Alan had studied business and played football at the University of San Diego, and now he was rising through the film and

TV ranks at the agency. We saw each other again the following week-end when he invited me to watch him play in the Hollywood Softball League at Balboa Park. Then he came back to my house for lunch and a relationship blossomed. It happened that easily. I would pinch myself whenever I thought about Alan. Not only was he breathtakingly handsome, he was also a kind, warm, generous, funny, easygoing guy. I'd lucked out.

Then this lovely new romance was interrupted by inquiries from the tabloids; they wanted to know my reaction to Rob's new girl-friend, Princess Stephanie of Monaco. Assuming that I must be heartbroken there was another princess in my love story, they asked if I was okay.

Rob and Stephanie had spent ten days together early that September in Paris, apparently falling instantly and madly in love, which shouldn't have shocked anyone since they were virtual look-alikes. He had also recently told Joan Rivers, then subbing for Johnny Carson on *The Tonight Show*, that Stephanie was his fantasy woman. Stephanie had then reciprocated through the press.

I instructed my publicist to say I had no comment, but truth be told, I could not have cared less. I was falling madly in love with Alan, who was not a shameless creature. I was bothered, though, when Katie called me one day after Rob's royal romance had hit high gear, with tabloids reporting that he and Stephanie had exchanged rings and were already planning to wed (not true). She wanted to throw a party for Rob and Stephanie, and she asked, "Is that okay with you?"

That was the beginning of a distance between us. I was pissed. Here was my best friend, a girl I let myself trust, and she was suddenly as swept up by the whole stardom thing as anyone else. In retrospect, I don't think our friendship would have taken such a hit if I'd said, "Dude, are you crazy? That's the most hurtful thing you've ever said to me."

But I wasn't mature enough to tell her how I felt. Instead, I said,

"Do whatever you want." Of course, I didn't want her to do anything. My damage.

In the meantime, I made the movie *Blood Vows: Story of a Mafia Wife* and then agreed to a small role in the movie of the week, *Penalty Phase*, after its director, Tony Richardson, called and asked if I'd sign on to play opposite Peter Strauss. Like *Blood Vows*, it was another step in the direction of more adult roles. I agreed and flew to Oregon.

The producers put me in a beautiful little Victorian home out in the country, and my day-to-day routine was pretty relaxing because I didn't have to work every day. The downside of that was I had too much time on my hands, and I got bored and lonely. Alan came up to see me, but he couldn't stay long, and almost as soon as he arrived, I got upset at the prospect he would have to leave. Okay, I didn't merely get upset. I worked myself into a state, as I was capable of doing back then.

On the day he was scheduled to fly back to L.A., we went out to lunch. As we ate, I thought, *If I can get really sick, I bet he'd stay with me.* An hour later, I complained of an excruciating pain in my stomach. Within an hour of that, I was in the emergency room at St. Vincent's Hospital, being wheeled into emergency surgery for a severe bout of appendicitis. My white-cell count was through the roof.

It was all very dramatic and scary. As I went under, the anesthesiologist warned that I would feel pressure on my throat. I was able to ask why and hear him explain it was a nurse pressing on my throat to make sure I didn't choke on my own vomit, since I'd recently eaten a cheeseburger. The next thing I knew I was waking up, my appendix was gone, and Alan was at my side, saying he'd stay an extra day. It was a large price to pay for a small victory.

After a few days in the hospital, I returned to work just in time for my big seduction scene with Peter. He stepped out of the shower to find me waiting for him wearing nothing but panties—and an enormous bandage across my stomach. Not only didn't I feel sexy, I was scared to death to stand there with my boobies exposed to Peter and my panty-wearing butt facing the camera. To get through it, I drew smiley faces on my bandage. They caught Peter off guard, and that tiny distraction took the edge off for me.

A few nights later, like an idiot, I went out with a couple people from the crew, stayed out way too late, drank way too much, and within forty-eight hours I was sicker than I'd been when I first went into the hospital. Unable to sit up for more than a few minutes at a time, I managed to finish my last scene, and then I flew home. Somehow I survived the plane ride and got to my house. I remember Rob coming over and the next thing I knew I was being driven straight to Cedars-Sinai Medical Center.

Delirious from fever due to a rampant case of strep that had invaded my entire body, I barely recognized Rob, who was very gallant in coming to my rescue even though he was still seeing Stephanie. Once he knew I was okay, he went back to his *other* princess. Then Alan took care of me.

Two months later, he took me to Tahiti for a proper rest. It was fall, and I thought we had been deposited in paradise. We had a hut on the beach. We woke up at sunrise, went to bed at sunset, and in between we ate, snorkeled, made love, napped, rode horses, drank, and made love again. It was a perfect place to decompress, a perfect place to be in love with a truly wonderful guy.

Around the holidays, Rob called me from a Porsche dealer and said he needed my help. I had read the Princess Stephanie thing had imploded, as it inevitably was going to do, and he was back in L.A.

"You need my help?" I asked.

"I'm buying a 928 and I'm scared shitless to sign the paperwork," he said. "You have to help me."

"First of all, I haven't spoken to you in how long?" I said. "And why do I have to help you? Why can't you do this?"

"I'm begging you," he said. "Please, Melissa? I've never bought anything like this in my life."

I understood; this was considerably different than the Mustang he had purchased when we were first together. But his request was also completely absurd—so absurd that I sped over to the Porsche dealer and sat with him as he signed the papers. Afterward, Rob said he needed to talk to me. I knew what he wanted, what he was going to say, and I didn't want to have that discussion. But he pleaded with me to change my mind and eventually broke me down.

We met up again later that day. I spent the few hours in between preparing my responses to all the apologies and entreaties I knew he was going to make. But it turned out Rob had more than forgiveness on his mind. He knew he'd been an asshole and admitted to breaking my heart far too many times. But he had, he explained, just been through the most insane experience of his life ("I'm sure you read about it," he said sheepishly; I said I had). Then, looking like a man who'd just walked back into his life after being given up for dead in a far-off land, he said, "I'm back! I'm here. I'm me!"

"What is that supposed to mean?" I asked.

"I'm not going to live without you," he said. "I swear to God, this time it's different."

"Really? What makes it different this time?"

"Because this time"—suddenly he dropped to one knee—"I want you to marry me."

He caught me totally off guard, and I froze. "You what?" I asked.

"I am formally asking for your hand in marriage," he said. "Will you marry me?"

I was at a complete loss. I stammered things like "Well, hold on now" and "I have to take care of a few things before I can give you an answer." I was totally thrown! I thought about Alan. I flashed on his family, whom I'd met on a recent trip to New York. I made a lot of strange sounds. I grunted and moaned. I did everything but say yes or no.

Finally, I said, "Rob, it's just too much. Go away. Give me some time and I will give you an answer."

So he roared off in his new Porsche and I collapsed on my bed and twisted myself into a knot, a position I stayed in quite uncomfortably for the next few days. I felt like I was in a dream. I didn't know if I was coming or going. I didn't believe Rob had actually proposed. Nor could I understand why. I even called him and said, "I'm going to ask you this again: are you seriously proposing marriage?"

"Yes," he said.

"I mean *marriage*," I said.

"Yes."

"Within a year of asking me, you're prepared to be married to me, because I'm not going to be engaged for decades and decades."

"Right."

"You're prepared for this?"

"Put any conditions on it you want."

"You mean this?"

"Yes," he said. "Do you have an answer?"

"Honestly, I still can't wrap my brain around this," I said. "You have to give me more time."

I really didn't know what the hell to do. In the meantime, I had a special man in my life who was calling me throughout this quandary and asking me to dinner and movies, asking me to hang out with him as we had been doing, and asking me if he could bring me soup or just sit with me when I told him that I'd been lying low because I wasn't feeling well.

Each time I found myself inching toward calling Rob with an answer, a voice in my head screamed at me, *Don't do it. You already have a wonderful guy. He's sweet. He's caring. He adores you. You're going to break his heart and then you're going to be sorry.*

The last thing in the world I wanted was to break someone else's heart, especially Alan's. I knew too well the misery of heartbreak. The thought of possibly doing so was almost more than I could bear. I didn't eat or sleep. I talked to my cats. I asked my dog for advice. I looked heavenward for a sign from my dad. I also talked to my mother, repeatedly asking her the same question each time: *What should I do?*

She finally threw up her hands and said, "It's up to you. Who's going to make you the happiest?"

She was right. I had to quit torturing myself and make a decision. I got out a piece of paper, titled it "The Pros & Cons of Marrying Rob Lowe," and made a list.

seventeen

WHAT FRESH HELL IS THIS?

After a great deal of soul-searching, the choice was clear. I had invested real time and effort into my relationship with Rob and if he was telling the truth, I was in. I knew we were young, but I also knew he was the man with whom I wanted to spend the rest of my life. He was the one I wanted all along.

Before I gave Rob my decision, though, I needed to break the news to Alan. I wanted to be as grown-up and considerate as possible. E-mail and text messages didn't exist back then; I wouldn't have delivered the news in such a cold manner, anyway. I wasn't going to do it over the phone or by letter, either. Alan deserved better. He deserved to hear me explain in person why I was making this extremely painful decision.

I went to his apartment, praying it would go all right. Unlike Rob, who I'd seen cry and scream (hey, he's an actor, there's histrionics and drama), Alan was very even-keeled and reserved. He wore his emotions as neatly and carefully as his necktie. I wanted to vomit, but I felt like I had a grip on my feelings as I told him that I had been forced to make a difficult decision after Rob had suddenly come back.

Alan's face was like stone, but I saw his eyes begin to melt as he uttered a scared and hesitant "Yes?"

"Back into my life," I continued.

"Yes?" he said.

Before I could get into the details, Alan began to cry. He realized what was happening. I felt like Alexis Carrington, just a colossal bitch. I wanted to run home, crawl into bed, and instruct my mom to tell Alan I was breaking up with him, tell Rob I would marry him, and then set up the wedding so all I had to do was show up. I didn't want to be a grown-up having this conversation, which quickly turned heartbreakingly sad and teary.

"What are you going to do?" Alan asked.

I told him, and he started to cry even harder. Then he pulled himself together and said he didn't know what to tell me other than he hoped I would be incredibly happy. That made me cry hardest of all. I spent the night—both of us wanted one last night together—but leaving the next morning was torture. I had to drag myself away from this wonderful guy, and then I chastised myself the whole way home. I knew I was behaving like an utter moron.

At home, my answering machine was full of messages from Rob. Unable to reach me, he wanted to know where I was. I called him back. He wanted to know if I'd made a decision yet. He said he was losing his mind. I told him that I loved him very much and had a decision, but I needed a couple more days before I saw him. When we finally got together, I was blunt about my reservations. I threw all the clichés at him, including the one about leopards not being able to change their spots.

"But I'm convinced people can change," I said. "And maybe you are willing to change. Maybe this is a turning point for us. Maybe the fact that you have to cough up some dough to put a shiny rock on my finger will add to the fact that we have this commitment. I don't now. But I'm not going to walk away from six years of my life, and I want to give this a chance, so . . . yes, I will marry you!"

After breaking the good news to our families, our biggest challenge was picking out a ring without seeing our engagement splashed across the tabloids. We snuck into a Beverly Hills jewelry store one day without attracting the attention of any paparazzi. I'd always loved jewelry, but I had no idea what the good stuff cost. The price tags shocked us. Not that I saw any rings I liked; all of them were too big or too gaudy or both, and too expensive. They ranged in price from twenty thousand to two hundred thousand dollars. Ridiculous! But like most women, I was able to summon a reserve of stamina and stay with the hunt until I found the perfect ring for me, a dainty sparkler with eleven baguettes and five marquise diamonds, all under a carat, shaped like a crown and set in white gold. I showed it to Rob and tried it on.

"This is the one," I said.

"It is?" he said.

I nodded.

"I don't know how much it's going to be," he said.

"Well, ask, stupid."

"You're sure you really like it?"

"It's perfect."

"Based on what I've seen," he winced, "this is gonna hurt."

"Maybe," I said, grinning.

The ring was priced at twenty-five hundred dollars, still a significant sum but not anywhere near the hit we had anticipated. As we left the jewelry store, we were met by a group of paparazzi, who had been tipped off we were inside picking out a ring. Amid the whir of snapping cameras and questions about our engagement, we hopped into Rob's Porsche and sped off to safety.

Suddenly and implausibly, Rob and I looked downright stable. Tom and Rebecca had split; so had Emilio and Demi; in fact, Emilio had fathered two children with Carey Salley, with whom he had an on-again, off-again relationship. At a New Year's party thrown by Alana Stewart in the house she got in her divorce from Rod, I spotted Ryan O'Neal and Farrah Fawcett and thought, *Well, they're a couple. They've made it. If they can do it, I think Rob and I can be okay.*

Thinking back to that moment of naive optimism reminds me, at least in tone, of the scene in *Postcards from the Edge* when Meryl

Streep comes home and Shirley MacLaine is waiting up for her, drinking, in pajamas with a turban on her head. They have an argument, and Shirley says, "You know, it could have been much worse. You could've had Joan Crawford or Lana Turner for a mother." And Meryl says, "What, those are the choices?"

Ryan and Farrah were our control couple? My North Star?

What was I thinking?

Per Rob, the next step was moving in with him. He wanted me to move from my mother's guesthouse into his mother's guesthouse.

However, his was more than fourteen feet away from the main house, and he had redone it in *American Gigolo* style, bachelor pad chic, featuring black lacquer cabinets, leather furniture, glass bricks, Bang & Olufsen electronics, and a splash of neon light. By contrast, my place was done with funky, comfortable furniture tending toward the style that would become known as shabby chic, with beautiful art nouveau accents. I also had three cats, Sylvester, Cairo, and her son, Dr. Murray Schwartz, as well as my dog, Sidney Beagleman. Rob had a cat, too, an Abyssinian named Bob Love.

I didn't see how the hell my stuff was going to blend with Rob's. Nor did I see how we were going to share his closet, which already overflowed with designer clothes and wardrobe from his various movies. Also, he didn't have a doggie door for Sidney. But every time I raised a new obstacle or problem, Rob told me not to worry, that we'd figure it out, and we did.

We worked out more than just living arrangements. In one of our conversations, we divulged to each other what had been going on while we were apart. I told Rob that I'd been seeing someone very seriously, but had ended it for him. He told me about the craziness of his relationship with Stephanie. After everything was finally purged, I said, "So let me ask you a question about you and Stephanie."

"Yes?" he said.

"What is it like fucking yourself? You guys are clones. What's it like?"

He just smiled his adorable Rob grin.

"You noticed?"

"Who didn't," I said. "I mean, she's clearly not just any other seashell, is she?"

After agreeing on a summer wedding date, Rob left for St. Augustine, Florida, where he began making *Illegally Yours,* and I turned my attention to actual wedding plans. I pored through bridal magazines, looked for dresses, and met with wedding planners, florists, and caterers to get ideas. Rob and I talked numerous times a day. He was more into the guest list, a monster task that began to resemble an awards show seating chart with all its nuanced complications. One day he said if we were going to have Francis Ford Coppola, we needed to invite Oliver Stone, too. I pointed out that we didn't know Oliver. Rob said, "Yeah, but we really should."

There were many similarly nutty conversations. Like could we invite Demi and still have Emilio? Could we invite my friend Leilani's sister, who had had a less serious thing with Emilio but a thing nonetheless? Judd or his ex, Loree? On and on ad nauseam. At one point, I felt like we had to invite everyone or no one, because it seemed as if everyone in Hollywood, at least those we knew, had slept with one another. Us included. It convinced me that one day way in the future, the industry will be run by one little banjo-playing mogul with an exceptionally high forehead, little beady eyes, and webbed fingers. The quintessential product of celebrity inbreeding.

In the meantime, Rob was having a great time in St. Augustine, hanging out with Colleen Camp and the crew. But he didn't completely get director Peter Bogdanovich. During rehearsals, Rob called me, perplexed. Peter had told him not to have orgasms during sex while he was shooting the movie. I said, "What?"

"Yeah. He said you lose a lot of energy that way, and it's a problem. So you can't let yourself come."

"You're not listening to him, are you?" I asked.

"No," he said.

"But wait. I'm not there. So what does it matter?" (Ha-ha.)

I visited a short time later and we had a nice time. Peter graciously opened his set to me anytime and I did all the touristy things in St. Augustine. Then I flew back home and hung out with friends. I was really determined to be good. Both Rob and I had multiple flings in the past, but I was going to make sure my behavior was as changed and chaste as he said his was. No John Cusack moments for me, no temporary fixes. I was Suzy Homemaker, planning my wedding, and as far as I recall, Rob was rolling along nicely, too.

Till then, I had been partying heavily. But I turned over a new leaf after accompanying my friend Lauren to a twelve-step meeting. A manicurist, Lauren was my primary coke connection. She also smoked bales of weed, and one day, feeling like her life was unmanageable, she decided to get sober. At her meeting, I introduced myself as a normy, but I left thinking my life would be infinitely better if I gave up drugs. Not alcohol, I didn't consider that a drug; a beer or a cocktail was fine. But I felt like I was doing a lot of coke. I'd recently missed an audition because I'd woken up after a too-brief sleep looking like shit. That was enough of a reason for me.

As I did with so many things, I got way too involved too fast. I went to meetings, became a life raft for people who were sinking in their own lives, put my name on phone lists, went out for lots of coffee, and had people to my house. It was a nice network of people. They were all a little dark and fun. My life did become a little bit more peaceful, too. I could focus on other people's drama instead of my own.

It was temporary, though. After finishing *Illegally Yours*, Rob flew straight to New York and began production on his next picture, *Masquerade*. I visited at the beginning, and I got a good vibe from director Bob Swain and Rob's costar, Meg Tilly. Rob had rented a lovely home in the Hamptons, and we had a great time there. During the day, we hung out at the beach and took funny videos of each other with the camera his parents had given him for Christmas, and at night, we hit the hot restaurants and clubs in the city.

Charlie Sheen was also in town shooting *Wall Street*. One night Charlie, Rob, and I were at a club with Oliver Stone, tucked away in a corner booth where the shadows fell a little heavier to afford more privacy, and the music wasn't quite as loud so we could actually have a conversation. Oliver was ranting about the terrible quality of television, going on and on about how the networks put on nothing but crap and in the process turned the culture into crap, and blah-blah-blah.

At one point, I saw out of the corner of my eye a group of girls staring at us from across the club. They had that look in their eyes. The celebrity-chasing photographers are called paparazzi. I call the people who stare across the room the recognazzi. These ones were in their early twenties and attractive. I watched them work up their nerve and walk up to our table. I thought they were going to ask for Rob's autograph. Rob sort of sat up straighter, getting ready to sign, shameless creature that he was, while Oliver went on with his diatribe and Charlie listened. But the girls looked past both of them and directly at me.

"You're Melissa Gilbert, right?" one of them asked.

"Yes," I said.

"Oh my God," one squealed.

"We've been watching *Little House on the Prairie* our whole lives," another one said. "We even watch the reruns."

"Growing up, I wanted to be just like you," the third chimed in. "I dressed as you for Halloween."

They excitedly recalled their favorite episodes and told me more memories they had of loving the show. Everyone at the table got quiet. Oliver looked at me curiously; I don't think he had any clue who I was. The girls, in turn, didn't seem to be bowled over by Rob or Charlie, and had no time for Oliver. Nor did they care. After they left, I flashed Oliver a grin and said, "And that is the power of television."

• • •

I returned home feeling pretty damn good about life. I heaved a sigh of relief at the decision I'd made to marry Rob. It seemed he had clearly changed. With our wedding plans moving along, I celebrated my twenty-second birthday with Katie Wagner and our producer-friend Brad Wyman. Since all of us were Tauruses, we called it the bullshit party.

I broke my vow to not do drugs that night and went on a two-day bender in Las Vegas with a group of friends that included Leif Garrett. Flying home, after not sleeping for forty-eight hours, I thought I saw the writing on the wall, and it scared the shit out of me. After that binge, I vowed to never do cocaine again.

Rob asked me to come back to the Hamptons to be with him, and I couldn't get there fast enough. I put the grizzled feeling of excess behind me and fell into an easy, loving, relaxed rhythm of visiting Rob on the set. We bopped around the Hamptons and hung out at night. We couldn't have had a better time.

After a couple of weeks, I bid him good-bye and went home to continue wedding preparations. I looked for a dress, met with the wedding planner, and relaxed with my girlfriends. I wasn't sure why, but I felt run-down, tired, cranky, and just plain blah. I was at our home in Malibu when I noticed my breasts were particularly tender. Then it hit me. Oh shit, my period was late!

I grabbed my Filofax and started counting days. It turned out I was about a week late. I bought a home pregnancy test, then tossed and turned through the night, waiting for the morning, when the instructions said to take the test. At the first glimmer of sunlight, I leapt out of bed, ran to the bathroom, and took the test.

It was positive.

I was pregnant.

My heart raced and my hands shook uncontrollably. I laughed and cried at the same time. My brain didn't know what to think, so it thought everything:

A baby.

My baby.

Mine. And Rob's.

Our child.

Oh God, the wedding! We would have to move the wedding date up! No way was I walking down the aisle with a bulging stomach and a train of whispers.

What was Rob going to say? I tried to imagine his reaction. How happy would he be when I told him the news? Surely he would be happy. Right?

My mind wouldn't stop. I was going to be a mother. I was going to have a family of my own. I made an appointment with my ob-gyn, who confirmed that I was pregnant, gave me a big hug, and sent me on my way with a handful of pamphlets and prenatal vitamins. My life was about to change in ways I couldn't begin to imagine. It was going to be exactly the way I had dreamed. I was beyond happy. I wanted to tell Rob the news in person, so I left the next day for the Hamptons. I arrived and slipped contentedly into his arms, thinking, *This is the man I love, the man I am going to marry, the man I am about to tell a secret that will make our lives perfect.* He held me and told me how happy he was that I had come back to be with him, how badly he had missed me, and how much he loved me.

That was my cue. With my cheek pressed against his face, I whispered, "There's more. I'm pregnant."

Silence.

I pulled back from him just enough to see his face. "Rob?"

He walked away from me and sat down on a patio chair across the room. I sat in the chair opposite him and said something along the lines of, "I know. It's a lot, and not something we planned. But we have time to prepare. How difficult can it be? People have been having babies forever."

I prattled on until I saw the look on his face change from shocked to positively panic-stricken.

More silence ensued. It was like I had stepped into a bottomless pit. I felt the terror of falling and no one to catch me.

Finally Rob cleared his throat, and with his voice trembling and tears in his eyes he said very softly, "I can't be a father."

"What?"

"I can't be a father," he said in a firmer voice.

Before I could respond, he said, "I can't be a husband." He had tears running down his face. "Melissa, I can't be a boyfriend right now either."

"What does that mean?" I asked. "I don't understand." I stared at him. "You have to tell me exactly what you mean!"

Rob started to cry.

"I am so sorry," he said. "I'm so sorry. I just can't do it. I can't do any of it. It's over."

"Over?"

"I'm so sorry," he said.

I walked over to him, put my arms around him, and we cried together. Both of us knew this time it really was over. Done. Finished.

I wanted to go home, but it was too late for me to get back to JFK and catch a plane and frankly, I just didn't have the strength. I stayed the night with him. I don't think I slept a minute. I watched Rob sleep while my mind replayed and analyzed what seemed like every moment of our relationship. Frustrated, I then stared into the darkness, as if I might find a window through which I could see what would happen next.

Rob was so lucky; anytime things got rough, God bless him, he would go to sleep. While I was as worked up as a supercomputer ablaze with blinking lights, he was fast asleep, curled up facing me, breathing rhythmically, and looking beautiful, contented, peaceful, and blissfully unaware of what lay ahead.

The next day was a blur. Before getting on the plane, I called home and rallied my girlfriends and my mother. They began the process of moving me back into my mom's guesthouse. I was a walking zombie. Everyone helped me unpack. Periodically my mother or one of my girlfriends would shove food in front of me and order me to eat, since I am the type of person who loses her appetite when going through any emotional upheaval. None of them knew I was pregnant.

Later that night, after everyone left and I found myself alone, I began one of the great cries of my lifetime. It was a full-on wailing, the kind of tear-filled purge that comes from deep inside. It was the kind that leaves you dehydrated, exhausted, and cleansed.

When it was over, I began to deal with the most difficult decision I had ever faced. What the hell was I going to do?

The way I saw it, I had three choices: (1) keep the baby and become a single mother at age twenty-three; (2) give the baby up for adoption; or (3) get an abortion.

Within days, the matter was complicated further by the press. Somehow the tabloids had sniffed out our breakup; their reporters circled like vultures. Headlines cropped up everywhere I turned. One said, "Jilted!" Another screamed, "Left at the Altar!" Lovely. Whatever decision I made about this pregnancy, it could *maybe* be kept private if I chose option three. Otherwise it would be splashed all over the place. My decision was also colored by the effect my image had on young girls.

For days, I felt like the world was on my shoulders. I had never been as torn or as scared in my life. I couldn't eat or sleep. My fuse was short. I snapped at my mother and at my friends, all of whom thought my moods were related solely to the breakup with Rob. I still hadn't told anyone what was really going on, and wasn't about to until I had reached a conclusion.

Finally, I began to see things a bit more clearly. I eliminated one option—having the baby and putting it up for adoption. I had never wanted to be anything but a mother myself. I had been drawn to babies from the time I was a little girl obsessed with my baby dolls, and I'd felt like a surrogate mom to Sara when she was a baby. I always knew my ultimate role in life would be that of mother.

Furthermore, I wasn't about to repeat my birth mother's decision. I would never give up my own child. Never. It wasn't a question. It would never happen. How would I keep my pregnancy a secret anyway? The only way I could keep something like that private would be to move to Outer Mongolia. Even then . . .

No, adoption was not and never would be an option. I understood why it was for other people. Just not for me.

This left me with two choices: being a young single mother or having an abortion. I researched both subjects. I processed the information. Rob, the only other person who knew, checked in on me. I gave him credit. He assured me that he would honor whatever decision I made and help in whatever way I needed.

I also prayed to God, to my father, and to all the angels who might possibly hear my pleas to help me find my way.

I would love to say that I did finally reach a conclusion, but I didn't need to. I woke up one morning and began spotting. Scared, I finally told my mother what was going on and she took me to my doctor. He did an ultrasound and told me that I was having a miscarriage. I went home in a daze and let nature take its course. I called Rob and told him what had happened. He seemed relieved. We made an attempt at a conversation but it was too sad.

My mom was amazing. She held me while I cried, brought me soup in bed, and stayed with me until I fell asleep.

A couple of days later I went back to the doctor with a fever. Things were not going well and I had to have an emergency D & C. It was done in my doctor's office with a local anesthetic, and it was painful. Coupled with my broken heart, the whole experience was agony and gave me some very real and scary insight into what an abortion must be like. It was horrendous, but it was over.

There was nothing left for me to do afterward but go home and face reality. I had lost the baby and my relationship with Rob.

Now I was completely, totally alone, and it hurt like hell.

A BRAND-NEW START OF IT

eighteen

THE HEART OF THE MATTER

In the weeks after that, I didn't function well. I rolled along as smoothly as a car with three flat tires. My self-esteem bottomed out. I felt unmoored and adrift, which I hated, since I saw myself as much stronger and more self-reliant than those women whose happiness was dependent on having a man in their life.

I was embarrassed, too. Fool me once, shame on you. Fool me twice, shame on me. Fool me five or six times . . . damn! My friends comforted me, though, and my sister made me laugh. I dove back into AA meetings with a renewed zeal and determination to get my footing back, and indeed, I found some comforting fellowship there, including an interesting guy named Danny Sugerman.

Everyone in L.A. knew Danny, and most had a story about him. He was that kind of guy. He had long, dark hair, angular features, and wire-rimmed glasses. A friend of his once wrote that Danny took quite literally the quote "The road of excess leads to the palace of wisdom," and it was true.

At age twelve, he began answering fan mail for the Doors. He was a fan and hung around their offices, and Jim Morrison took a liking to him and had their manager hire him. After Morrison died in 1971, he became the band's manager, a task he undertook for nearly thirty years. For better or worse, Morrison was the biggest influence on his life. Danny's first book, *No One Here Gets Out Alive,* was a biography that painted the rock icon as more mystic poet than macabre addict. Not surprisingly, Danny was a little like that, too—dark, funny, smart, mesmerizing. Whatever doors Morrison had opened for him—and there were plenty—Danny not only walked through them, but he also felt obligated to share his experiences.

During this time when I was floundering, I had some deep, fascinating conversations with him about life and pain and the ability to come through both smarter and wiser. "One of the wonderful things about human beings," he later wrote in his book *Wonderland Avenue,* is that "we can and often do change, not always gracefully and not often willingly, but occasionally just like that, in a snap, we change. Sometimes fast, sometimes slowly, sometimes for no reason at all or maybe a hundred and fifty."

Such philosophizing was music to my soul; I needed to hear it, and Danny's years of battling heroin addiction as well as his relationship with Morrison provided him with an endless supply. His stories fascinated me. I was a sponge for all the lessons he needed to share in order to feel whole himself. I'd never talked with anyone as seriously about the big issues of life. I felt drawn to him.

He, in turn, gravitated to my injured soul, to my neediness. My pain was something he related to, and I had plenty of it. I was fragile. I cried at the drop of a pin. I questioned who I was as a woman. I felt unlovable and undesirable. I didn't see any meaning to my life. It was all just misery.

In addition to psychological woes, I was hobbled by a week of horrible and ultimately debilitating pains in my lower right side. After examining me, my doctor held up an X-ray in front of my face and pointed to the problem: a large cyst on my ovary. I went in for surgery, but with a great deal of trepidation about the pain medication I would need afterward. Between all my AA meetings and the talks I'd had with Danny about heroin, morphine, Dilaudid, and other shit he rammed up his veins, I worried I'd end up doing the same thing.

But everything went fine. I recovered in the fancy eighth floor at Cedars-Sinai Medical Center. I regulated my pain medication with a PDA, or patient directed analgesic. Basically, when I pushed a button, it administered a squirt of morphine or Demerol into my IV. I tried to go fifteen or twenty minutes longer than necessary to prove to myself that I wasn't a junkie. I wasn't. Downers were not yet my drug of choice anyway.

One day I heard a sharp knock on my door, and before I could say "Come in," it swung open and Danny walked in carrying a stack of books.

These books, he said, were full of information I should know. They ranged from poetry to rock biographies. Danny rattled off titles and the names of authors, including Rimbaud ("the original rock star," he said), Allen Ginsberg, and his friend Pamela Des Barres. I devoured her memoir of life as a groupie, *I'm with the Band*, and picked through the other material.

I was entranced by Ginsberg's epic *Howl*—how could I not be sucked in by the opening lines, "I saw the best minds of my generation destroyed by madness, starving hysterical naked / dragging themselves through the negro streets at dawn looking for an angry fix"? Danny then pointed me to works by Jack Kerouac and William S. Burroughs, and from there, he turned me on to music by Lou Reed, Iggy Pop, and the Cure. It was as if I'd gone to college with the Brat Pack and now Danny was providing me my master's in counterculture.

As he nursed me through my recovery with wheat germ shakes, we began having an affair. In retrospect, it was a risky thing to have done. Danny was an ex-junkie, and we were having unprotected sex. I was not in a good place psychologically. The breakup with Rob had left me traumatized, and I was lonely, scared, and desperate to be loved. And although Danny had been sober for a long stretch, you only had to scratch the surface to find that crazy, dramatic, addictlike behavior.

Danny and I were the perfect codependent couple. Empathetic to a fault, self-centered, and overly dramatic. Danny was sure that one day we would get married. Swept up in the drama and romance of his proclamation, I agreed. We toasted ourselves with champagne. One night, Danny did a couple lines of blow someone had given him, then turned to me and said, "It's cool. I'm not doing heroin."

I nodded my approval. In reality, I could not have been more clueless. No, that's not true. I had read *Wonderland Avenue* and so I was familiar with the dark Danny who appeared with the flip of a switch, the Danny who was always on the precipice of despair and death. I was drawn to that drama. But I also knew it was just a phase.

Late that summer, I went with him to New York to see a show by Echo and the Bunnymen. The English rock band had provided a faithful cover of the Doors' song "People Are Strange" for the *Lost Boys* movie soundtrack, and the Doors' keyboardist Ray Manzarek, who Danny managed, was playing with them in concert.

While we were there, I received a call from my agent in L.A., asking if I'd be interested in auditioning for a new off-Broadway play called *A Shayna Maidel*. He explained it was the story of two Jewish sisters who reunite in 1946 following a twenty-year separation. One was a survivor of a Nazi concentration camp, and the other had grown up in America.

I was moved by the bare-bones description. I was also intrigued by what doing the play would mean, namely, moving to New York. I'd never lived away from home before. In addition to the challenge of doing something new, I'd be getting a fresh start. I wasn't getting feature work. I didn't have anything tying me to home. As I told my agent, it sounded exactly like the kind of opportunity I needed.

"I have to warn you," he said, "this is off-Broadway. There's very little money. Like five hundred bucks a week."

"I hope you enjoy your ten percent." I laughed. "And don't spend it all in one place. I'm still interested."

Years earlier I had auditioned for one of Joe Papp's Shakespeare productions at the Public Theater, and I'd choked. Not a word came out of my mouth. But this time was different. After reading *A Shayna*

Maidel, which I thought was an extraordinarily written piece, I walked into the audition full of what-do-I-have-to-lose determination, not to mention that little voice in me whispering, *Watch this,* and damn if I didn't get the role. I was shocked—beyond shocked, in fact.

Danny had already gone back to L.A. and in the interim, I began talking to Rob, who was doing a play in nearby Westport, Connecticut. He had a few days off and wanted to visit me. I made it clear I wasn't going to start up another relationship. He still wanted to remain friends, as did I, and we agreed to try to pull it off. So he came into the city and stayed with me for three days. He helped me look for an apartment, and we used the time together to talk ourselves into a good place.

On our last night there, we were about to walk into the hotel lobby when I recognized the band just inside the door. I grabbed Rob and pulled him back.

"No, you can't go in there," I exclaimed. "The Bunnymen are in there."

He had no idea what I was talking about.

"Are you nuts?" He laughed. "What the hell are the bunny men?"

I explained as I dragged him around the block to the hotel's back entrance. From then on, the "bunny men" became a private joke of ours. If we crossed paths, he would ask if the bunny men were there.

The ensuing days were full of chores. I found a furnished apartment in Gramercy Park, met with playwright Barbara LeBow and director Mary Robinson, and began the process of blowing off Danny, which was cruel. But I couldn't handle another face-to-face. I delivered the final blow over the phone when I was back in L.A. and busy packing all my belongings.

After a going-away send-off, I flew back East with my dog, Sidney, and my cat, Sylvester. My apartment wasn't going to be available for a month, so the three of us stayed in my friend Tom Hulce's apartment. He had left menus from nearby restaurants on the table, and on that first night Sidney, Sylvester, and I ate Chinese takeout. Then I sat in bed all night and listened to sirens and the other sounds of the city, shaking, crying, and thinking, *Oh my God, what have I done?*

I felt like I had bitten off more than I could chew. I was pathetic.

How pathetic was I?

I woke up the next day with the single-minded goal of finding a City National Bank where I could break a hundred-dollar bill. I didn't have anything smaller and didn't know I could go into any store and get change. I thought I had to go to a branch of my bank. I knew how to do many things, including how to write checks and use credit cards, of which I had many at my disposal. But I had no idea where to break that hundred. Who doesn't know how to get change? As my Papa Harry would say, "What kind of moron doesn't know from this?"

When I finally realized that I was never going to find a City National Bank, or any bank open at that early hour, I walked into the nearest bodega and asked the guy behind the deli counter if he could break my hundred. I was sweating and practically in tears. I told him that I had to get to rehearsal. Like he cared. He said he'd break it, but I'm sure he thought I was crazy. Or maybe not; it was New York City, after all.

I was so grateful. On my way out, I had a revelation. I wondered if all the bodegas and neighborhood markets were like this one. I turned back to the guy who'd helped me.

"Can I get change here again?" I asked.

"Yes," he said. "But you better buy something, too."

With change in hand, I could catch a taxi to rehearsal. (The subway was beyond me then.) I was determined to make a good impression by getting to the theater early. I knew that people had a preconceived notion of TV actors, particularly those who were celebrities, as I was at the time. They expected them to show up late, bring an entourage, and make demands. I wanted them to think of me as I saw myself: a hardworking, accessible, anticelebrity actor.

However, I got to the Westside Arts Theater on Forty-third Street so early it was still locked. I sat outside on the steps. Eventually a beautiful blond woman who I recognized from auditions came walking up and in a sweet voice asked if I was waiting for rehearsals. Her name was Cordelia Richards, and she was playing my sister's best friend. She sat down next to me and we bonded immediately. She could trace her lineage back to the *Mayflower*. She had gone to Brown and been housemates with John Kennedy Jr. and Christiane Amanpour. Now she lived in a loft on Bleecker Street with her boyfriend Will Patton, a brilliant actor himself.

The whole play had just six characters. My sister was played by Gordana Rashovich, whose backstage warmup consisted of drinking a coffee and a coke, chain-smoking cigarettes, and biting her knuckles till the skin peeled off; then she'd file over the area with an emery board to keep the skin smooth. She was an interesting woman and a very talented actress. The rest of the cast included Joan MacIntosh, Paul Sparer, and Jon Tenney, whose dashing good looks and talent crashed down on me like a falling piano. I was smitten before he made me laugh, which he did often and effortlessly. I always go for the funny.

We began a lovely little romance, which we tried to keep others from knowing about to avoid distracting people from the work we were doing. We shared a cab to rehearsals if one of us spent the night at the other's place, but we had the taxi stop a block or two away from the theater and one of us would get out to walk the rest of the way. One day, as Jon hopped out, we heard someone exclaim, "Gotcha!" It was Cordelia, who was standing right there with a giant grin plastered across her face.

"Don't say anything, okay?" I asked.

She gave me a look and said, "Like everyone doesn't already know what's going on?"

Before I left L.A., my mother had said she couldn't believe I was going to be one of those actresses running to rehearsal with a cup of coffee, a bagel, and my scarf trailing in the breeze. Nor could I believe it when I actually stepped into that role, slipping on pedal pushers and ballet flats in the morning and buying my coffee and bagel across the street from my apartment before hurrying to the theater.

Rehearsals were grueling, but I was determined to make a go of it. My advisors back in L.A. warned the play could be a flop. I didn't believe them—or care. Not only did the work push me creatively to exercise new muscles, I enjoyed my newfound independence in New York City. Every day seemed full of possibility. If there was a gallery opening, I was in. A nightclub opening, I was in. A sweet affair with Jon Tenney, great, I was all for it.

Did it hurt the play when the romance ended at the tail end of rehearsals? No, we remained a tightly knit group of friends. After shows, we ate dinner together at Le Madeleine, the French bistro next door to the theater. On Mondays, when the theater was dark, my New York pals would meet for southern home cooking at Live Bait, a joint on Twenty-third Street, and then we danced till the wee hours at Heartbreak. We called Monday nights "Bait and Break."

For opening night in late October, I called in the troops for moral support. Along with a coterie of agents, my mother and Sara flew into town. So did Rob, who I wanted there not only for the confidence he would give me by being in the audience but also to show him what I could do. I thought we nailed the performance, and the reviews showed the critics agreed, including the New York Times, which called Gordana's and my performances "beautifully matched" and said "the play introduces New Yorkers to a talented dramatist." Not bad for a TV personality.

My mother and Sara returned to L.A. a few days later, as did Rob. Right after he left, I received a call from my publicist, who said a young actor who was starring in Scooncat, another off-Broadway production, had seen me in A Shayna Maidel and wanted to know if I would be his date at his opening night. I asked who this actor was,

wondering if he was some creepy person. She said he was the step-
son of Eve Ensler, who'd written *Scooncat,* and he'd been in a couple
movies.

"He was just in *Interview* magazine," she said.

"What's his name?" I asked.

"Dylan McDermott," she said.

"Hmm."

"He's kind of sexy," she continued. "He's really good in the play
he's doing. I think you guys might actually get along."

I wasn't able to see his show because I had a performance that
same night, but I met up with Dylan at the after-party, thus beginning a short-lived but very enjoyable fling that was over by the holidays. My mom and Sara spent Christmas break in Russia on a
school-sponsored trip, but I flew home anyway and spent Christmas
Day with my godparents, Charlie and Mitzi, who took me to a party
at Ann-Margret's house. The next day I was hanging out at their
house again when Rob called looking for something to do. I was flying back to New York that night, but Charlie and Mitzi screamed at
him from the background to come over. A short time later, he showed
up. Before either of us knew what was going on, they convinced Rob
to fly back with me.

"Don't make her go back by herself," Mitzi said. "Take her back
there."

"Stay a day or two," Charlie added.

"Just grab and go," Mitzi said enthusiastically. "Grab and go."

With nothing else planned, Rob escorted me back to New York,
packing only an appetite for adventure and a toothbrush we bought
at the airport. He stayed with me for the next couple days. The fun
we had together made it clear to me that I had the opportunity to re-
kindle our relationship if I wanted to. Our special chemistry was still
intact and both of us were vulnerable over the holidays, which had always been a good time for us no matter what had happened before.

As much as it pained me, I came to the conclusion that we
couldn't be together in the same room unless we were really going to

be *together,* and that was impossible because neither one of us was ready to make that commitment, especially Rob. I made it clear to him that, despite the genuine love and affection and attraction we had for each other, I didn't think it would ever work out between us.

Rob left feeling very sad. I felt it right in my gut, and in my heart. We were parting forever as lovers. The day he left we stood holding each other outside of my apartment building. I'll never forget clinging to him as it began to snow, saying good-bye. I knew we would always have our memories, and more important, I hoped we would always be friends.

It was a sweet end to our sweet love story.

nineteen

NEW YORK STORIES

A few days after New Year's, I was hanging out with my friends Howard Goldman and Glenn Zagoren. Howard worked in the modeling world and Glenn was a tycoon who tooled around Manhattan in a chauffeur-driven Rolls-Royce. Howard, or Howchie as I called him, always dated the most beautiful, leggy creatures, the kind of sexy, out-of-the-pages-of-*Vogue* specimens who made me feel like a garden gnome when I stood next to them. He said he wanted to introduce me to a guy he knew, but he was reluctant to set up the meeting because "almost all the couples I've set up on blind dates have ended up married."

"Howard, please," I said, laughing. "Like I'm going to marry someone. I'm still in the throes of the world's longest breakup with Rob. Maybe another nice little fling would be good, but the last thing I'm going to do is marry someone."

"I'm just stating the facts," he said. "You can do whatever you want with the information."

"Go ahead and introduce me," I said. "But I guarantee you that I'm not going to be interested. Maybe for a little of the old in-out, in-out, but I'm not getting married."

"Okay," he said. "But I see you two together."

"Well, who is he?" I asked.

Howchie described this guy who was a playwright from Texas. The following Monday night, a group of us met for dinner at Live Bait. I had a bunch of friends with me that night, including Judd and Katie. Howard arrived with Glenn. Finally, the artist formerly known as Chester Harry Brinkman III sauntered past the bar and up to our table. I didn't see him until Howard said, "He's here."

I turned around and saw this long-haired, very handsome man, a better-looking version of Dennis Quaid, who, I later found out, was his first cousin. He introduced himself as Bo, Bo Brinkman. He wore a long cashmere coat, a pair of worn jeans, and cowboy boots. A cigarette dangled from his lips. I could already smell the intoxicating scent of booze and nicotine. He was gorgeous, and he had danger written all over him.

Discovering someone new who looked like that was nearly always a fun if not fascinating endeavor, and my initial conversation with Bo turned into one that I knew I'd remember. It wasn't combative, but we traded questions and answers with a serve-and-volley sort of zing. He tested me because I was a TV actress doing theater, which struck him as wrong.

There was something else. Years earlier, when he was living with Dennis Quaid and Dennis was living with the actress Leah Thompson, Bo had coached Leah for her screen test for *Sylvester*. She had come home afterward and said, "I can't believe I lost the part to that fucking Melissa Gilbert." So now he was meeting that fucking Melissa Gilbert.

As the evening wore on, everyone drank and ate and had a great time drinking, drinking, and drinking. Bo thought he could outdrink everyone. But I showed him that Texans had nothing on the Irish. We walked up to the bar at one point and a guy sitting on the stool muttered something to Bo I couldn't hear. A moment later, though, I heard a thump. I turned around and the guy was splayed on the ground. Bo stood over him, having just punched the guy in the face.

"What the fu—" I said.

"He was saying rude things about you," he said. "I put him in his place."

I think the guy had said something along the lines of "Are you going to take her home and fuck her?" It was the kind of stupid stuff that is too often said at bars late at night by people who've been drinking. Now the poor schmuck probably had a broken nose and I, an even more pathetic creature, thought I had found my Prince Charming. Bo had defended my honor by punching a man. Rob didn't know how to change a lightbulb, let alone punch someone in my defense.

Besides being shocking and exciting, the altercation proved a powerful and sudden end to the evening. All of our friends got up from the table and scrambled out of the restaurant, some running to Glenn's Rolls-Royce, others shouting quick good-byes and disappearing up the street, where they climbed into taxis. I said good night to Bo, who then went back to the apartment in the West Village he shared with his girlfriend, a model named Larissa.

It wasn't what I would term an auspicious way to begin a romance. But it was the beginning.

Like Danny, Bo was part of a world that was completely foreign to me. He had his own theater company and they put on plays in a basement space below a bar called the Trocadero on Charles and Bleecker. He wanted to be a lot of things over the years, but the first thing I knew he wanted to be was Sam Shepard. He smoked *and* chewed tobacco because he'd heard Shepard did the same thing.

The plays Bo wrote were dark, twisted, and very sexual, like Bo himself. He was a guy who on first meeting knew what you looked like naked. Everything about him was right there. He worked with a feverish intensity and drew from past experiences he'd had working on a tanker and at an oil refinery. When I met him he was earning money by restoring landmark buildings in New York; that he could build things with his hands reminded me of my father.

He was a big, complicated storm of personality, like one of the hurricanes he talked about having survived, and I was completely swept up by it. Almost immediately my life was consumed with Bo. Every waking moment was about him. Where was he? Where were we going to go? What were we going to do?

Six weeks after we met, Bo proposed and I said yes. All of a sudden I was putting together a wedding with Glenn and not telling anybody else other than Cordelia. I found an antique-style wedding dress at a boutique in the East Village and I bought a pair of shoes and made a silk flower wreath, both of which I tea-stained to match the dress. On February 21, the night of the deed, or rather the event, I had a show, and a few of my close friends, as well as Bo's sister and a couple of his friends from high school who flew in from Texas, were told to gather at Le Madeleine for dinner. Right before Cordelia and I ventured over from the theater, everyone was let in on the secret: they were going to be guests that night at our wedding.

Per arrangements Glenn had made, all of us were loaded into cars and taken to someplace on Long Island, where we marched into city hall, signed papers, and exchanged I do's in front of a justice of the peace. Just as the justice said, "Mr. Brinkman, you may kiss the bride," a group of firemen burst into the room wearing their fire-fighting garb, including protective masks, yelling something about a gas leak. We hadn't heard an alarm, but they instructed us to evacuate the premises immediately.

As they whisked us outside, I broke into a cold sweat. I thought for sure it was a sign from God telling me that this marriage was a mistake and doomed from the get-go. We were ushered into waiting fire trucks, at which point we were informed the whole thing was a prank concocted by Glenn, who worked with those guys as a volunteer fireman. With sirens blaring, the trucks took us to the firehouse, where the firefighters and their families hosted a family-style reception with champagne, pigs in a blanket, and chips and sour cream and onion dip. Then we went into the city for a fancy dinner in a private room at a restaurant where more friends joined us.

I went to the ladies' room, and as I came down the stairs afterward in my full wedding garb, with flowers still in my hair, I ran into Howard Stern's radio show cohost, Robin Quivers, who was going up the stairs. I had originally met Howard and Robin through Danny, and I had called into their show a few months earlier, around the time my play opened, as a surprise when Rob was a guest. Robin hugged me and said, "What's with the getup?"

"I just got married," I said.

Robin did a double take. I could see her mind hard at work. She kept up on all the latest celebrity gossip and I knew there hadn't been any mention of my relationship with Bo, let alone an engagement.

"Does Howard know?" she asked.

I put my hand to my forehead and said, "Oh, fuck—no, he doesn't."

Well, I knew the King of All Media would know soon enough. Robin congratulated me and went to the ladies' room. I returned to the table and told Bo that we should anticipate a call from Howard Stern in the morning. When we finally got back to my apartment that night, I called my mother and told her that I'd gotten married to Bo. Her response? "That's nice." There were no other embellishments or explanations. I think Bo and I finally fell asleep around four in the morning.

Two hours later, the phone rang. I let Bo answer and only heard his end of the conversation, which went something like this: "Who? Just a minute while I check. Is your name Melissa? Some guy named Howard wants to talk to you. Hold on." Then I said hello and Howard asked if I'd gotten married last night. "I did?" I said. "Oh my God, I was so drunk. Wait a minute, Howard." I turned to Bo and asked, "Did we get married last night?" He said, "I don't know."

At that point, I ended the little charade in a fit of laughter and gave Howard all the details. Within no time, the Associated Press picked up the story and soon it was everywhere. Not until way later did I learn that Rob was with Judd in New York at the time and very hurt by the news. So was Judd. I wouldn't see or hear from Judd for nearly a year.

I didn't need too much hindsight to know that I failed to handle the situation as well as I should have. Despite the conversation I'd had with Rob precipitating his departure after Christmas, I apparently still needed to make it clear to myself and to him that it was over, really over, between us. Which, by the way, it wasn't. So what did I do? I married a stranger, someone I didn't know at all.

God bless my mother. If I'd been my child, I would've killed me.

From day two, our marriage was a challenge fueled by alcohol, insecurity, and the unfamiliarity of two people who barely knew each other trying to merge their lives and work. I would love to say that I wish I'd spent more time getting to know Bo before we married. But then I probably wouldn't have married him. And if I hadn't married him, I wouldn't have had an amazing kid.

But first things first. Bo moved out of his ex-girlfriend's apartment and into mine. As soon as I got a couple days off from the play, I took Bo to L.A. and introduced him to my family and friends, which I was eager to do. My mother hosted a reception at her house. Rob showed up and brought Chynna Phillips, then enjoying stardom with the singing group Wilson Phillips. As soon as I saw him my guts twisted into knots. I thought, *What the hell are we doing? I am married to a guy I barely know and there you are with that beautiful woman and we should be together.* When my dog, Sidney, saw Rob and began jumping up and down and whimpering, I walked away and avoided Rob the rest of the night. Thankfully he and Chynna left early.

That wasn't the only uncomfortable moment during the trip. Before we even arrived, I made it clear to my mom and Uncle Ray that Bo would be involved in all the decisions in my life, including my finances. That explained why she greeted me on my first day back by insisting I put my signature on a quit claim document, giving her complete ownership of her house. I guessed at some point my money had been used to help buy it. At the same time, and unbeknownst to me, Uncle Ray sat Bo down and made it clear that he was skeptical of Bo's rapid appearance in my life, and he wasn't going to let him ride my well-respected coattails to a career of his own.

"You better know that from the beginning," he said in a very stern Louis B. Mayer–like manner. "So you have absolutely no bearing and no meaning in her life as far as I'm concerned."

I was livid when I heard about that sit-down. It started me down the path of separating from my longtime manager and also untangling myself from my mother. I was almost twenty-four years old, and it was time for me to take more control of my life anyway. Back in New York, I dove into work, play, and my new marriage with renewed gusto and independence. Bo had written a movie based on his play *Ice House*, a twisted piece about a Texas oil field worker who wants to break into the music business in L.A. He had raised enough money to start production.

I agreed to star in it with him as his ex-girlfriend. It required me to juggle both the play and the movie. After I would finish at the theater, we would shoot all night. A chunk of it was done at the Chelsea Hotel; other parts were shot guerrilla-style around New York and on the streets of L.A. Only at twenty-four could I have maintained that kind of crazy schedule. I found myself writing checks to keep the production afloat, more than a hundred thousand dollars by the time all was finished.

But I didn't care, not then anyway. Bo was passionate about the work, and I felt I was doing something new, raw, and exhilarating. Two things about it were really rotten, though. It was a nonunion project, and I didn't realize I was violating Screen Actors Guild rules by working in it—something I would get fined for a year later and rue many years down the line. And it was one of the worst movies ever made.

But that latter fact wasn't immediately apparent to us. We were, as they say, so into it we were out of touch. Our lives were full, crazy, occasionally stupid, and sometimes amazing, which motivated us to add another project, a baby. From the moment we got married, we knew we wanted to start a family. If others thought we were rushing things, too bad. I had wanted a child of my own since I was three years old. I also thought it would cement Bo's and my relationship.

In late spring, I left *A Shayna Maidel*, returned briefly to L.A. to shoot the TV movie *Killer Instinct*, and then focused on getting pregnant. Each month, I thought I would end up pregnant, and then I would not see a line in the pregnancy test and ball up with disappointment. I worried about the effect surgery may have had on my ovaries. I had no patience then; that's something I'm only learning now. Finally, while I was doing a play at Bo's theater company, I started to have a funny feeling that something might be stirring inside me, but I didn't rush out and do a test as I had the previous months. Maybe I was distracted by the play.

The show was a series of one-acts. I was in one titled *Big El's Best Friend*, which was about two women who shared a room and an obsession with Elvis Presley. It costarred Susan Astin and James Gandolfini, who may have been making his acting debut on that basement stage, and we were having a great old raucous time together. Such a sweet group of people—until everyone started to drink. At one point, we referred to ourselves as the black-eyed production. Everyone had a black eye. Susan and Jim had gotten in a fight and given each other shiners. Bo had brawled with someone on the street. One of the actors in one of the other plays had walked into an open kitchen cupboard. Then one night when Bo and I were sound asleep, he'd bolted upright, screamed "Get away from me," and elbowed me square in the eye. I'd never been struck like that before, and though dizzy with pain, I still had the presence to shriek, "Thank God it wasn't my nose!"

A little while later I took my black-eyed self to the doctor for a blood test. Lo and behold, the nurse came in and said I was pregnant. Unfortunately, I hadn't dragged Bo with me. After so many negatives, I hadn't seen the point, so he was at FAO Schwarz with his fourteen-year-old niece, Corbett, who was visiting us from Texas. But I was exploding with excitement. I had to tell someone. I called my mom, who started to cry from happiness (I think). I told her not to say anything to anyone because I hadn't told Bo yet.

Eventually I had him paged at the toy store and gave him the good news. He was ecstatic and we celebrated that night at Windows on the World. We had a wonderful evening and got back to the apartment as the phone was ringing. Bo answered. It was my mother, who congratulated him on the baby news. He asked how she knew. She said that I'd called her right away. He gave me the silent treatment for the next three days. I couldn't figure out what I'd done until he finally said, "I can't believe you told your mother you were pregnant before you told me."

I was shocked.

"Dude, you were in FAO Schwarz," I said. "Do you know what it took for me to find you there? I had to tell someone. I told my mother. It's not like I called up Liz Smith. And I told her to keep it quiet until I told you."

"So you told her that I didn't know?" he asked.

It was a no-win situation, like most arguments with Bo. But he calmed down and everything was great. He was consumed by post-production on *Ice House*.

It was fall, and I set about nesting and being pregnant. We moved to a four-story brownstone on West Twelfth Street between Washington and Greenwich streets. The family that owned the building occupied the top two floors, and we took the bottom two. Our courtyard in the back boasted the tallest tree in lower Manhattan, and all the neighbors had little kids and babies. For New York, the building was idyllic.

And so was my pregnancy, though I was nauseous through my first trimester. I never understood why it was called morning sickness. I was sick all day. I'll spare the details of those first three months; just know they were miserable and mollified with saltines and ginger ale.

On the other hand, I was excited by every little change, feeling, and sensation that happened as a new life took shape inside my tummy. I knew the experience of creating a new life was special, as close as we get to experiencing a miracle, and I took time to appreciate each little change in my body. I got curvy. I developed a little belly. I suddenly had boobs, which was totally foreign to me, and yet fantastic. I was happy to stay home and cook or meet friends for dinner and then go to bed early, which wasn't on Bo's agenda.

Such differences were a bone of contention between us until I gave him the green light to go out with his friends and get into whatever mischief he wanted. That didn't mean I gave up fun. In September, I threw Bo a birthday party at a friend's restaurant. I pulled out all the stops by renting out the joint, bringing in a DJ, and making sure the special menu included all of Bo's favorites. It was a good time until Bo and one of his buddies, after drinking too much, knocked over tables and got completely out of control while doing Monty Python's fish-slapping dance.

Mortified and angered by their wanton destructiveness, I left the restaurant, went home and gathered my clothes and crackers, and spent the night at my friend Lauren Holly's apartment. I returned the next morning, but Bo gave me the silent treatment for a couple days. I let it slide. I wanted to keep the drama to a minimum. I gave him a long leash—he could do whatever he wanted. As far as I was concerned, my existence was about nurturing the baby.

The only part of my pregnancy I didn't enjoy was the baby shower my mother threw in L.A. With practically every woman in my life there, from my grandmother to my second-grade teacher, it should have been a high point. But Bo, who was supposed to videotape the ladies-only celebration, was a no-show. He disappeared without telling me where he was going, let alone that he had gone.

I felt humiliated and embarrassed in front of all my friends and family.

I finally located him at his friend's house. He had gone on a bender. The next time my mother asked me about his whereabouts, something she had done repeatedly through the party, I thought the hell with it, and I told her and everyone at the shower exactly why my husband wasn't there. There were gasps.

"Huh?"

"Just leave it," I said.

When he finally showed up later that night, we had a huge fight. At the end, he vowed to never do anything like that again. We took the train back to New York and were able to do a lot of healing and re-connecting during the cross-country trip.

The last month of my pregnancy was pretty easy. I enjoyed my birthing classes, led by a cool-looking Jamaican woman with dreads, I shopped for blankets and onesies, and I studied the spectacle that my belly had grown into.

As my April 20 due date neared, I put my family and friends on alert. It seemed like a false alarm, as that day came and went and other days ticked by without any signs of me going into labor. The phone rang all day with people asking if there was a baby yet.

There wasn't. The baby, who we knew was a boy, appeared con-tent to stay where he was. If I hadn't felt like I had an elephant inside me, I would have enjoyed having him there. It boggled my mind to think that a whole person was growing inside me. It was all the proof I needed to believe in miracles. I would watch my stomach in total amazement as an elbow moved or a foot pushed. I would talk to him, read to him, sing to him, and at night I would curse him out for get-ting the hiccups as soon as I tried to fall asleep. He was like clock-work. Except for when it came time to make an appearance.

I was scheduled to see my doctor for a stress test on May 2. The day before, I started to nest like crazy. The urge hit me from out of nowhere. I cleaned and straightened my home as if every cell in my body had been reprogrammed. I was mystified by it, almost amused by my inability to control my behavior. I had forgotten that right before going into labor, a woman's body often releases a hormone that makes her want to get things in order before the big change that's about to occur.

While lying in bed late that night, I heard a popping noise from within my body and a moment later I felt water. My stomach went down slightly. I told Bo that my water had broken. We called our mothers and my doctor and decided to wait until my contractions were five minutes apart before going to Beth Israel hospital. I was still energized at sunrise. Being the codependent that I was, I spent the morning preparing Bo snacks—sandwiches, yogurt, trail mix, juice boxes—all the stuff I knew he'd want while we were at the hospital. Every so often I would stop, hold on to the kitchen counter, and wince while having a contraction.

Around nine in the morning my contractions were strong enough that Bo took me to the hospital, which was an Orthodox Jewish hospital. I heard a lot of "oy, oy, oy" coming from birthing rooms; I got there and filled my portion of the hallway with F-bombs. By late morning, my mother, Cordelia, my friend Kate, and my mother-in-law were taking turns in my room, trying to distract me from the pain. A few hours later, my contractions were so strong I grabbed Bo and yelled at him to get my daddy. My doctor was in the room and told Bo it was fine for him to get my father. Bo said, "You don't understand. He's been dead since she was eleven." At that point, Dr. Essig leaned into me and said, "Melissa, you know the expression 'crazy with pain'? That's where you are now. I'd like to start the epidural."

Until that point I had wanted to deliver my baby without any pain medication. But as soon as he uttered the word "epidural," I said, "Great! I don't effing care. Just shoot me up. Now!" Sometime in the early evening, after I'd been in labor for twenty hours, and active labor for about twelve, my doctor informed me the baby still hadn't dropped and was starting to have heart decelerations. Almost apologetically, he recommended a C-section.

"I don't care if you have to pull this thing out of my nose," I said. "I want to see this kid. I'm ready. Just get him out of me."

I was awake but completely numb during the procedure. I could move my arms and hands, but nothing else. I was nervous I might fall off the operating table. I asked the doctor to tell me when he made the first cut, since I figured once I knew it didn't hurt, I could relax. Then I smelled something burning.

"What are you doing?" I asked.

"I'm making the incision," the doctor said.

"What the hell are you using?"

"I'm cauterizing as I'm cutting," he said.

"So that burning smell is me?"

"Melissa," he said, "will you please let me do my job and get this baby out?"

Moments later, after some pushing and pulling, the room turned quiet and I heard the doctor say, "Here he is." I couldn't stand being unable to see him, especially after Bo exclaimed, "Oh my God," and then I heard the baby cry for the first time.

"Bring him to me," I said. "He shouldn't be crying like that."

"He's fine," the doctor assured me.

We had already named him Dakota Paul, after Bo's grandmother and my father, and he arrived weighing just shy of eight pounds. When the nurse held Dakota next to my face so I could finally see him, I was overwhelmed by something I hadn't expected. "Oh my God," I gasped. "He looks . . . like me." I had developed the same mannerisms and expressions as my mother and my grandparents. But until that moment when Dakota was put in front of my eyes, I had never seen anyone who had the same physical characteristics as me. I didn't know anything about my birth parents or have a clue what they looked like. But Dakota looked like me. It was mind-blowing.

Well, he didn't look exactly like me. He had hair like Don King, hair that was so black and tightly curled and sticking straight up that Bo said, "Who fathered this kid?" But Dakota looked like Bo, too. With perfect, pink skin, he was the most gorgeous thing I had seen in my life. Bo thought so, too. In the home video of us in the operating room, from behind the camera Bo says, "Honey, the baby is beautiful." Then he adds, "But your stomach, whoa, it looks like the Holland Tunnel."

For the next two days, I nursed Dakota, spoke to him ("Hi, I'm the lady who has been talking to you for all these months"), and stared at him without sleeping. My mother and sister and Bo's mom took turns holding him. My friend Howard brought Judd, who was the first person outside the family to hold Dakota. Each time someone took the baby, I asked for him back. I was totally entranced by this child. Every breath. Every sound. I didn't want to miss a moment.

Finally, after warning me that I could go crazy if I didn't rest, the nurse gave me a sleeping pill. It put me out for three or four hours, half as long as they expected. They didn't understand that when he was right in front of me, I felt more complete, perfect, and fulfilled than I ever had in my life. To this day, I'm happiest and most content when all of my kids are at home. I don't care how chaotic it gets, who screams, or what breaks. I'm in my element. Everything in me relaxes, my shoulders drop, and I breathe easily. I first experienced that with Dakota. I entered what I call the baby bubble, and I was at peace even when the world around me began to fall apart.

twenty

NEWSFLASH: THIS PERSON DOESN'T YELL, "DO ME, DADDY"

I wasn't the only one fascinated by the changes new motherhood brought. About six weeks after bringing Dakota home, a time when I was consumed with nursing and pumping, keeping ledgers of Dakota's eating habits, bathing him, dressing him, and watching every second of his extraordinary little life, Bo and I attended the New York City premiere of *Great Balls of Fire,* Dennis Quaid's tour de force portrayal of the turbulent life of rock pioneer Jerry Lee Lewis.

It was a beautiful June night, and I enjoyed getting dressed up for the first time in months. I couldn't remember the last time Bo and I had gone out. I wore a sexy black strapless bustier dress, which was perfect for a red carpet event, but not so perfect, I realized, for a nursing mom. My attitude? Tough. I stuck in a couple of round, absorbent breast pads so I didn't leak and went to the gala.

By the end of the movie, though, my boobs were enormous. Since this was my first time away from home, I hadn't anticipated what would happen after my milk let down. At first I thought, okay, I can handle this. But it kept happening and they kept getting bigger. By the time we got to the after-party, they were enormous and rock-hard. If I hadn't been enjoying myself, I would have gone home. But Bo was hammered and I wanted to visit with friends. Johnny Depp was sitting beside me; we'd known each other for a while at that point, and when I turned to say something to him, he leaned toward me and stared at my boobs with a stunned and innocent curiosity.

"What are you looking at?" I asked.

"I'm sorry," he said, embarrassed and pulling back. "I've never seen anything like those in my life."

"I know," I said. "I don't know what to do about them."

"What's happening with them?" he asked.

"It's milk," I said.

"Milk?"

I gave Johnny a quick primer about being a nursing mother. He asked several questions, and finally he asked if he could touch them. I said, "Yeah, do whatever you want." For the next two minutes, I sat there with Johnny Depp holding my breasts as I chatted away with other friends around the table.

With Dakota making me happy to the core, my life in New York couldn't have gotten any better—and it didn't. One day as I was taking Dakota to a checkup, I was standing on Hudson Street, trying to hail a cab. I had the baby in a snuggly, a backpack on one shoulder, a portable stroller slung over the other, and a car seat in one hand. As I juggled all that stuff, I projected a few years forward and wondered what we were going to do when Dakota wanted to ride a bike or throw a baseball.

I started to think about moving back to L.A. Bo had once lived there and hated it so much he swore he'd never live there again. I pushed the idea more seriously after a crack house sprung up in the midst of our family-oriented neighborhood and some of the mothers were being held up as they took their children to and from school.

I also wanted more support from family. I didn't have a nanny, and sometimes, as much as I loved my baby, Dakota pushed me to the edge of sanity.

One night in particular, he cried for four straight hours, most likely from a bout of colic, which was unusual for him. His nonstop wailing was like torture, the new mother's version of waterboarding. When I couldn't find Bo to help me, I called Cordelia, who was going through a breakup with her boyfriend, and got her to come over and sit with Dakota while I took a much-needed walk around the block, during which even the crack-addicted muggers kept their distance from me.

I had never felt as crazed, but the walk helped me to recenter myself. A few days later, though, I was even crazier.

It was the Fourth of July, and we had friends over for a barbecue that was a perfect, all-American celebration. As Bo cleaned up the kitchen, I said good night, put the baby down, washed my face, and went to bed. Around three in the morning, I heard Dakota wake up, hungry. It was one of the rare occasions when I was simply too tired to nurse him, and with the baby in my arms, I went downstairs to get some pumped milk from the fridge.

The first floor was all one giant space, with the kitchen on one side and the living room on the other, and the stairs were on the living room side. My eyes weren't fully focused as I walked toward the kitchen. It was dark except for the TV, which was on, and the sofa was right in front of me. On it I saw Bo having sex with a woman.

For a moment, I thought I was dreaming. I shook my head and blinked my eyes to make sure I was awake. Bo was indeed screwing another woman. He stopped and turned toward me.

"What are you looking at?" he snarled.

I didn't know what to say. How does a person answer that question?

I walked past him, got the milk out of the refrigerator, warmed it up, and went back upstairs as he continued to screw that woman on my sofa. In hindsight, I can't believe that I didn't grab him by the scruff of the neck and throw him out the door. But I didn't know what to do. There's not a chapter on that situation in *What to Expect When You're Expecting*. As I fed the baby, I heard the front door open and close, then a stomp-stomp-stomp up the stairs. The bedroom door flung open and Bo stood at the foot of the bed like an angry bull.

"What's your problem?" he asked.

"I'm not going to discuss it while I'm holding the baby," I said. "We'll talk about this later."

"No, we're going to talk about it now."

"No," I insisted. "Later."

After I had fed Dakota and tucked him back in his crib, we did have the conversation. I could see that Bo had been drinking heavily, and I was doubtful that talking would help. But I wanted to know how he thought what I'd seen was my fault. I couldn't imagine what kind of convoluted, Bo-centric idiocy I was going to hear. He didn't disappoint. Bo explained it was because I hadn't had sex with him and he needed to get laid. I was dumbfounded. I pointed out that I'd had a C-section two months earlier and neither my body nor my mind was ready for an amorous romp.

"Aside from the fact that this person"—I gestured at myself— "doesn't yell, 'Do me, Daddy,' I just can't imagine such a thing right now."

I explained my whole body's purpose was to nurture and feed a newborn. My brain was hyperfocused on the purity and sanctity of motherhood. Sex was the last thing on my mind. The last thing I could imagine myself doing.

Bo cried and said he was a terrible person. Maybe not terrible, I said, but what he did was pretty messed up. I had no idea how messed up until he offered to tell me exactly what had happened. According to Bo, after finishing the dishes, he was flipping through the TV channels when he began watching *The Robin Byrd Show,* a sex program hosted by the porn actress on public access. The show was filled with advertisements for 800 numbers to call to speak to hookers. He got so horny he called one.

"Wait a minute," I said. "You were screwing a hooker? In my house?"

"Yeah," he said angrily. "What's your problem?"

"My problem?" I said. "Wait a minute. I'm going to make a phone call."

I don't know what came over me or where I got the idea, but I called Bo's mother in Texas and told her the situation: that her son thought I had a problem because I was upset after finding him having sex with a hooker on the sofa in our living room while I was upstairs with our two-month-old child. Then I handed the receiver to Bo, who was speechless.

The middle-of-the-night drama was so absurd that I couldn't even cry. In AA, they talk about moments of clarity and spiritual awakenings, moments when you realize that your life is out of control and you have to change it. Looking at Bo, I had one of those moments. I realized I had to get out of my marriage. I had to leave him. In fact, I never should have married him. I didn't even like him anymore.

I realized I had an even bigger problem when I went back upstairs and checked on Dakota. How could I leave Bo when we had this kid? I didn't want my precious son growing up without his father the way I did when my parents divorced. I wasn't going to do that to my child. Or if I did, I knew I was first going to try everything possible to avoid it.

Although Bo begged for my forgiveness, I didn't give it that night or the next. It took me a long time to get over what he'd done, and basically, the way I got over it was by telling him that I was done with New York. We were going to move back to L.A.

We decompressed in Sun Valley, where we hooked up with my mother, who was vacationing there. During that stay, for the first time in my life, I asked her about my birth family. We had spoken about it in cursory ways when I was little. Then years passed when I never gave it a single thought. But now, inspired by Dakota's resemblance to me, I was curious to know if there were any more people out there who looked like me. If there were, I wanted to meet them.

Before returning to L.A., she gave me a last name for my birth father, Darlington, but professed to not know any other details. A few weeks later, after we had visited Bo's family in Texas and arrived in L.A., where we rented a house on one of the "bird" streets in the Hollywood Hills, Bo hired a private investigator to search for more information. I was costarring with Scott Valentine in the TV movie *Without Her Consent*, the last project under my production company's banner, when the PI unearthed a copy of my original birth certificate.

Obviously I didn't need confirmation that I existed. Nor was I looking to replace my mother or memories of my father; they would always be my parents. But I had never heard any details about my arrival in this world, none of the kinds of stories I would be able to tell my own child. I was eager to read that birth certificate for myself. I discovered that my father's name was David Darlington and my mother's name was Susan Alabaster. As for my name, it said "Baby Girl Darlington." What kind of name was that? I tried to imagine the conversation between the nurse and my birth parents.

"Do you have a name for her?"

"No, just put down Baby Girl. We don't want her."

Of course, such a conversation may not have occurred. Either way, I was good with Baby Girl, my name for the first twenty-four hours of my life. Rob had called me Baby Girl soon after we met. The other nicknames people had given me over the years included Half Pint, Mel, Merv, Smelly, Lissa, Lizard, Bunny, Mouse, Franchise, Wissy-do, Whisper, Gem, Fancy, Melodious, and Poopsidoodle. Baby Girl was one of the better ones.

The PI wasn't able to turn up any additional information on either Darlington or Alabaster, which we thought sounded like an assumed name (and we turned out to be correct), and Bo and I on our own would randomly call information in different parts of L.A. looking for David Darlington, to no avail. I don't know why, but it never dawned on me to look beyond the city.

After a few months of getting nowhere, we abandoned the search on all fronts. Our lives got too busy, and the PI was ridiculously expensive. However, in the back of my mind, I knew that one day I would pick the search back up. I might not find them or get the answers I wanted. But somehow I understood that just asking the questions could be equally if not more beneficial.

Soon after, while I shot *Without Her Consent*, we leased a lovely house in Sherman Oaks. Bo packed up our belongings in New York and drove them to the white house with blue shutters and a white picket fence, previously owned by my pal Tracy Nelson. It was in perfect condition, and we were able to move right in, along with our new nanny, Rosa, her daughter Linda, my dogs, Sidney and Maggie, and my cats, Sylvester and Christmas. Soon we added a stray Lab that Rosa found and named him Brando. I don't remember if I knew how much Bo drank or if I overlooked it because that was easier while I was working long hours on the movie, but life was pretty manageable.

In the fall, I got ready to leave for Hong Kong, where I was starting my next project, *Forbidden Nights,* a big-budget movie for CBS about an American schoolteacher who takes a two-year assignment in China and must confront major cultural obstacles after she falls in love with one of her students. Talk about being out of your element. Production actually began outside of Hong Kong, in one of the new territories, about an hour outside of the city. Everything was either a mall or it was still turn-of-the-century backward. Aside from me, the cast was either Asian-American or Asian, and the crew was mostly Brits and Australians. One man seemed to control everything from the equipment to the trailers; I suspected he was connected to the Triad mob.

I had a nice bus to change in, but unlike the luxury Winnebago I had on my previous picture in L.A., this one didn't have a bathroom. Instead, I was directed to a porta-potty, except this one was sans potty; it was just a squat hole. I wasn't ever going to be known as a prima donna, but I drew the line at a squat hole. If I needed a toilet, I asked to be driven to the nearest hotel.

Others felt the same. Being fish out of water, the Aussies and Brits got together every night in someone's hotel room for a meeting of what someone dubbed the RPPS, the Rape, Plunder, and Pillage Society. Basically, it was the name given to the room where everyone would gather to eat, drink (not me, since I was still nursing), carry on, and unwind after a day of really impossible shooting, crowd control, and culture shock. They were a fun group of people who served as a social life raft, and ultimately they did provide much-needed support.

One day we were shooting in the middle of some small town's square that was doubling as Beijing's Tiananmen Square. Like others on the crew, I was dispirited from feeling isolated and adrift, lost in a foreign country where not even the Chinese takeout tasted like the Chinese takeout I was used to. All of a sudden I looked up and saw Monty Python's Terry Jones walking toward me. I thought I was hallucinating. What would he be doing out in the middle of nowhere in China?

I had always been a devoted, or rather devout fan of *Monty Python's Flying Circus*. From behind me, I heard one of the English grips shout "Oy." Without missing a beat, Terry drifted over to our encampment, eager to say hello to people who spoke with an accent similar to his. He spent the rest of the day with us and stayed through that night's RPPS gathering. We traded lines from *The Holy Grail* and *The Life of Brian*, and he did the Silly Walk with us. One of the highlights of my life will always be the memory of standing in that room with Terry and singing "The Lumberjack Song."

Bo, who was on location with me, had a great deal of time on his hands, so he found a tailor who made him a new wardrobe of custom suits and shirts, complete with his name embroidered in his signature on the cuffs of the shirts. One night I was eating dinner with Rosa and Dakota when Bo returned and said he had a surprise for me. He had me close my eyes and hold out my hands. When I opened my eyes again, I saw a Cartier box in front of me. Inside was an eighteen-karat gold ladies' panther watch. I had carried on about wanting this watch for years, ever since Rob had gotten the men's version years before. Unlike Rob, I didn't have the stones to pay that kind of money for a watch. I have a feeling that when Britney Spears got engaged to K-Fed, she felt the same way I did at that moment: I had the watch I wanted, but I was also concerned that I had just bought myself the watch without my knowledge.

I said thank you and let Bo know I was thrilled. The deed was done. I owned the watch. But then he said, "Look what I got." He pushed up his sleeve and revealed a brand-new Rolex. Although smiling, I thought, *Oh my God, I am working my ass off in a foreign country with nothing but a port-a-squat toilet and this guy is spending the money I'm making as fast as I make it.*

Bo's drinking was more of a problem than his spending. At the next night's RPPS, he had a little more than he should have and, thinking he was funny, snatched a stuffed dog from the daughter of one of the crew guys. After saying "We have a beagle and sometimes he drives me crazy," he began punching and stomping on the toy dog. He was out of control, and the little girl was in tears. Embarrassed, I dragged Bo out and sent him back to our room.

After a couple more awkward episodes, he was banned altogether from the RPPS gatherings. That's when he decided he would have his own fun, and then things really got out of control. One night I went to the RPPS, hung out for a bit, then went to my room. When I woke up in the morning, Bo wasn't there. Nor was he back at the end of the day.

After dinner, I went to the RPPS and asked the guys what I should do. A bunch of them who knew Hong Kong said they would make calls and find him. That reassured me, but when I woke up the following morning, Bo still hadn't returned. At that point, I panicked.

I was in Hong Kong, breast-feeding my kid, depleted of strength and energy, and now I was also sick and nervous. It was surreal. Almost like I was living in one of my Lifetime movies.

When I walked back into the hotel that night after work, Bo was waiting for me. I didn't know whether to hug him or hit him. He said he had hooked up with some British sailors and ended up on a two-day bender. Though relieved he was safe, I told him that I couldn't handle dealing with him or even worrying about him. I wanted him to go home and get sober. He broke down in tears, said he was sorry, and agreed he needed help.

"I'll leave," he said.

"Good. Let's get you on the next flight."

Then it was as if a switch went off inside him. What about his suits? He insisted he couldn't leave until his custom-made suits were finished. He phoned the tailor and found out they wouldn't be ready for a couple more days. Rather than argue, I said fine, he could wait for the suits. But he couldn't stay with me. He had to find another hotel. I couldn't work, take care of Dakota, *and* worry about him.

I felt horribly guilty, hateful, and hurtful for sending him away, but he seemed to understand. In hindsight, I think I did the right thing. I received nothing but support from the crew that night at the RPPS. A few of them generously said their wives would take turns with the baby if I needed help. Around ten o'clock, I went back to my room and began to get ready for bed when the phone rang. It was Bo, and he was out of his mind, screaming at me.

"You're not going to take my son," he said. "I know what you're planning to do, you fucking bitch. I know this is just the beginning of the end. You're sending me away so you can divorce me, take everything . . ."

I don't know whether the conversation escalated or de-escalated, but Bo accused me of using him solely to father a child and swore he was going to see me dead before I took his son. He was quite graphic about it.

"I'm going to fucking kill you," he said. "I'm going to take our son. And I'm going to leave. And I'm going to leave you dying in a pool of blood."

Even though I knew that rage was fueled by alcohol, or maybe because it was, I took Bo seriously. I called in several producers and members of the crew with whom I was close and told them what had happened. They phoned the police. They moved Dakota, Rosa, and me to a new suite, and stationed guards outside the door and at the hotel's various entrances. Then, in case Bo managed to circumvent all those barriers, our key grip, David Nichols, slept on the floor at the foot of my bed.

As it turned out, Bo never showed up. After a thorough search, the police found him passed out in some hotel room with a large samurai sword next to him. They basically ushered him out of the country, and my godfather, Charlie, met him at the airport in L.A. and checked him into rehab.

Somehow the tabloids got wind of the story, which I denied for months before finally admitting to a *TV Guide* reporter with Bo at my side that he had a "tendency to lose control of himself" when he drank and that following a difficult time, "I asked him to leave Hong Kong and get help."

What I didn't describe was the relief I felt after he left and how that subsequently opened up the floodgates of an *Oh my God, what have I done with my life?* string of questions. I couldn't believe what I saw in the mirror. My hair was dyed black, I had lost weight, my eyes were permanently bloodshot, and I was alone with a baby and a nanny in this far-off land. I shook my head in disbelief. Who had I become?

I needed a life preserver, and I found one in David Nichols. I hung on to him for the rest of the shoot. From Sydney, he had a sane but carefree attitude about life that I needed, and I might have had a complete breakdown if not for his joyful, peaceful, and reassuring presence. We talked endlessly about what I was going to do when I got home. His answers were always to the point. He said, "Figure out what you want in life, what you want for yourself, and what you want for your child. Nothing else matters. Where do you want to be? What do you want out of your marriage? What are you willing to put up with?"

They were all excellent points. We would sit down after work and I would write list after list, trying to figure out what I wanted. I never got a chance to thank David for the help he provided, but I've remained eternally grateful. He helped me find the strength to stand up for myself. He also started me on the process of realizing that I, like many people, could have everything I had ever wanted in life but still be missing the things I actually needed.

twenty-one

No, No, No, We're Not Going to Do That

Bo was in rehab when I got home and we started to see a therapist together. I also began attending Al-Anon meetings. After he finished rehab, he moved into the Oakwood apartments, where he would have his encounter with Shannen Doherty. I was convinced that most of his problems stemmed from substance abuse, and if he stayed clean and we kept going to therapy, we could give Dakota a two-parent home. It wasn't the best decision, but I thought for Dakota's sake, I would do what I could to put our relationship back together.

It seemed to be working. We were still separated when the holidays rolled around, and I took Dakota to my mother's house for Christmas Eve. Despite my share of moments in the past when I wanted to strangle my mom, this was one of those times when her crazy zest for life and cockeyed wisdom made perfect sense to me, and I realized I would be absolutely lost without the love and nourishment she provided my soul.

Buoyed and hopeful, I invited Bo to Christmas dinner. My whole family was there, including my grandparents, who, at my mother's insistence, agreed to be in the same room together. We had a warm, wonderful night together. As Bo prepared to go back to his Oakwood apartment, I felt a swell of emotion in my heart and invited him to come back home with us after the first of the year. He was sober and doing well and I wanted to try and continue down this path and make our marriage work.

That May, we celebrated Dakota's first birthday while I was working on *Joshua's Heart*, a movie about the effect of divorce on children. We relaxed with new friends Jack Scalia and his wife, Karen, and Sandy and David Peckinpah, all of whom had kids around the same age as Dakota. We went on walks together, arranged play dates, threw impromptu barbecues, and began the tradition of a rotating Christmas Eve dinner.

Sandy and I developed a fast and intense friendship, almost like we had been connected in a previous life. To this day she remains my best friend.

Life was almost normal. I had turned into a working suburban mom. We rented a way-too-large, way-too-expensive home in Hidden Hills, an exclusive community in the west San Fernando Valley that Bo had wanted to live in ever since going to a party there years before. That house was way beyond our grasp financially, but it meant the world to Bo and it was a fun neighborhood. Our doors were always open and we always had houseguests, mostly Bo's friends and family.

I also exercised my independence in ways I never thought possible. First, I fired my longtime manager, Ray Katz, and then I called my mother and told her that I was ending our contract. Splitting from Uncle Ray was scary and breaking away from my mother was unpleasant and gut-wrenching, but necessary if the two of us were going to have a good relationship. I was no longer a child. I needed to take control of my career, along with my life, and that's what I did.

That fall, Leslie Landon got married. Like me, Leslie had grown up considerably since our last days on *Little House*. She had earned a master's in clinical psychology from Pepperdine University and practiced marriage and family counseling. I was so proud of her. And her wedding to Brian Matthews, held at a church in Westwood, was a beautiful affair.

The first person I saw there was Michael Landon. Quite a few years had passed since we had seen each other, but we bridged that gap instantly with hugs and kisses. It felt so good to have his strong arms wrapped around me again and to breathe in that familiar Mike smell, and I was filled with warm memories. He asked about Dakota and said, "You know, Half Pint, in the weird world of Hollywood, he's kind of my grandchild."

I knew what he meant and smiled broadly.

"When do I get to see him?" he asked.

"We'll make plans," I said. "We'll figure it out."

He said they were skiing over Christmas, but we'd make arrangements when they got back. He wanted me to bring Dakota to the house and spend time. Like a parent, he gave me a stern look and said he needed to see me more often. In February, I called to schedule that get-together and spoke to Cindy, who said they still had a full schedule, but promised to call me back when they settled in. In early April, Leslie called and said she wanted me to hear some news directly from her before I heard it on TV. I stopped and braced myself for I didn't know what.

"Dad's got pancreatic cancer," she said.

"What did you just say?"

"Inoperable cancer of the pancreas and liver."

I sat down.

"What does that mean?" I asked. "You have to explain to me what that means."

I could hear her take a deep breath.

"Well, he's going to try every treatment possible, but Schmoe"— her nickname for me—"you have to know it's not good."

"What does that mean?" I asked.

"He's going to fight," she said. "You know he's going to fight."

A few days later, Mike invited the press to his house and revealed his illness and determination to fight it. It was so characteristic of him to deliver the news on his own terms and try to keep the tabloids from printing rumors. I watched the press conference on TV. To me, he looked the same as he had at Leslie's wedding. Maybe he was a little thinner. If he was, it was a negligible difference, perhaps the result of healthier eating and more exercise, which I thought might indicate he was winning his fight.

May began yet again with celebrations: Dakota's birthday on the first and mine on the eighth. The night after my birthday, a little weary myself, I sat up in bed with Bo and waited for Mike's appearance on *The Tonight Show*. I'd heard he was going on to tell off the tabloids for the sensationalized and inaccurate coverage of his illness. If one were able to give the middle-finger salute on television, he would've done it. Instead, he came out and said, "It didn't do a helluva lot of good to hold the press conference." His good friend Johnny Carson agreed. Mike was most miffed about one particular story that maintained he wanted to have another child, which would have been his tenth, so his wife would have something to remember him by.

"I have nine kids, nine dogs, three grandkids, one in the oven, three parrots—and my wife, Cindy, needs something to remember me by?" he said.

Johnny told Mike that he looked good.

"I feel good," Mike said.

I didn't buy it. He had lost a significant amount of weight since the press conference and much more since Leslie's wedding. Though, in a turquoise shirt and khaki pants, he was as handsome as always, and he even professed to still work out, he looked completely different. His big, strong chest was gone. His voice was also thinner. Even his humor seemed forced to me, and that wasn't Mike, though I did laugh when he acknowledged his alternative therapies included coffee enemas.

"I invited Johnny over for one," he cracked. "But he wanted cream and sugar and I'm not pouring."

Johnny then complimented his hair.

"I had my roots done yesterday," said Mike, who had been dying his hair since before his days on *Bonanza*.

"You're kidding," Johnny said.

"For this show?" he said. "Sure. Two blood transfusions and my roots done."

I thought the most poignant moment of the show came at the end when Johnny invited his other guest, George Foreman, back after his next fight in August and Mike said he would also come back then. I nearly burst into tears because I realized that Mike knew there was no chance he would be back then. Whatever he was doing to fight the Big C, as he called it, he knew he was going to die.

I did, too, and that was beyond anything I could comprehend. As far as I was concerned, Mike was the biggest, strongest, toughest, most determined person ever. If I had done the math and counted up the cigarettes and vodka he had consumed, I would have seen it add up to liver cancer. But I had been in denial up till the point I saw him with Johnny.

Then everything changed. I had not been able to say good-bye to my own father. I wasn't going to screw this up. I turned to Bo and said, "I think I need to see Mike as soon as possible."

"Let's work it out," Bo said. "Let's make sure you see him."

A couple days later I was inventing excuses why I couldn't see him. I was scared. I didn't know what to say, what not to say, or how to say good-bye to this person who had played one of the most pivotal roles in my life. Finally, at Bo's insistence, I came around and we set up a time to see Mike. Then that was repeatedly postponed, as Mike either had complications requiring emergency treatment or was trying some alternative therapy.

At each juncture, I received a new update, and each time the prognosis was worse. It was always a variation of "He's fighting but it doesn't look good." In early June, he basically said good-bye to fans in an interview that ran on the cover of *LIFE* magazine. About a week later, we finally set up a time to go out to his house. Knowing he was declining, I didn't want to take away any precious moments his family could spend with him, but selfishly, I needed to see him.

On the morning we were scheduled to go, I sat on the bedroom floor playing Super Mario Brothers. I was like a gaming fiend. Every time Bo said it was time to leave, I pleaded with him to let me get to one more level. I didn't want to come out of that make-believe world. Finally, Bo turned off the TV and practically carried me to the car. He put Dakota in his car seat. I was useless.

Once we arrived at Mike's house in Malibu, I realized that I had never been there before. He had moved in after his divorce and that had been an unusual time for all of us. His house was breathtakingly gorgeous, a true palace for a man who had conquered the world on his terms. He had a beautiful saltwater swimming pool that Dakota jumped in almost immediately. The views went on forever.

Inside, I said hi to Mike, who was lying on a couch in the family room. I'd never seen anyone as sick as he was then. He was extremely thin and frail. He looked twice his age. His hair was white and his skin was gray; all of his color had vanished. It was like he was almost invisible.

A crowd of family, children, nurses, attendants, and helpers bustled around him. He was hooked up to a drip, which I assumed was morphine. I gave Cindy a basket of spa treatments; I figured the last thing she was doing was relaxing or taking care of herself. Since I had heard Mike say the one thing he wanted to do was laugh, I brought a tape of my grandfather and Jerry Lewis making crank phone calls back in the 1960s, the entire Three Stooges collection, and a fart machine.

We made small talk until Bo brought Dakota in the room and put him in my arms. Dakota was now two and a big, adventurous toddler, but he was perfectly calm as Mike pulled him close and gave him a kiss. Then someone told Dakota there were horses in the backyard. He wanted to go see them, and Bo volunteered to take him. Nerves caused me to chime in that we should all go. Bo gave me a look and very pointedly said, "I will take him to see the horses. You stay here."

I don't know if what happened next was planned or an accident of fate, but I sat down on the coffee table next to Mike and everyone else left the room. It was almost as if someone had said "Let them have their time." I held his hand and pretended not to look at him. The TV was on, and both of us stared at it in silence. If he was like me, he was not just remembering but feeling all the time we had spent together—way too much to ever articulate—pass back and forth in the flesh of our hands.

I didn't know what to say. A part of me felt like holding hands and being together was enough. Then he turned his gaze from the TV to me. His eyes were like blankets wrapping themselves around me, and whatever he was thinking made him smile. Finally, he said, "I want you to know, I've seen everything you've done."

"You have?" I said, genuinely surprised.

"Oh yeah." He smiled. "I've watched every movie. Every one."

"You have? Really?"

"Yeah." He was quiet for a moment or two. He appeared to be remembering something. Then he said, "I always knew it."

"You knew what?" I asked.

"I knew you would be the one."

I couldn't contain the tears anymore. I'd been trying so hard not to cry, but they just overflowed.

"No, no, no," Mike said. "We're not going to do that."

"Okay," I said, sniffling and wiping my eyes. I recalled when, as a little girl on the set seventeen years earlier, I was unable to cry on cue and Mike had taken me aside, looked me straight in the eye, and said, "Do you know how much I love you? I love you so much."

Now we weren't doing that. We weren't going to cry. Instead, he pulled me toward him and we hugged. Nothing else needed to be said. That hug was more than enough. That's all he wanted. And that was pretty much all I was capable of.

Out of the corner of my eye, I saw someone in the kitchen doorway gesturing for me to get up and go in there. It seemed urgent. I told Mike that I'd be right back. He was sort of drifting in and out at that point anyway. I was met in the kitchen by a nurse, Bo, and Dakota, who was crying hysterically. One of the horses had bit his fingers. I looked at his hand; his fingers were smashed, but kids' bones are very soft, and after a couple of minutes they looked normal again and he seemed all right. I was worried, but when one of Mike's nurses got Dakota to reach for a balloon that had been attached to a flower arrangement, I knew he was fine.

I told everyone that I didn't want Mike to know what had happened. It would just upset him. A little while later, I went back into the family room and sat down next to him again. He asked what had happened. I shook my head. "Nothing."

"No, I heard something happened to the kid," he said.

"One of the horses bit him." I shrugged.

"Was it bad?" he asked.

"No, he's fine," I said. "His fingers were kind of smashed, but he's in the kitchen digging through a bowl of goldfish crackers."

"Oh, thank God," he said. "If something bad had happened, I'd feel just awful." Then he grinned—that unmistakable Michael Landon grin—and added, "Wait a minute. I'm dying of cancer. How could I possibly feel worse?"

Soon after, he drifted back to sleep and I said my good-byes.

•   •   •

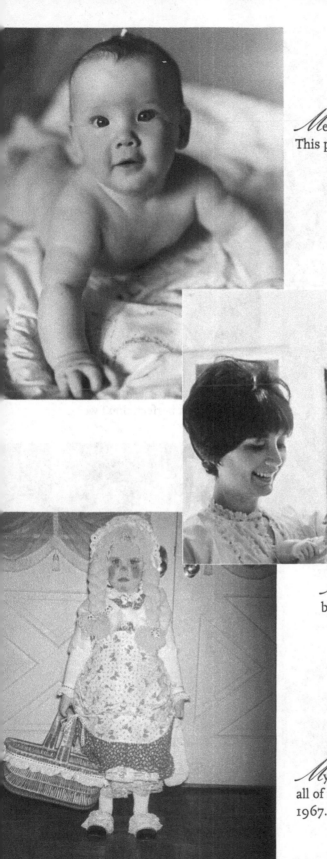

*M*e, approximately eight months old. This photo was taken by my dad.

*M*om, Dad, and me, the fattest baby EVER, 1964.

*M*y mom loved Halloween. She made all of my costumes. This one is from 1967. I look very serious for a doll!

Me and William Windom on the set of *Gunsmoke*.

My mom, me (in my *Saturday Night Fever* suit), Jonathan, Tricie, and Sara in Hawaii in 1979. We look perfect, don't we?

My Pa directing *Little House* in 1975.

My mom, Auntie Lynn and Michael Lando: and my grandma at my brother's bar mitzvah 1980.

Me with Victor French on set, 1975.

*M*y Super Celebrity Sweet 16!
Victoria and Ed McMahon, me, my
aunt Dotty, my mom, and my
grandma.

*S*eventeen and deadly at the
Night of 100 Stars.

Me at my eighteenth birthday party with friends, including Katie Daly, Chad Lowe, and Michael Landon Jr.—what a motley crew!

Senior prom with Mike Jr. My makeup was done on the set of *Splendor*.

*R*ob and me, happy and in love, 1981. I can't get over what babies we were!

*W*ith Rob, circa 1986. I really love this photo of us, *Courtesy of Peter Borsari Photography.*

My Alan Greenspan (not the Chairman of the Fed). *Courtesy of Toby Greenspan Zneimer.*

*L*auren Holly, me, and Katie Wagner at Bo's Birthday party in 1988 (while I was pregnant with Dakota).

*B*o and me bringing Dakota home from the hospital in New York City. All I wanted to do was get inside and curl up with my son.

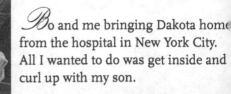

*M*e and Bo celebrating Christmas at my mom's in 1989, after our first separation.

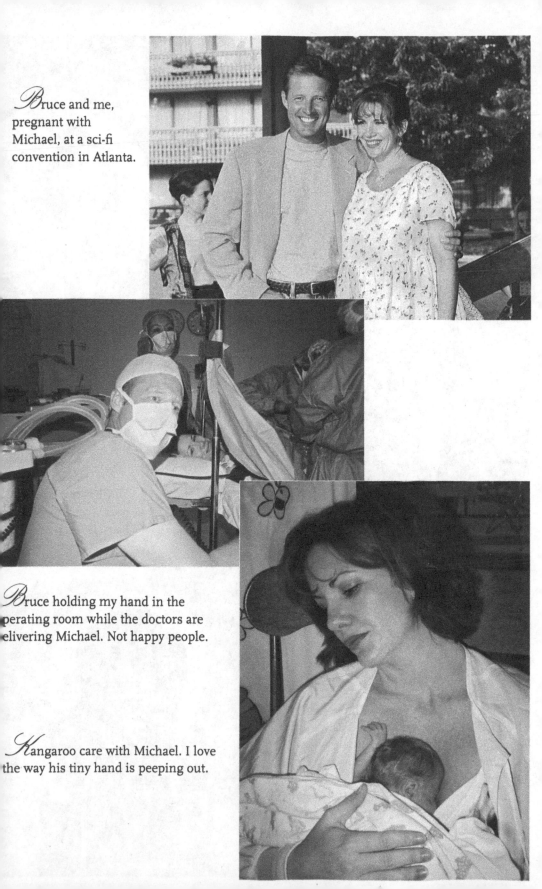

*B*ruce and me, pregnant with Michael, at a sci-fi convention in Atlanta.

*B*ruce holding my hand in the operating room while the doctors are delivering Michael. Not happy people.

*K*angaroo care with Michael. I love the way his tiny hand is peeping out.

Bruce and me celebrating on the night of the SAG election recount results. All hail the conquering heroine!

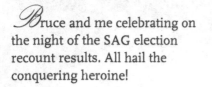

Bruce and the boys on Christmas, 2007. (FROM LEFT: Lee, Michael, Sam, Dakota, and Bruce.)

Visiting Walnut Grove with the cast of *Little House: The Musical* in a really silly reproduction covered wagon. (CLOCKWISE, FROM TOP LEFT: Jenn Gambatese, Kara Lindsay, Kevin Massy, and me.)

A week later I was with Dakota in the family room, which was really his giant playroom, as he scampered around, listening to his records and playing with balloons. The TV was on, tuned to CNN as it was every day. We were in the midst of the first Gulf War, but I wasn't paying attention to the coverage, I was having fun with Dakota. Then the anchor came on and said that actor Michael Landon had died. I may have screamed; I don't recall. But Bo immediately rushed into the room and asked what was wrong. I pointed to the TV screen, which was showing a retrospective of Mike's career.

Bo scooped up Dakota, who was crying because I was upset. I was inconsolable for a few minutes, and then something in me switched. I needed more information than I was getting on TV. Maybe, I thought, CNN had it wrong. I became obsessed with finding Leslie and hearing for myself what had really happened.

Honestly, I don't remember if I called her or she called me, but at some point that day we talked for a long time. She told me about the unusual things that happened during the last twenty-four hours of Mike's life. He had seen the proverbial light that guides people onto the next phase of their journey. He had seen his late mother waiting to comfort him. As a family, they had shared moments that, on hearing them, didn't lessen my sadness but reassured me that death isn't a horrible, scary thing as much as it is a transition to something else.

Still, I was heartbroken. My mother came over and my sister, sweet thing, brought me a milk shake. After that, my phone rang off the hook with requests from reporters wanting a comment. It seemed everyone in the world wanted a quote. Yet I was incapable of communicating.

I finally gave my publicist a statement, something about Mike's contribution to the world and a hole in my heart. Then I fell into a deep depression. I stayed in bed with the shades drawn. Anytime I got up and tried to move around, it felt as if I was moving through mud. I walked around dazed in my pajamas for days until Bo came home one day with two puppies and said I had to housebreak them. He told me that with a two-year-old and two puppies, I had my hands full. Bless his heart, he knew exactly how to gently get me up and moving.

About a week later, Kent McCray, who'd been an executive producer on *Little House,* called and asked if I would deliver one of the eulogies at Mike's funeral. I said of course, no question. The second I hung up, I regretted it. What the hell was I going to say? Scratch that. There was so much to say. But how was I going to stand up in front of his family, his children, his friends, and talk about him without bludgeoning everyone with my feelings?

In my opinion, part of the responsibility of delivering a eulogy is to try to bring some comfort to the people who are grieving. It wasn't about standing in front of everyone and bawling like a self-absorbed idiot, which was what I pictured myself doing. How could I not get up there and just cry?

I found it impossible to write a eulogy that articulated my relationship with Mike, what he meant to me, and also what his loss meant to me. I tried numerous times without success. Finally, on the night before the service, I managed to gather my various attempts—a bunch of notes—into a concise form. Then I prayed to Mike to help me through it. It also helped that I was married to a playwright, who gently nudged me forward. By midnight I was done, and then I spent the rest of the night tossing and turning, terrified of what would happen the next day.

The service itself was a blur of familiar faces who, like me, were doing a relatively fair job of keeping their emotions in check. I saw Luke Tillman, our special-effects guy who was missing multiple fingers, which had always amused me as a kid. (Why was the guy in charge of our special effects missing fingers?) I saw Melissa Sue and Karen Grassle. Ernest Borgnine was behind me. I sat with the other speakers, including Mike's business manager, Jay Eller, who recalled how after Mike was first diagnosed he had warned Mike that he could lose his hair if he did chemotherapy. And Mike said, "Jay, don't worry. I'm rich. I'll buy a hat."

Then it was my turn. I walked up to the little platform with a huge lump in my throat and I began to read what I'd written the night before. I managed to get through my remembrance by focusing with laserlike precision on two people, one on each side of the room: former president Ronald Reagan and singer Al Jarreau. Since I didn't know either one of them, I was able to deliver my eulogy without feeling an emotional connection. If I had looked at Karen, Melissa Sue, or one of Mike's kids, I would have ended up a puddle of tears.

Afterward, we made a brief stop at the postmemorial reception at the Landons' house in Malibu. I was able to spend some one-on-one time with Mike's family and some of the *Little House* cast and crew people. There was a lot of hugging and crying, but there was also a lot of laughter as we all shared stories about Mike's fantastic sense of humor. It was very comforting to be around people who'd known Mike so well and loved him as much as I did, if not more.

The rest of the year seemed to be taken up by requests for quotes to media outlets and shows doing Michael Landon tributes. Even when Bo and I were performing one of his plays at the Barn Theater in Kalamazoo, Michigan, I flew back to L.A. for a tribute to Mike at the Emmy Awards. That was when I ran into Shannen Doherty on the side of the stage. Aside from that pissing me off, I was upset that Mike never got an Emmy while he was alive. He was never even nominated. What was it that Marty Sheen had warned me about Hollywood?

Of course, Mike would have told me that stuff wasn't important, which I had learned years earlier. He had his priorities straight. That's why I responded with a quote every time a request came in. But eventually I reached a point where it felt like too much.

One day I was with Sandy and David Peckinpah when yet another show called and asked me to talk about Mike. I wanted to turn them down, but David urged me to think otherwise.

"You better do as many of these as you can," he said. "After all, Michael Landon is not going to be dead forever."

I had never heard such a sick and twisted comment in my life. It made me laugh. Mike would've laughed, too.

twenty-two

GETTYSBURG WAS MY WATERLOO

In early 1992, Fox ordered seven episodes of *Stand by Your Man*, a sitcom starring me and Rosie O'Donnell, a young comedic talent just coming into her own. She had won *Star Search*, played Nell Carter's neighbor on *Gimme a Break!* and who knows, if *Stand By Your Man* had taken off, she may not have had time to make the movie *A League of Their Own*, which accelerated her trajectory toward stardom.

But our show, a remake of the British series *Birds of a Feather*, was canceled less than two months after it debuted in April. It was too bad. From all the TV movies, the public knew I could cry. I wanted to show people that I had a sense of humor, too. Rosie saw it. Of course, she could make me laugh until I almost peed.

After we finished the pilot, I got a call from two guys with a business that helped adoptees reunite with their birth parents. Bo had hired Troy Dunn and Virgil Klunder a few months earlier, and after much digging, they had located my father, David Darlington, in Las Vegas, and they said my mother was not Susan Alabaster, the name on my birth certificate, but a woman named Kathy.

In photographs they sent soon after, I saw a strong resemblance to Kathy but not much to my father, whose phone number was included in the packet of information. I stared at the number as if it were the key to a long-lost treasure chest. I needed a day or two to work up the courage to call. A man picked up on the second ring. He confirmed he was David Darlington, and when I asked if he had given a child up for adoption in 1964, he paused and then said, "Well, I think it was '63. But yeah."

"No, it was '64," I said, as my entire body trembled from nerves. "And it was a girl."

"Yes, it was a girl," he said.

"And . . . and that baby was me," I said.

After a long pause, he said, "Oh my God."

He asked who I was and what I did. I told him that was the weird part and to brace himself.

"I'm an actor," I said.

"Really?"

"Yes. And I'm on television. I was on a TV series for ten years when I was a kid and I've done a number of movies for television."

"Well, what's your name?" he asked.

"Melissa Gilbert," I said.

There was another long pause.

"I know who you are," he said.

"Yes, you do, and no, you really don't," I said.

As if the conversation wasn't already weird, it got weirder when he asked me about work, Michael Landon, and other celebrities. He was like any person on the street. And I answered a few questions before interrupting to say that I would like to meet him. He was instantly amenable to that as well as to the date I suggested. I told him if he and his family wanted to see what I looked like now, they could see me the night before I would meet them on *The Tonight Show.*

"We'll watch you," he said excitedly. "And then we'll see you in person."

I have been doing talk shows since I was nine years old. I get a little nervous for a second before I walk on, but once I'm out there, I could care less. This time was different. I was terrified to walk out and talk to Jay Leno, who had recently taken over for the newly re-tired Johnny Carson. All I could think about was the whole Darling-ton clan gathered around their TV, watching me with brand-new eyes. It was the stiffest, worst interview I've ever done. I owe Jay an apology.

I woke up early the next morning and got on a plane with Bo and Dakota. We checked into a hotel room off the Strip to avoid any chance of the press getting wind of this very personal, poignant mo-ment in my life. I paced nervously across the room, checking my watch and waiting for David Darlington, my birth father, to show up. As soon as I heard a knock on the door, I opened it and found myself standing opposite a very tall man who immediately opened his arms wide and gave me a hug. All I could say was "Oh my God, oh my God."

It was an incredible moment, though it was also one of the strangest I had ever experienced. The whole time I was looking at him, hugging him, and saying "Oh my God," a voice in my head was saying, *Don't be crazy. You're not related to this man. He looks nothing like you.* I was also saying to myself, *This is the man who gave you away. No, he didn't give you away. He just couldn't keep you.*

It was insane. My head was filled with more voices than a debate club. And all I could say was "Oh my God." Then he asked if he could have a drink. It was noon. To me, that was a bit early for a drink. But I was scared shitless and thought a drink was probably a very good idea.

The two of us went to the bar and had Bloody Marys. I showed him a photo album of my life that my mother had prepared for the occasion. I'm sure she was secretly petrified that I might fall in love with these people and dump her. But she had shown me nothing but support in my quest for information and answers. And she needn't have worried anyway.

As we relaxed, I learned that David Darlington was a sign painter in Las Vegas, not a Rhodes Scholar as my mother had always told me. As for Kathy being a prima ballerina, I found out over the course of the afternoon that she had indeed been a dancer, but not a balle-rina, and like David, she'd had three kids of her own when they got together.

But these were not the Bradys. It turned out Kathy had died in 1980 after years of nagging injuries stemming from a serious motor-cycle accident she and David were in shortly after my birth. Later that night, I ate dinner at David's house, where his daughter Bonne shed more light on the family history, which included an unsettling amount of alcoholism and cancer.

Sadly, it was not the warm, loving, we've-been-waiting-for-you-to-show-up fantasy I had entertained ever since initiating the search for my birth parents. There wasn't any meaningful discussion about my origins, my first twenty-four hours in this world, or whether, despite giving me up for adoption, either one of my parents had ever wanted me. Whenever I asked a question, David's recall was fuzzy. The best and most memorable part of the whole night was the warm spinach salad with the hot bacon dressing. It was delicious.

Reality was a tough pill to swallow after believing for twenty-eight years that my birth parents were quite different from what I encoun-tered. Not only was that bubble unceremoniously burst, but David by the end of the evening insisted that I had been born in 1963, not '64 as my birth certificate said, which made me a year older!

By the time I got back to my hotel room, I was crying like a hys-terical, inconsolable five-year-old. I couldn't catch my breath. Bo didn't know what to do, so he called my mother. She got on the phone and listened to me recount what had happened and how terri-bly disappointed I was by the outcome. Then she let me cry until I ran out of gas.

"This is part of your journey, Melissa," she said. "You had to do this for you. And now you've done it. You can do what you want with what you know. Most important, you can move on."

In addition to being right, she was very clear, supportive, and helpful, a life raft in a time of need, as only a mother can be. Through tears and sniffles, I told her how much I loved her and that good or bad, nobody would or could take her place in my life—ever.

Then I pulled myself together and focused on how to handle the situation going forward. I wouldn't say meeting the Darlingtons was a Pandora's box, but I had created a mess that needed management. I didn't want it to become a story in the *National Enquirer*. I arranged to see them for brunch the next day before we left and I laid the cards on the table. I said the information we had shared belonged to them as much as it did to me. They could talk about it with whomever they liked, including the tabloids, who would probably pay for their story. But I cautioned that those same tabloids and papers had reported on my life for almost twenty years and already knew everything about me. If they came forward, they would be opening their lives to the same scrutiny. "They will dig into your pasts," I warned. So I advised them to not talk about our fateful connection if there were things in their pasts they didn't want out in the public.

Nothing ever made it into the press.

After our trip to Vegas, Bo got a role in *Gettysburg,* the first in a planned trilogy of features on the Civil War bankrolled by billionaire history buff and media mogul Ted Turner. It seemed like the perfect big break. Bo's friend Ron Maxwell had signed on as director and Tom Berringer and Marty Sheen headlined a fine cast. When he left to shoot the movie, our lives were fairly well ordered in the new, smaller house we had moved into. Dakota was doing well. We had horses in the backyard.

Some things had changed. Bo was drinking a little here and there, which I thought may have been a byproduct of the pain pills he took for a knee surgery he'd endured following a ski accident. He'd stopped going to meetings, too.

Then there was the feeling within the house. With Bo on location, it was peaceful. I recognized it took two to whip up a tornado of drama, but I kind of liked the way things worked when he was out of the equation. As a result, I was full of excuses when Bo called and asked me to visit him in Gettysburg. Dakota was in preschool, and there was too much going on for me to leave. Bottom line: I didn't want to go.

While there are much better ways to communicate disaffection in a marriage, one thing was clear: problems that we hadn't dealt with for years were coming to a head. I don't think either of us was con-sciously aware of what we were doing. Then one day my publicist and friend Colleen Schlatter called and said the *National Enquirer* was working up a story on Bo. She said they had photos of him drink-ing and carousing, as well as women leaving his hotel room in the middle of the night.

I asked her to try and hold them off from running the story, which she somehow managed to do. I didn't have to fly to Gettysburg and get my own photos of Bo. When one or both people in a relation-ship drink to excess, it can be damn near impossible to tell the differ-ence between reality and the stuff you make up in dreams. So I hired a PI. I wanted a definitive answer because I could feel the end of our marriage getting perilously close. If I was going to blow up my child's life, I first wanted concrete evidence.

And I got it. The detective called from Gettysburg with news that Bo was definitely drinking; he had pictures of him serving drinks at a bar and getting wasted. He also had photos of girls going in and out of Bo's hotel room.

Armed with that information, I took Dakota to visit his father, and after Dakota went to sleep I confronted Bo on the first night we arrived. We went back and forth a while before he finally owned up to everything. I had already decided that Gettysburg was going to be my Waterloo, and I matter-of-factly told Bo the same thing. I was finished—and it wasn't even about the drinking or fooling around.

"I'm done," I said. "I'm going to take responsibility for my life. I am unhappy. I am not functioning on all cylinders because I'm so miserable. I'm sucked into drama that I can't stand and I can't get out of—and I want out. I don't want to do this anymore. I'm not going to do it anymore. It's over."

Bo stomped his foot and clenched his fist out of frustration like a four-year-old and screamed, "I didn't do anything."

"Believe that all you want," I said. "But I did stuff, too. I contributed to this unhappiness. I own up to my half, and I'm done."

I stayed for a couple days so Bo and Dakota could have a good visit. I watched one of the battle scenes. I also visited with Marty Sheen. It seemed like I was in an alternate universe. Everybody on the movie knew what Bo had been doing, and there I was, the moron wife with the kid. I hated every second of it, but it was important to me that Dakota have some time with his father.

Back in L.A., I began the process of moving Bo out of the house. My goal was to make it as easy as possible on everyone. Joint custody of Dakota was fine; Bo had been restoring a 1952 pickup, and I told him to take the truck, take his clothes, take the cactus, take everything. Take it all. He didn't owe me anything, and I didn't want anything.

After *Gettysburg* wrapped and we had been separated for a couple months, Bo moved in with Ron Maxwell, who had rented a home in our gated neighborhood, and I began the process of legally unraveling the marriage, which wasn't difficult since we agreed on joint custody and had more debts than assets. I regrouped by diving into my favorite role, that of mom. I drove Dakota to school and arranged play dates with friends. My whole life revolved around kids and horses.

Through the tending of my horses, I met a woman named Cindy Bond, who had horses too. She introduced me to Kitty Ogilvy. One night Kitty and her husband, Ian, hosted a barbecue, and I was talking to her when she said, "God, I wish my ex-husband would date someone like you instead of the bimbos he's been going out with." I knew her ex-husband was Bruce Boxleitner. I immediately flashed on the picture of him I used to keep in my junior high school locker.

"Well, give him my number," I said.

"Okay," she said, nodding, "I will."

At the time, Bruce was shooting movies, traveling, and enmeshed in his own drama with an ex-girlfriend and a soon-to-be ex-girlfriend, plus some peripheral hysteria with additional girls that occupied his spare time. Though he didn't seem to be in the market for another relationship, Kitty told him that she had met an attractive, intelligent woman who she thought he should take on a date. But when she told him that person was me, he said, "Are you crazy? She's twelve years old!"

"No, she is in fact twenty-eight years old," Kitty said. "She's a total hottie, and she lives here in Hidden Hills."

"Yeah?"

"With her son."

"Really?"

"And you should take her out."

"You think?"

"I do."

Several weeks passed, and I was getting on with my life as best as possible when Kitty called and said Bruce wanted to know if he could call me. I was surprised by the question, since I had already told her to give him my number, which was tantamount to an open invitation. But she explained that Bruce, who also resided in our neighborhood, was kind of old-fashioned in that regard. He wanted to double-check. I assured her it was okay if he called.

A short time later, the phone rang. Since I knew it was Bruce, I answered in what I considered to be my sexiest voice. His voice was way better. To this day, his voice still kills me. It sounds like whiskey and cigars, and it is flat-out sexy without him even trying. We made small talk before he asked if I wanted to go out sometime.

"Sure, I'd love to," I said, trying to play it cool.

"When are you available?" he asked. "Dinner? Lunch? What do you want to do?"

Normally I would have been shy and reticent about such an invitation. Given the state of my life at the time, I didn't feel at the top of my game. In fact, I had stuffed most of my self-esteem in drawers with my summer clothes and had been living like a semirecluse in baggy sweaters for the past few months. So I am not really sure where my response came from, but I somehow channeled some forties film-star moxie and said, "Well, I'm not doing anything right now. How about lunch?"

Bruce laughed.

"Okay," he said. "I'll pick you up in about fifteen minutes."

I grabbed my nanny, Gladys, by the arm and raced with her up stairs, taking clothes off, putting others on, and asking her what looked good. We were going to the Cheesecake Factory and I didn't want to look too dressy or too casual. I couldn't wear sweats, but a dress was too much. I finally settled on the right combination of jeans, a T-shirt, and cowboy boots, which was and still is my uniform. I put on mascara, pinched my cheeks, and waited for Bruce.

I was peering out the bay window in the kitchen with Gladys when he pulled up in a little convertible Mercedes. He didn't get out of the car as much as unfolded himself from it; it was so small, and he was so tall and lanky. Gladys turned to me and said, "Oh my God, he's handsome." I agreed. Then the doorbell rang. I smiled at Gladys and chirped, "I'll be back when I'm back."

Lunch could not have been more comfortable. Within fifteen minutes, Bruce and I were laughing as I recalled the first time we had met, which he didn't remember. It had been on a *Battle of the Network Stars* in 1981. Rob was with me, and I introduced myself to Bruce between swim races after having stared at him for most of the day. Bruce had said he knew exactly who I was; his then two-year-old son, Sam, who was with him, watched *Little House*, which he called "the horsey car show." Then Bruce was summoned to an event.

"You said you had to go and patted me on the head," I said.

"I did?" he said with a wince.

"You were also wearing a Speedo," I said, smiling. "That wasn't lost on me."

Smiling sheepishly, Bruce laid his cards on the table, explaining his personal life was complicated. In an apologetic tone, he said his hands were full. I understood. In case he hadn't read it in the tabloids, I reminded him that my five-year marriage had just blown up. I wasn't even officially divorced. We laughed at each other over spinach and artichoke dip and by the time we paid the bill we knew there was an attraction and that something was going to happen. The question was when.

I wasn't prepared for that attraction, and it blew me away. I didn't necessarily want to be alone, but I thought it might be nice to have a series of friends with benefits. I had a child in my life and the last thing I wanted was to get involved with someone.

Yet as cliché as it sounds, I knew Bruce was *the guy*. Did I know the straits and narrows we would have to navigate, indeed survive, before we would get to that place of happily ever after? No, I had no idea. But things happened right away that convinced me my gut was right. On the way home from lunch, I asked him to drive me to Saks while I went to the Clinique counter and bought face cream. He didn't come in with me, but he greeted me with a patient smile when I got back. In the driveway, I invited him to a screening of my latest movie, *With a Vengeance*.

"I have no idea why I'm asking you," I said. "But it feels right—and I think we'll have a good time."

"I'd love to," he said.

Going to those types of events with Bo had been unpleasant. He was terribly insecure and became upset if I had a conversation with someone other than him or forgot to introduce him. He also forbade me to disagree with him in public and once left me standing in the middle of Benedict Canyon because I had taken exception to something he had said at the dinner table. But the screening with Bruce was different. As I chatted with people, Bruce asked if he could get me a glass of wine and some cheese and fruit on a plate.

I was stunned. For years, I was Rob's appendage, and then I was the woman who was trying to build up Bo. Now I was with a guy who was absolutely my equal, someone who understood my responsibilities that night and decided he was going to make it easier for me. It got even better. At one point, I lost track of Bruce's whereabouts. When I looked around, I saw he was involved in his own conversation. He knew people, and if he didn't know them, he introduced himself.

Moment by moment, I was falling for this guy whom I'd known for only a day. Then came the pièce de résistance. The movie ended and we went back to Bruce's for some coffee. I was mesmerized when I walked into his house—it was a major, man-size house, which he owned, at the end of a cul-de-sac (he also owned the barn with horses across the street). From the way I gawked and gazed at each room, you would have thought I had never seen furniture before. I was impressed at how together he was. Also with the way he offered me freshly brewed coffee. Instead of taking it, though, I pointed toward the ceiling. He looked up.

"What?" he asked. "Do you see something?"

"You have a chandelier," I said.

He gave me a questioning look.

"No, you don't understand," I said. "You have a chandelier."

"Yeah, it's nice," he said. "Real antlers, too."

I couldn't articulate it, but that chandelier was so symbolic to me. It meant he had a home that he owned and a career that was flourishing. He was a full-grown man, confident, sexy, smart, independent, and together. Bruce was a grown-up but he still had that bad-boy glimmer in his eyes. He was trouble. Trouble with a capital *T*. I had finally met my match.

EXACTLY WHERE
I NEED TO BE

twenty-three

GABLE AND LOMBARD: THE TV VERSION

Bruce has since told me that when I opened the front door the day we first went out to lunch, he knew we were going to be together. He didn't say how long he thought we were going to be together. To him, together meant going to bed. He was juggling several women, all of whom were viciously vying for his attention. But those women were dispatched within the second week of this redhead entering his life, and we enjoyed each other's company dressed and undressed.

Because both of us had children who had been through our separate marital storms, we kept them out of the equation for a long time, and we determinedly kept our relationship out of the public eye. Aside from the physical attraction, I liked that Bruce was his own man. He was opinionated. We had been in the industry for almost the same amount of time, and we shared an appreciation of home and family.

During the early days of our courtship, he would saddle up his horse and ride over to my house. From the trail, I would hear him yell, "Hello, the house!" I would walk out on the balcony, wave, and then saddle up my horse and we would go on a ride together. One day we were sitting on our horses out in the middle of the Ahmanson Ranch, and I said to Bruce, "This feels very Gable and Lombard to me."

"Yes, it does," he agreed.

"But the TV version," I added.

We had a lot of dinners at my place, and we spent a lot of nights at his house. Bruce was amazed he was dating someone who could cook. I was still impressed by his chandelier. I drank coffee back then, and I enjoyed waking up to the sound of him grinding beans and then bringing me a fresh-brewed cup of coffee in bed, where we'd watch the news and snuggle. Of course, that was the extent of Bruce's ability in the kitchen. He could grind beans and brew coffee. He could also pour a mean bowl of cereal. That was it. There was no cooking. Period. Hasn't been to this very day.

In that blushy, getting-to-know-each-other time, we would sit up in bed at night and drink red wine, eat brie cheese on French bread, and talk for hours and hours about absolutely everything. One of the first subjects we tackled was our pasts. There are versions people tell each other. Sensing our relationship could be long-term, Bruce and I were thoroughly honest. We agreed that neither one of us would walk into a room and be surprised by something, or someone, we didn't know about.

On our first public date, we went to the premiere of Francis Ford Coppola's *Bram Stoker's Dracula*. It was right after we had gone through our lists together. We walked into the theater, sat down, and both of us at the same time half-jokingly asked, "Is there anyone in here that one of us didn't sleep with?"

I was head over heels for him when I left to make the movie *Family of Strangers* in Vancouver. It was my second movie with Anna (Patty Duke). It also starred William Shatner. I had been warned that Shatner could be difficult on the set. One person went so far as to call him a nightmare. I loved him instantly.

Actually, the movie's director was the nightmare. Maybe it was his bad toupee. Someone said if I walked up behind him and held out a handful of nuts, his hair would jump out and try to eat them. The man had a hedgehog on his head. At different points during the shoot, he made both Anna and me cry. However, he hit a roadblock with Shatner.

We were doing a scene where he was supposed to be watching television and change the channel with the remote control. During rehearsal, he refused to do it. The director pleaded with him to change his mind, but Bill refused. He said he would gladly walk across the room and change the channel. He just wasn't going to use the remote. The director explained that getting up from the sofa would break up the scene. Bill didn't care.

"I'm not holding the fucking remote," he said.

"Why?" asked the frustrated director. "Why the hell won't you hold it?"

"I don't hold anything that looks like a phaser," he said. "Got it?"

I had to run off the set, lest I upset the poor schmuck director even more with my laughter.

Bruce was a ray of sunshine during that experience, though he hit me with a surprise on his first day visiting me. He said he had something to talk to me about. I always hate when people start a conversation like that, especially when they are as serious as Bruce was. It's a preamble for bad news. Bruce said he had seen Annie, one of his exes, a few days earlier. I was surprised, obviously. But I played it cool and very intentionally appeared calm and collected, even though I could feel the acid begin to churn in my stomach.

"How'd that go?" I asked as nonchalantly as possible.

"Well, I just wanted to make sure it was really over," he said.

"And?" I remained blasé, as if the answer would not faze me either way.

"It's really over."

"How do you know?" I asked, not daring to look at him; otherwise he might see that I was freaking out.

"Because the whole time I was sitting across from her, and she was going on and on about stuff, I could only think about you," he said. "I wondered where you were. I wondered what you were doing. I wanted to be with you."

That was it. I leapt into his arms, wrapping my legs around his waist, smothering him with kisses. Mine, mine mine . . . he was all mine!

I had that next weekend off and we snuck off to the Hastings House on Salt Spring Island, a gorgeous hideaway in an out-of-the-way cove that was like something out of a romance novel, it's so perfectly charming and peaceful. We were on fire for each other. It was intense, passionate, and hot. Then, back in Vancouver, we spent hours walking around Stanley Park and I realized we were even more compatible than I'd thought.

Bruce had been back in L.A. for a couple weeks when he called and said he had been out to dinner with friends and run into his ex again. It had been an ugly scene, he said, but the gist was that he was lonely. Since I had Saturday and Sunday off, I offered to fly home and spend the weekend with him.

"Really?" he asked.

"If you're lonely," I said, "yeah, I'll come home for the weekend."

"No one has ever done that for me before," he said.

"I don't think I've ever done that for anyone before," I replied. "But I'm willing." I spent a lovely weekend with Bruce, then went back on location.

It sounds like it was all moonlight and roses, perfect and beautiful, but there were glitches along the way. Sometimes I would drink too much and say something out of line. Bruce, who's half Irish, knew how to argue right back, especially when alcohol was involved. We didn't clash on the epic scale of Colleen Dewhurst and George C. Scott, but on occasion we rattled the walls.

I was hesitant but hopeful when we began getting the kids together. Bruce and I had different parenting skills, but the family meet-and-greets went pretty seamlessly. I credit the boys, my son Dakota and Bruce's boys, Sam and Lee. They got along like long-lost best friends. As I told Bruce then and many times since, the best gift he has ever given me are his remarkable sons.

Only one person had a difficult time with our relationship, and that was Bo. He came over to my house one day to pick up Dakota and flew into a rage after seeing a copy of the *Hollywood Reporter* on the table with Bruce's address on it. He threw open the front door with such fury that the doorknob punched a hole in the wall, then he fishtailed his truck across my front lawn and took off.

The melodramatic craziness continued a few nights later when he called and screamed at me until I cried. Bruce was there at the time, and he grabbed the phone. I could only hear his side of the conversation, which went something like this: "Son, son, son . . . leave the lady alone . . . son . . . yes, I am . . . yes, I am . . . in your bed . . . go ahead, because I've got a safe full of my own."

Bo blamed me for many of his problems, including his difficulty getting work in Hollywood. He claimed I had destroyed his career by calling him an alcoholic. That made me laugh. The entertainment industry may be the only business in the world where it's not only okay to be an alcoholic, it may be a requirement.

No, he had to take responsibility for his own behavior. But he wasn't ready to do that just yet.

In the meantime, Bruce earned raves from my friends, the Scalias and the Peckinpahs, and that year, we enjoyed a fabulous and loving Christmas and New Year's Eve. But the good times were too much for Bruce to handle. One night, as we watched TV at his house, he turned to me and said, "I hate to say this, but I think we're better friends than lovers, and I think we should just be friends."

I didn't understand. He might as well have punched me in the gut.

"Drive me home," I said.

"What?" he asked.

"Drive me home," I said. "I'm not staying here."

My house was only a few blocks away. We got dressed and in the car he said, "I think I just put my foot through the Rembrandt."

"Oh, you did worse than that," I said.

A few days after his blunder, Bruce attempted a rapprochement. We had plans to go on an all-expenses-paid celebrity ski vacation to Austria, and he called and asked if I still planned to go with him. I did not respond kindly. I wanted to know how he saw my role on the trip—as his ski valet, his pal, his golf partner . . . I rattled off a long list of possibilities. He begged me to let him come over and talk.

Within minutes, Bruce was at my house, pleading with me to forgive him and explaining that he was scared to death about getting into a serious relationship. He was already a failure at marriage, he said. He didn't want to tie the knot again. He didn't want more kids. He didn't want to get deeper into something he thought he would eventually screw up, so he got it over with.

"But here's the problem," he said. "I can't not be with you. So what are we going to do?"

"Did I say I want to get married? Did I say this was for the rest of our lives?"

Even though I had a sense that it would be for the rest of our lives, I realized my big, strong cowboy was a scaredy cat when it came to relationships. I could imagine him breaking into a rash when he heard the word "commitment." I thought about what pussies men are and I wanted to laugh; but I didn't.

Instead, I told him that we should just take it a little bit at a time and see where we ended up. In the meantime, I advised him to just live the dream. I told him that over and over. Don't worry. Just live the dream.

"I don't know what the dream is, but live the dream," I said. "It can all be yours, whatever you want."

We went to Austria, and we were having a good time up until the point when I learned that Bo had filed a report with Child Protective Services, claiming that my nanny was abusing Dakota. Apparently the guy who took care of my animals said he had witnessed it when I wasn't around. It didn't seem possible to me. But as I said to Bruce, what if it was true? And if it was true, what was I doing in Austria?

I became hysterical. I burned up the long-distance phone lines, trying to regain control of the situation. If Bo's intention was to make me crazy, he did a good job. I downed glasses of wine and schnapps. I took my frustration out on Bruce. We got into one of our big knock-down, drag-out fights and didn't speak to each other for two solid days.

I was a mess until we got back home. Then I fired the nanny, got my lawyer involved, and waited for more bad news. I was like one of those women in Westerns, standing behind the front door with a rifle and waiting for the bad guys to show up. Just to add to the bizarreness, I went into the hospital for some elective surgery. Okay, I went in for a boob job.

I thought about canceling the surgery given the circumstances. But hey, the procedure had been scheduled for months and I didn't see how postponing it would help. In fact, I thought new boobs would make me feel better. I was pretty comfortable with my body, but Dakota had destroyed my breasts after nursing for more than a year. Bo had once described them as socks full of marbles with knots at the top, and I was so uncomfortable about the way my boobs looked that I rarely took my shirt off around Bruce.

So I had the surgery, and two days later, the investigator from Child Protective Services showed up at the house to interview me. Her timing couldn't have been worse. When she arrived, I was in the midst of having a severe reaction to the pain medication and residual anesthesia. I wanted this woman to think I was normal and my home was a paradigm of well-being. Instead, I looked like the psycho, junkie actress who got new tits for Christmas.

Apparently that was acceptable. The complaint went away after her investigation, as it should have. There was no story. It was bullshit. My chest healed without a story to tell, either. I was glad I went in for the lift, perk, augmentation—whatever you call it. Bruce was even happier. For months afterward, he asked, "How are the girls?" Then he asked how I was. I was great. With my new boobs, I had the body I had wanted my entire life.

I played a cop in my next movie, *With Hostile Intent*. Bruce came to the Florida set to visit and enjoyed seeing me in a uniform. At the end of the shoot, Dakota was also on the set with me.

Like many working mothers, I had my hands full trying to juggle my job and my number one role, being a mom to my nearly four-year-old son. One night he was cranky from what looked to be a bite on his stomach. By the next afternoon, he had a full-blown case of the chicken pox. I called my mother and asked if I had ever had the chicken pox. She cavalierly said I had, which was a relief. I took care of Dakota, letting the poor itchy kid sleep in my bed and waking up with him several times to reapply the Caladryl lotion.

Dakota healed and flew back to L.A. with Bo's mom, Lou, aka Moomoo. A couple of weeks later the film wrapped and I got on the plane to go home. A half hour into the flight, I started to feel achy and sick. I looked at myself in the lavatory mirror and my face was blotchy with spots. By the time we got home, my entire body was covered with them, head to toe. I called my doctor, who said, "You are going to be one miserable puppy." He was right; I was. He also warned me to call him if I got a headache. If that happened, he said it could mean the chicken pox were in my brain. Oy!

They didn't go there. But I had them everyplace else, including my new beautiful boobs. I had a fever and my face was swollen up like I'd just done ten rounds with Mike Tyson. The therapy was to keep me sedated—on Benadryl, Valium, and Advil—with mittens on my hands so I wouldn't scratch. I was swollen and totally out of it when Bruce came over to watch the Academy Awards with me. He had a bout of pink eye. Drooling, with pustules all over my face and wearing flannel jammies and mittens, I turned to him and said, "Gable and Lombard, my ass."

• • •

After my chicken pox cleared, I went to Toronto for the movie *Shattered Trust: The Shari Karney Story*, the real-life story of an attorney who, while representing a woman in an incest case, learns that she was molested by her father as a small child. Because I'd been doing so much traveling—three locations in six months—I arrived muddled. On my first day there, they dyed my hair black. I got up in the middle of the night to go to the bathroom, flipped on the light, saw a raven-haired woman in the mirror, and screamed. It was me.

I got back home soon enough, but within a month I left with Bruce for New Orleans, where we costarred in the movie *House of Secrets*, an eerie thriller about a woman who suffers after killing her abusive husband. It was the first time Bruce and I worked together and we had a blast. I was the suffering wife, he the abusive husband. NBC knew full well they were casting a real-life couple; they wanted the play in the press.

It was a violent movie, and Bruce and I had to get physical with each other, which was surprisingly fun. Doing violent stuff on film is so much easier when you really trust the actor you are working with. I was far more uncomfortable shooting our love scene. I felt like that was too personal and private to share with other people.

There was one sequence toward the end of the movie that called for me to wear a sheer, sexy nightgown. They made me a beautiful light green silky nightie, and I could wear nothing underneath but a skin-colored thong. Not a problem for me with my new boobs.

Interestingly, the network gave specific notes about my breasts. They wanted to see shape but not color. Which was another way of saying they wanted to see my tits but not my nipples. Because of the sheerness, I couldn't wear breast petals, the little pads that make nipples disappear under clothing. Instead, my boobs needed their own hour in the makeup chair.

For one of the scenes, I had to run down Bourbon Street at night in nothing but my nightgown. At 2:00 a.m., the time we shot, Bourbon Street was a wild, fun, frenzied zoo, and the police were out on a blue flu strike that night, so there wasn't an officer in sight. I was supposed to be terrified as I fled down the street, thinking that Bruce was stalking me from beyond the grave. But instead, I was just trying not to crack up, because as I ran there were a bunch of guys with wedges of cheese on their heads and carrying Hurricanes, running alongside me and screaming, "Hey, Half Pint, show us your tits!"

On one of our days off we had a crazy night out on the town, whose high or low point, depending on your perspective, came when Bruce pushed me into a strip club for women called Cajundales. I knew it was time to leave when I was yanked onstage by a male stripper and saw a woman with no teeth in the front row turn to her friend and say, "Ain't that Melissa Gilbert from *Little House on the Prairie?*" As I hurried out, I saw Bruce in the back of the club, laughing his ass off at me.

The last few weeks of the shoot, Bruce and I stayed in a cottage at a bed-and-breakfast in Covington, Louisiana. It was a magical time for us. We'd come home from work and drink wine while listening to the frogs and bugs making a wall of sound outside while we decompressed and debriefed. Then we'd make love, sleep, and start all over again the next day.

I was determined to bail myself out of the quarter-million-dollar debt I had when Bo and I split. We'd lived beyond our means for way too long. It was so bad that at one point, my then stepfather, Manny Udko, who owned a fantastic jewelry business, offered to loan me money. I loved Manny, he was a mensch. He had a great warmth and charm and he was generous and fiercely protective of those he loved. When he and my mom first got together, I loved listening to his stories about growing up in Boyle Heights in L.A. and how, as a young man, he hung with real gangsters, like Meyer Lansky and Ben

(Bugsy) Siegel, and he remained a true friend years after he and my mom split.

My goal was to pay Manny back, dig myself out of the debt, and be able to buy a house of my own, so I crammed one more movie in before the end of the summer. It was a stinker called *Dying to Remember* that Ted Shackelford and I shot in Vancouver. There are a few reasons to do a movie: the location, the script, the director, the cast, or the money. The best projects have all or more than one of those elements. This was one I did strictly for the money.

It was so bad that Ted and I entertained ourselves between scenes and during rehearsals by inventing alter egos for ourselves: two pompous, overly stuffy English actors, Cecil and Gwenny.

Some unpleasantness with Bo crept into my life again during production, and Ted calmed me down one day by telling me that he had gotten divorced years before and had a deal with his ex-wife to pay her a percentage of his earnings. They didn't have any children, so he just stopped working for a while. I thought that was hilarious.

On September 21, the one-year anniversary of my first date with Bruce, I had to be in New York for press and talk shows. To celebrate, Bruce came with and we went out to a romantic restaurant on the East Side. We were enjoying ourselves when Bruce suddenly leaned over the table to ensure privacy and said, "What would you say if I asked you to marry me?"

I was jarred by the unexpected question.

"What would you say if I said yes?" I replied.

"Oh, I'd be happy," he said.

"Okay, then," I said.

"So I guess this means we're engaged," he said, stopping just short of making it sound like another question.

"I think it—yeah, that's what it means."

"No, we are. We are now engaged."

I excused myself to go to the ladies' room and called my friend Sandy. I repeated the conversation I'd just had with Bruce and asked her to translate it for me.

"Am I engaged or not?" I asked.

"It sounds to me like he asked you to marry him," she said. "But I'm not a hundred percent sure."

"Well, I'll just go with the flow and assume he did ask me," I said.

When I returned to the table, Bruce suggested we go ring shopping the next day. I guessed that made the engagement official. I reminded him that Manny was a jeweler who would save us money. Instead, we picked out a little pear-shaped cubic zirconia and Bruce slipped it on my finger, making it official. I loved that ring. I had worked my ass off for it.

We called family and friends and very quietly rolled out the news. When the lease on my house was up, Bruce insisted I move into his place rather than get my own home, as I had planned. Despite my reservations, the move felt right. We had weathered storms and breakups. We knew each other well. We weren't kids—I was twenty-nine, he was forty-three. We were good to go.

And then the shit hit the fan.

twenty-four

DATES WE WILL NEVER FORGET

The next movie I was offered was about a doctor in Vermont who artificially inseminated dozens of women with his own sperm, fathering more than a score of children. I had many reasons for turning it down. I thought the script was awful, I didn't want to tackle another project after making four pictures back-to-back, and it was close to Christmas. I passed four times. Each time, the producers offered more money. Finally, my team, Marc and Erwin, called together and told me to sit down.

"You really don't want to do this movie, do you?" they asked.

"No, I don't," I said.

"Would you change your mind for half a million dollars?"

"That's crazy money," I said. "I'm still trying to dig myself out of debt."

"That's why we told you to sit down."

"Oh God," I moaned. "Hold on."

I yelled to Bruce, who was upstairs. He knew I'd turned down multiple offers. "It's up to half a million. What do I do?"

"You get on the plane tomorrow," he said. "And you make it work."

I did. I went to Toronto and starred in *Baby Maker: The Story of Doctor Cecil Jacobsen* with Tom Verica and George Dzundza. For five weeks, I thought, *Lord help us all!* The silver lining was that I developed a really close friendship with Tom Verica, who introduced me to Vietnamese food, pho in particular, and led a day trip to Niagara Falls. The time flew by until the end. Then, early in the morning on December 19, Bruce called, extremely upset. He said that my best friend Sandy's sixteen-year-old son, Garrett, was dead. I turned ice cold.

"What?"

"I don't know any more," he said. "All I know is that Trevor"— Garrett's little brother—"called here crying, 'I don't have a brother. My brother is dead.' And there was screaming in the background."

I called Karen Scalia, who confirmed the horrible news, but details were still sketchy. Garrett had just returned home from boarding school. He was excited to help his family prepare for Christmas, and now he was dead?

I finally got a hold of Sandy and listened to her wailing, keening grief with a sense of helplessness that made me physically sick and desperate to be home immediately to help her.

She said Garrett had come home with what they thought was the flu and they took him to the doctor. He had a terrible headache the night before, and he never woke up. It turned out he had meningococcal meningitis, which the doctor had missed, though Garrett hadn't presented the normal symptoms and it was such a virulent killer that it wouldn't have mattered.

For the last three days of shooting, I was a wreck because I couldn't be with my best friend at a time when she needed me most. I was also unable to get on a commercial flight that would get me into L.A. the night before the funeral. Through my manager and agent, someone spoke to Treat Williams, who had a charter service, and thanks to him, I was able to go directly from the last scene of the movie to the airport. I didn't know Treat personally but he sent me a lovely food basket for the trip, and because of his generous heart, I was able to be with my dearest friends when they needed me most. I will forever be grateful to him for that. I flew home wearing my wardrobe and makeup. Sandy and David had asked me to speak at the service, so I was able to write my eulogy on the plane.

I sat up that night with Bruce, Jack, Karen, Sandy, and David, who said he wasn't going to cry the next day in front of everyone at Garrett's funeral. Of course, he was the first one to break down. I remember helping Sandy's other girlfriends get her dressed for the service, and as we were trimming the veil on the hat she was wearing, she broke down, repeating over and over that we should be dressing her for his wedding, not his funeral.

To this day, I have not witnessed grief so deep or so raw. I spent the next several days with Sandy. It was god-awful. When I tried to explain what was going on to Dakota, who used to play with Garrett's sister (and my goddaughter), Julianne, he asked, "Will Garrett get better if we give him hot chocolate?"

I said no and sat down with him for a long talk about heaven and what happens when we die, but no explanation made the tragic loss any better or easier to understand or accept. I didn't know how to make sense out of such a loss, and I wasn't sure I ever would. It was a horrible time that left each of us indelibly bruised deep within our soul. We canceled our annual Christmas Eve dinner and never had it again. I helped Sandy wrap Christmas presents and cried with her. Bruce bristled at me for getting too involved in someone else's grief, but that was the way it went with me. Now he's used to it.

I didn't have much of a Christmas spirit when we woke on the morning of the twenty-fifth to open presents, but I mustered enthusiasm for Dakota's sake and tried to make it as festive as possible under the circumstances. After all the presents had been opened, Bruce handed me a little box. I thought I knew what was inside. We had discussed making my little pear-shaped CZ into a real ring.

I opened the box and instead found a huge oval-shaped diamond ring that Bruce had designed with Manny. It was gorgeous and extravagant. Bruce was scared to death to give it to me. He didn't know how I'd react.

I burst into a full-bodied laugh, something I hadn't done for days. I was amazed Bruce had been able to pull off the surprise. It caught me completely off guard, and I loved it.

That ring was my light at the end of the tunnel. He slipped it onto my finger as tears streamed down my face. I was living the dream. I envisioned our wedding and life together. It filled me with hope and joy.

On January 17, 1994, our lives were shaken again, though this time it was a 6.7 magnitude earthquake that struck at 4:30 a.m. and made our world seem like a speck of dirt on a string suddenly pulled so tight that everything on it fell off. Seventy-two people died in that quake, more than nine thousand were injured, and damage across Southern California totaled more than $20 billion.

The Northridge epicenter wasn't that far from our community, but we were among the fortunate. Our house was seriously damaged, but not red-tagged as uninhabitable. Like everyone else's, our nerves were frayed, and each aftershock put us more on edge. Beyond that, all of us were okay.

Looking back, Bruce and I handled ourselves quite differently throughout the crisis, and that in itself produced aftershocks in our relationship. He emerged with his pith helmet and knife, waiting for looters, while I was either more fatalistic or practical, depending on your perspective. I figured if an aftershock was going to kill us, there was little we could do about it.

I had just seen my best friend walk through the worst thing a human being had to endure, the loss of her child. I wasn't going to make myself crazy over a bunch of broken stuff. Even when I saw valuable antiques in pieces, I would shrug and say, "It's not a life."

But Bruce didn't like that nonchalant attitude, as he called it. A distance began to develop between us and then one night we had our worst fight ever. It was so bad that I took the dogs and stayed at my mom's. I thought we needed to go to our corners and cool off. When I returned the next morning, I found Bruce sitting in the kitchen waiting for me. He said he wanted me out of his house. I sort of half giggled, thinking he was joking. He wasn't—and he refused to talk about it.

"Are you kidding me? There's nothing to talk about?" I asked in a rising tide of disbelief and anger.

"No, there's nothing to talk about," he said. "I want you out."

I was stunned, hurt, and confused. Though his house was full of my furniture and belongings, I gathered my clothing and toiletries and moved back into my mother's guesthouse. It was the craziest, most maddening situation. I gave him a couple days to cool off before calling again and asking if he wanted to work out whatever was bothering him. He didn't want to talk. Nor did he want me back. He just kept repeating that it was over. I was incredulous. *Over?* He answered, ice cold, "Yes, Melissa. Over." And he hung up the phone.

I was so incensed that I thought, *Fine, we'll do it your way.* I hired movers to box up my belongings at Bruce's house and move them into storage, leaving him with a bed, a futon, and a television. I also put my engagement ring into my safe. Somehow, amid the days I spent weeping about having landed with my four-year-old son back in my mom's guesthouse, I was cast in *Sweet Justice,* a legal pilot for NBC, and soon after, I had my Scarlett O'Hara tomorrow-is-another-day moment, only stronger. I had a child to consider. He needed stability, something solid. Something he and I could count on . . . we needed a home of our own! Having made a ton of money on all those TV movies, I went out and bought my dream house, an adorable Cape Cod–style cottage with green shutters and a white picket fence.

As we were about to close, Bruce called and said he was about to leave for India and Montreal to work on a miniseries that would keep him away for four months. When he asked what was new with me, I told him that I was about to shoot a pilot in New Orleans. Then I said very calmly, "Oh, and I bought a house."

"You bought a *house?*" he asked. "So it's really over?"

"No, no, no," I said. "You're not going to do this to me. You ended it. I am doing what I need to do to take care of myself and my son."

"Look, can we just have dinner before I go to India?"

"Fine," I said.

At my suggestion, we met at an Indian restaurant that had been a favorite of ours, but dinner was a disaster. We got in a huge fight and I left, wishing him a good time in India. Before I took off for New Orleans, I started therapy. As I told my therapist, I didn't want to live at the beck and whim of some guy. I didn't want anyone other than me to be responsible for my happiness. Clearly, my way wasn't working, and I was searching for a better course.

So I dove in, wanting to fix things and aware it wasn't going to be overnight. But the feeling that I was at least addressing the problem by asking the right questions carried me through the *Sweet Justice* pilot in New Orleans. Well, that and the fact that the cast was fantastic. Ronny Cox, my dear friend, played my dad, the gorgeous Jason Gedrick played my ex-boyfriend, and my wardrobe consisted of Armani suits . . . lovely!

From New Orleans, I was to go to Wilmington, North Carolina, for the TV movie *Against Her Will: The Carrie Buck Story*. I picked up Dakota and our nanny, Rosa, who had been staying with Bo in South Carolina at Tom Berringer's, and we stayed in a beautiful beach house throughout the filming, where my costar and friend Marlee Matlin helped me celebrate my thirtieth birthday. On my birthday, thirty red roses were delivered to my door, along with a card that said, "Happy Birthday. Thinking of you. Sending you love. Bruce."

Knowing Bruce as I did, I recognized it was a miracle that he remembered my birthday. That he gave a shit was even more miraculous. And the fact that he figured out a way to call his sister from India and make sure she sent me flowers showed me the depth to which he was thinking about me. Later in the day, he called, which I found out was quite a feat from where he was in India. We caught up long enough for Bruce to tell me that his trip was life-changing—no embellishment, no I miss you, just that it was life-changing—and for me to tell him that in a few weeks I would be back in L.A. and starting another movie.

Setting up my new house with Dakota, whom I adored and worshipped and found endlessly entertaining, was a thoroughly gleeful experience. It was a personal triumph and brought a sense of independence that was exhilarating to say the least. As I was settling in, I began work on *Cries from the Heart*, my third movie with Patty Duke, and was entertaining the idea of escalating a flirtatious friendship I'd struck up with George Clooney, when Bruce and I began talking frequently and rather intimately on the phone. He had called after moving to Montreal from India. A very healing initial conversation led to others, and finally I agreed to fly to Canada for the weekend.

I got to Montreal and had an extraordinarily romantic reunion with Bruce, who was shooting when I arrived. I napped in his trailer, as I'd flown all night and was exhausted. On his lunch break he climbed into the bed in that trailer beside me and we made love for the first time in months. The tone of the weekend was enhanced when we went back to the hotel and found the producer had sent champagne and strawberries to his beautiful penthouse suite. I showed Bruce a rough cut of my pilot. We talked, made love in a beautiful four-poster bed, and then as we sat up and talked some more, we could see fireworks out the window, lighting up the night sky in celebration of Bastille Day. But it was like they were for us.

By this time, I had heard Bruce confess that he'd kicked me out of his house and sabotaged our relationship because, in his words, he was a scared moron. He was panic-stricken that we would get married and have a child, and then he would find a way to screw things up, resulting in more children with parents who had split up. Then he played me a song. Bruce is not an overly romantic guy, but I could tell this song had a real impact on him. It was Marc Cohn's "True Companion." He said that hearing it is what had turned him around.

"I heard this song and all I could think of was you," he said. "I can't put anyone else in it. Nor do I want to. This is it—forever and ever."

I went back home, opened my safe, pulled out my ring, and put it back on my finger. Bruce returned soon after and then was cast in *Babylon 5*. Then NBC picked up *Sweet Justice*. I don't know that we fell back into a relaxed, normal life as much as we were swept up by the business of doing series and planning our wedding, but I was busy and happy. That was the other thing that had happened in Montreal: I made it clear I wanted a date, not an ambiguous reengagement with a wedding to be determined in the future.

"Call it," Bruce said.

"Let's pick something that neither of us will ever forget," I said.

"Fine."

"How do you feel about January first?" I asked.

"Can you pull it together that fast?"

"Pull what?" I asked. "We're not having a big wedding. I just want family. We could probably do it at my mom's."

"Really?"

"Really," I said. "Are you good with that?"

Bruce nodded. "Let's do it." Then he paused. "But tell me again—what's the date?"

Other than the fact that it was next to impossible to get roses and hydrangeas in Los Angeles the day before the Rose Parade, wedding plans could not have gone smoother. The ceremony took place in front of the fireplace in my mother's living room with about forty-five guests, including family on Bruce's side who had flown in from out of town. Votive candles gave the house a soft, romantic glow, the music was perfect, and the Jewish ceremony included five minutes of standup from the rabbi and his brother that left all of us laughing and crying.

At the end of the evening, a decoy limo zoomed down the driveway to a chorus of fake good-byes, distracting the crew of paparazzi that had waited all night in the street for us to leave. Then Bruce and I hopped in his Ford Explorer and drove to my house without anyone following us.

Dakota was being dropped off at Bo's, so we had the place to ourselves. I had prepared the bed with fresh linens and rose petals, readied an ice bucket with champagne, and set out a negligee that I thought guaranteed our first night as a married couple would be memorable. Instead, we sat on the living room sofa and talked in a state of disbelief, wonder, and joy about how we had gone all the way.

"I married you," I said.

"You married me, and I married you back," Bruce said. "That means—"

"You're my husband."

"And you're my wife."

Such iterations went on for hours. Sometime around three in the morning, we finally fell asleep in each other's arms. Our honeymoon lasted all of the following day and then we were both back at work. But I wasn't about to complain given what happened to me the day I returned: I was at an event for NBC affiliates, promoting *Sweet Justice*. George Clooney was also there. He apparently saw me giving interviews across the room and went up to my publicist, Colleen, and said, "You know your client broke my heart."

"What do you mean?" Colleen asked.

"She went and got married," George said.

He couldn't have given me a nicer wedding present. What woman wouldn't want to hear that from George Clooney? But, my God, how I loved my husband! After all the work we had done together and separately to get to this point, I knew he was exactly what I wanted. I thought marrying him was proof that I could indeed live life on my terms—the good, the bad, and the surgically enhanced.

Then, of course, I was reminded that every time you think you are in control, God taps you on the shoulder—or kicks you in the ass, depending on what you need—and shows you who's really in charge.

twenty-five

DAYS OF MIRACLES
AND WONDER

Bruce and I were busy shooting our series. We stayed at my house during the week, when both of us worked, and we bunked at his place in Hidden Hills on the weekend. My hours on *Sweet Justice* were often in the fourteen- to sixteen-hour range, excruciatingly long by any standard, and I blamed Cicely Tyson for the delays, as did everyone else in our otherwise outstanding cast.

Her mesmerizing performance in *The Autobiography of Miss Jane Pittman* was a gold star on her résumé, but she was extremely difficult. She insisted everyone call her by her character's name, though she never remembered the names of any of our characters. She rarely knew her lines. One day she kept everyone waiting hours because she didn't have the proper bra. Another time she slapped a director across the face. And still another time guest star Cotter Smith stormed off the set after a lengthy courtroom scene and fumed, "I'm never working with that woman again."

We had a giant makeup trailer where everyone gathered in the morning, listened to music, and drank coffee. Cicely would come in, turn off the music, dump the coffee because she hated the smell of it, and then make us sit quietly while she got her makeup done. I learned early on from my grandfather, whose mantra was "Don't start," not to start trouble. I was a team player; years later Aaron Spelling would refer to me as his quarterback. But this stuff with Cicely was out of control. Because of her, I was unable to spend quality time with my family.

She insisted on hiring a woman to help with wardrobe who was inexperienced, and I paid dearly for her lack of qualifications when she failed to wet me down properly for a scene where I was supposed to walk inside from a rainstorm. My feet went out from under me, and I landed flat on my back and head. I got my first ride in an ambulance that day. It was scary as hell. Production shut down for a few days while I healed, though ultimately that fall caused damage in my neck that would lead to surgery years later.

I finally snapped. I called NBC president Warren Littlefield and insisted he get a separate trailer for her and do something about the delays. Having grown up with Michael Landon, one of the biggest stars in TV history, who insisted that no one get their own trailers or any other special treatment, I never understood Cicely's divalike temperament.

Sweet Justice debuted the same year as *Friends* and *ER*. Early on, it was pretty clear the show wasn't going to make it, but we got in a full twenty-two episodes and I made some really great friends.

During hiatus, as we waited halfheartedly for the pickup that never came, I was cast as the lead in Danielle Steele's miniseries *Zoya,* a lavish historical romance based on a novel about a Russian ballerina/countess who flees the 1917 revolution for Paris and then America. Bruce also landed a costarring role as one of my husbands, though he wouldn't be able to join me until he wrapped *Babylon 5.*

To prepare, I vowed to get in the best shape of my life. I quit smoking, adopted a mostly vegan diet, and worked out with my childhood ballet teacher, who got me back up on pointe for the first time in fifteen years. By April, I felt wonderful. I was so healthy, in fact, that I got pregnant.

I want to say I was delighted, and I was, but truthfully, I was also mystified. We weren't trying, and there were so many barriers in place that either Bruce had supersperm or I had crazy eggs or it was a combination of both. A few days before I left for Russia, I was in ballet class and doing spins across the floor when I felt unusually dizzy. I stopped the lesson early, went home, and tried to figure out why I felt crappy. I flipped through the old Filofax and saw I was two weeks late.

"Of course," I blurted.

I immediately knew I was pregnant, but I didn't want to say anything to Bruce or my family until it was confirmed. After a blood test at my doctor's office, the nurse came in and said, "Congratulations!" I turned white and began to hyperventilate. I had to sit down. I was leaving in a few days for a three-month shoot in Russia and then Paris, London, New York, and Montreal. I would be gone the entire first trimester, playing a ballerina/countess from age seventeen to seventy. It was hard to fathom.

On the way home, I started making a mental checklist of the things I had to do to take care of myself now that I was pregnant, including taking vitamins and adding stuff to my diet. I had a little laugh as I realized Bruce and I would be shooting a scene where my character loses her virginity to his character. I was going to be playing a virgin while pregnant, whereas years ago on *Little House* I was a virgin playing a pregnant woman.

But there was a problem. I had to tell Bruce, who had the day off and was waiting for me at my Valley Village home. After I broke the news, he looked at me for an uncomfortably long time and then in a calm but firm voice said, "No." I said, "Yes, I'm pregnant." He replied, "No. You're. Not."

"I'm pregnant."

"No. No. No, no, no, no."

"Are you telling me I'm lying?" I asked.

"You can't be pregnant," he said. "How could you be pregnant?"

"Do I need to explain it to you?" I said sarcastically. "I think I have a pretty good idea how it happened."

"But—"

"I guess both of us are fertile people."

I saw that Bruce was on a slow boil and decided to wait it out while he cycled through his emotions, which he was entitled to do. First he accused me of getting pregnant to trap him into marrying me. Hilarious! I pointed out, of course, that we were already married. Then he began to pace, muttering to himself. I heard a lot of "Oh my God" and "How am I going to take care of this kid?" coming from him in a barely discernible, guttural mumble. Then he stopped and turned toward me, looking like a helpless ten-year-old boy in a jam.

"Another child," he said. "I'm not ready to do this right now."

"Look," I said. "Let's take a breath and just sit with it for a while. We'll see how you feel."

Two hours later I was sifting through clothes and starting to pack when Bruce came into the bedroom looking very different—almost satisfied with himself.

"Well?" I asked.

"I think it's time to call our parents," he said. "My baby is having a baby."

"Really?"

"Even with all the preparation in the world, you're never ready, so I might as well just roll with it," he said.

The rest of the evening was filled with joyous screaming and carrying on as we told our parents and our boys. A couple days later, I took off for St. Petersburg, Russia, by myself. Well, not by myself. I had someone else growing inside my tummy.

When I first heard I was going to be shooting in Russia, I was excited. I would be working with producer Douglas Cramer, who did everything first-class, and Diana Rigg, one of the coolest actresses ever (I mean, Emma Peel—come on, it doesn't get better than that). I also pictured myself drinking vodka, eating caviar, and whooping it up between visits to the Hermitage and other sites. Instead, I got there and my morning sickness was so bad that all I ate was porridge.

Plus, St. Petersburg wasn't at all what I expected. I thought it might be like Paris, only less sophisticated. But it was dirty and bleak. As for the people, what I saw was either extreme, ridiculous wealth or extreme, horrific poverty; either young girls in Chanel and Dior spilling out of limos with mob dudes trailing behind them, or an old woman with missing teeth pulling a cart down the street. I ate at one restaurant where an offering on the menu was "neck." Not whose neck or what kind of neck or how it was prepared. Just neck.

The highlight of my ten days there was shooting with the Kirov Ballet in the famed Mariinsky Theatre. Then we went to Paris, where I met up with Bruce, who played my first husband. It was his first trip to that romantic city, and luckily we found ourselves with an unexpected day off when the Russians held up all of our film equipment for some unexplained reason. I whisked him through the Louvre, down the Champs-Elysées, and up the Eiffel Tower, cramming three days' worth of sightseeing into eight exhausting but thrilling hours.

We were in New York for my birthday and Mother's Day, and then we settled into Montreal for the bulk of production on the miniseries. The director was an interesting guy, an ex-hippie sort with long hair. We had met privately before shooting and had a nice, flirtatious talk, and though I was married, I detected a you're-my-leading-lady-so-I-can-have-you kind of thing. But once he found out I was pregnant, every day was ridiculously adversarial.

On the bright side, Jennifer Garner played Bruce's and my daughter in what was her first job. She was especially beautiful, amazingly talented, and sweet. On the third day, Bruce and I predicted she would become a big star. I remember saying to him, "Just watch. She's something special." I am so very proud of her.

Despite all the hard work on the movie, we enjoyed some beautiful, peaceful early summer days in Montreal as well. At night and

early in the morning, when we had time for ourselves, Bruce and I
began trying to figure out what we were going to name our new baby.
I bought books full of baby names. We knew right away if it was a
girl we would name her Ruby. We also knew the middle name was
most likely going to be Garrett, since we wanted to honor Garrett
Peckinpah. But neither of us could come up with a boy's name that
we liked. Every day we riffled through the pages of the naming books,
as if a name we had overlooked would miraculously jump out.

It didn't. But one day I turned the page, looked up, and slapped
myself on the side of the head. Bruce asked why I was upset and I
shook my head and simply said, "Michael."

"Of course," he replied. "I can't believe we didn't think of it earlier."

We returned home in June and moved into my Valley Village
home for about a month while I gutted and redecorated Bruce's place
to make it more family-friendly and reflective of my taste. I wanted
to rent out my house, but I let Bo move in when I heard he didn't
have anywhere to stay. I thought I was going to be able to kick back
between July and the baby's due date on Christmas Eve; Bruce was
returning to *Babylon 5*, and I envisioned myself getting fat and shopping for baby things in his absence.

But the stress-free environment I craved didn't materialize. In
mid-July, my publicist, Colleen, called and told me to brace myself
for a scathingly bad cover story in the *National Enquirer*. I took a deep
breath and asked, "Again?"

She warned it wasn't like before. This time the tabloid quoted Bo
as saying I was a "deadbeat mother." They claimed Dakota ran up to
strange women on the street and asked them to be his mommy. They
said Bo had had to get up at night to feed him when he was an in-
fant. It also said I refused to take care of him when he had the
chicken pox, and I forced him to watch reruns of *Little House*.

Over the years the tabloids had called me manipulative, accused
me of having people fired on *Little House*, followed Rob and me like
vultures, and paired me up with people I never dated. But this was

beyond the pale. It planted a seed. For instance, Bruce's relatives in the Midwest didn't know this was untrue, and they received calls from people delicately inferring that maybe Bruce shouldn't be having a child with me. It was ugly. I decided I wasn't going to shrug it off and walk away.

I hired powerhouse attorney Larry Stein and sued the *National Enquirer* and Bo for defamation, invasion of privacy, and infliction of emotional distress. The suit would drag out for nearly three years. I went to a couple hearings and opened every facet of my life, including my entire financial history. I felt like I'd been pinned and dissected without anesthesia. The lawyers were cold, crude, and unflinchingly callous.

At one hearing in early September, I was plainly sick and uncomfortable. I asked my attorney if we could postpone the session for another day. After he made the request, the attorneys for the *National Enquirer* and Bo conferred with each other, and then the *Enquirer*'s attorney said, "We'll move forward. We have no sympathy for Ms. Gilbert."

I thought, *Okay, you motherfuckers, game on.* I was already committed to seeking justice, but at that point I vowed to see the suit through and win, come hell, high water, or severe nausea.

Unlike me, the tabloid had limitless resources and money. It was a mess, and it filled my otherwise perfect life with an unhealthy dose of daily stress. The stuff they threw at me was brutal. But I soldiered on, knowing I was in the right. On October 1, I had my baby shower. Five days later, I woke up and was lying in bed, plotting out my day, which I thought would include writing thank-you notes, when suddenly I heard my water break. I knew the sound. Then I felt wet. I thought—hoped—that maybe I had lost bladder control, as that happens to some pregnant women. I was still in denial when I stood up and watched water gush out of me. I thought, *This is wrong, very wrong.*

Thank God Bruce was home. I called out to him and I was crying and shaking when he ran into the bedroom. I said, "We have a problem." Though it was early in the morning, I called my doctor and had her paged. She called me right back, listened to me describe the problem, and calmly said, "Why don't you come into the office and we'll see what's going on before we get hysterical. Just have Bruce bring you in."

"Okay," I said. "When?"

"Right now. I'll meet you there," she said.

Thus began an unforgettable ordeal.

I felt panic surge through my body as soon as I stretched out on the examining table in her office and began the wait for my doctor to tell me what was going on. Tears dripped into my ears as she did a litmus paper test on the fluid and confirmed that my water had broken. She did an ultrasound and estimated Michael—by this time, we knew the baby was a boy—weighed about three pounds. She called ahead to Los Robles Regional Medical Center and told us to go straight there. I left her office shaking with fear but managed to mutter, "I'm not going to have this baby now."

At the hospital, they put me in a room and gave me an IV of magnesium sulfate to slow down the labor. The doctor came in and said they needed to keep the baby in me for at least a day, and in the course of that day they were going to give me three steroid injections to speed up development of the baby's lungs. They also put me in bed in the Trendelenburg position, but turned on my side, with my feet higher than my head, to remove as much stress as possible from my uterus.

Bruce and I called everyone and told them what was going on, and that we were in a holding pattern. The magnesium sulfate gave me a wicked headache, which wasn't fun. It also made my lips puff up, which I didn't mind. Around 1:00 p.m., I sent Bruce home to go for a run, pick up some of my stuff, and come back around dinnertime. My mother, Sandy, and my midwife, Sage, took his place. Sandy put makeup on me, saying I'd thank her later when I looked at pictures. It was also very comforting feeling her hands on my face.

A while later the doctor did another ultrasound, which showed that I had lost all my amniotic fluid. The head of the neonatal intensive care unit, Dr. Paul Hinkes, came in and explained that he wanted my doctors to do a C-section as soon as possible. Keeping the baby in me any longer, he said, posed numerous risks. He pointed out that Michael's heart rate was dropping, and he also cautioned that his lungs weren't going to be able to breathe on their own, so he'd have to be hooked up to a ventilator. Then he ran down a list of things that might be wrong with him after they got him out, such as a cerebral hemorrhage, blindness, a perforated intestine, or a hole in his heart.

At the time, none of these horrible things registered in me. They would later, for sure. But I didn't hear a word after he said "If he makes it through the first twenty-four hours, it's good. If he makes it through the next twenty-four hours, it's better. And if he makes it through the next twenty-four hours, we'll be okay." I just wanted to get him out. I said as much over and over. "Let's get him out."

By then it was four o'clock. Bruce rushed back to the hospital and got into surgical scrubs. On my way to the OR the nurses were kind enough to stop the gurney so I could see my mom and Sandy one more time. We all kissed one another, crying and repeating that everything was going to be fine. As I was wheeled into the operating room, I started to panic a little. Bruce put his mouth right next to my ear and kept whispering, "It's okay, baby. Everything's going to be okay." Both partners from my ob-gyn office, Dr. Ambe-Crain and Dr. Taylor, performed my C-section. There was also a respiratory therapist, a neonatologist, and the NICU nurse in the room. I'd had an epidural and was awake through the surgery. As with Dakota's birth, the doctor asked if I felt the first cut. I said no, and she said, "Okay, then, here we go."

With Bruce holding my hand, I listened to the doctors exchange procedural small talk. Then I heard one of them say, "Here he is." The other said, "Oh my goodness, isn't that silly." I asked what was happening and someone said he had reached his little hand out of the incision. Then it got very quiet, too quiet. I heard whispering, and then I began to get scared.

"What's going on?" I asked.

My doctor walked to the side of my head so I could see her and explained it was hard to get him out. There was no lubrication, she said, and he was hiding from them. She warned, "He might be a little bruised, but we'll get him out." Though it seemed like an hour had passed, it was only several minutes later that I heard them say, "He's out." I waited to hear him cry. I knew he would be okay if he cried; it would mean that he could breathe.

Sure enough, I heard a cry. It was barely audible, but it was the first glimmer of hope that things would be all right.

They whisked him to the side of the room and put him in an open incubator, where they began to work on him with practiced precision and determination. From where I was lying, I could only see his foot—one little blue foot sticking out from all the activity. Then his foot turned pink and I thought, *Okay, he's getting oxygen.* I heard another little cry, and the people in the operating room cheered.

"He looks so tiny," I said.

"He looks beautiful," Bruce replied.

They quickly put a breathing tube into his lungs and brought him to where I could see him. He was the tiniest thing, like a little bird that fell out of a nest. At just twenty-eight weeks, he already had a head full of blond hair. He also had Bruce's profile, his exact nose. He was unmistakably a Boxleitner. My God, he was so beautiful. He was also pink, and I heaved a sigh of relief. He certainly wasn't out of danger, but I had a feeling that he was going to pull through.

Bruce didn't know where to go. He wanted to stay with me, but ultimately, we decided he should go to the NICU with Michael. I told Bruce to watch him and take pictures while I was sewed up and taken to recovery. After a little bit, the neonatologist came in and reported that Michael was a fighter, but not out of danger. I gave him a steely look and said, "It's not going to happen. Nothing bad is going to happen."

I barely slept that night, and in the morning I called friends and relatives with the latest news before it hit the tabloids. I didn't want a repeat of what had happened ten years earlier when I had my appendectomy and it was reported in a dozen different ways by the media. As I later joked to *People* magazine, "I think my internal organs actually got higher ratings than my face."

After breakfast, I was taken to the NICU for my first visit with Michael. I was shocked by the way the tiny infants were laid out in open beds—Michael, in particular, reminded me of the frogs we dissected in high school. He was lying with his arms and legs spread out and attached to various lifelines. One line went right into his belly button and into his heart cavity. He had a pulse oximeter light on his foot, measuring his blood's oxygen level. He had one IV here, one there. A wire attached to the top of his head monitored his body temperature. He was the exact antithesis of the baby whose welcome to the world is a cozy swaddle in a warm blanket. It almost struck me as barbaric. And yet he was so serene, so peaceful. When I talked to him, he turned toward me and gave me a little peek out of his eyes. That's how he got his nickname, Peeker. I thought, *Okay, you're going to make it.*

Fortunately, Michael's next few days were unremarkable for a preemie, though there was nothing unremarkable about them for Bruce and me. Bruce has since confided that he refused to let himself become too attached to Michael in those first few days in case something happened. He didn't want to care in case our son died. He also later admitted that he had actually feared losing both of us on the operating table.

I was a focused soldier. On October 8, two days after giving birth, I was able to sort of hold Michael for the first time, along with the padding from his bed. The next day he was taken off the ventilator. On the tenth I went home, which was excruciatingly hard. Leaving my child behind, despite knowing he needed to be at the hospital, was gut-wrenching. My days fell into a blurry, methodical schedule. I got up, pumped breast milk, got Dakota off to school, went to the hospital, watched Michael, went back home, pumped some more, had lunch, checked in with Bruce, picked Dakota up from school, got homework started, pumped again, fixed dinner, spent two more hours at the hospital with Michael, came home, pumped one last time, and passed out. I was never as happy as the day I was actually able to hold him without the mattress pad.

We weren't out of the woods, though. Nine days after he was born, I showed up at the hospital and Michael had two big tubes up his nose. He'd been put on a CPAP, a special kind of ventilator, after having had trouble breathing the night before. They had to force air into his lungs because he'd been working too hard to breathe. I was assured he wasn't as uncomfortable as he looked, but I saw that and fell apart.

I was a jumble of emotions I couldn't begin to figure out. Walking in and out of the NICU every day with other parents worrying about their child's condition was a strange experience. We shared our love and fear in a communal silence that was like a fragile crystal bubble. It was as if we didn't want to shatter the status quo by talking. Monitors beeped, lights flashed, parents whispered to doctors and nurses, and in between all of us prayed.

If bad thoughts crept into my head, I would write out dosage charts for Michael's medications or I would make detailed lists of things I had to do. I had never been so purposeful.

One day I was at the hospital kangarooing with Michael— meaning I held him against my bare chest, with blankets on the outside, a practice adopted from Third World countries where modern NICUs weren't readily available. The idea was the mother's body would regulate the baby's temperature. Suddenly his temperature dropped and the two nurses monitoring his vital signs came over.

One nurse reached out for Michael and said it was time to put him back in his heated Isolette. Then the other, seeing the look on

my face, said, "Let's wait. Give her ten minutes." Within a few minutes, Michael's temperature regulated again. Then they took my temperature. It was 101. My body had heated up in order to provide him
necessary warmth.

I was aware that thirty-one years earlier I wasn't held like that,
nor was I wanted, but dammit, my kid was—and I just wanted to get
him home.

Michael thrived. On October 17, he received his first taste of breast
milk through a tube in his nose. Six days later, he fed from a bottle.
During this time friends and family would visit. His brothers made
drawings and cards that I taped around his Isolette. My grandfather
came to visit, took one look at the tiny boy, and said, "What's he
doing in that thing? He looks like he should be sleeping in a hol-
lowed-out melon." Things were not only on course but a little bit
ahead of schedule. I felt like I took my first deep breath in nearly a
month. I wanted to know when I could take him home.

I pestered the doctors and nurses with questions, showed them
that I knew all of his medications and doses, and had home nurses
and special lights for his jaundice all lined up to care for him at
home.

On November 15, Bruce and I were finishing breakfast and talking about the day ahead when the doctor called and said we could
bring Michael home. I screamed. Bruce canceled whatever appoint-
ments he had and we hurried to the hospital. Normally they don't let
babies leave the hospital until they weigh five pounds; Michael was
only four and a half. But I knew if I could get him home, tuck him
into my bed, dim the lights, feed him whenever he wanted to eat
(every two hours, it turned out), and just love him up all day and
night, he would do well. And that's exactly what happened.

Once I got him home, he blossomed. A nurse came every other
day and assessed him, and I took him to the pediatrician once a

week. On his first visit, he was in the seventh percentile for weight, if that. By Christmas, he weighed about ten pounds and was in the eighty-fifth percentile. The doctor marveled; I beamed. My little guy was an early overachiever, just like I'd been.

So much attention had been given to Michael that I wanted to get Dakota a special present for Christmas. When I asked what he wanted, Dakota said he wanted his dad and me to get along. Bo and I had had little to do with each other since I filed the lawsuit, and what interaction we did have was fraught with strain and tension stemming from the fact that I knew he had fabricated the story for the *National Enquirer*, which I held responsible for creating the stress that had caused Michael's premature birth.

But for Dakota's sake, I called Bo and invited him over to talk. Because nothing in my life ever happened the way I expected it to, he and Bruce hit it off immediately and I was pushed out of the equation. Their bromance robbed me of a chance to unload on him. And despite my considerable resentment, I dropped him out of the lawsuit without any satisfaction for the suffering he'd inflicted.

I continued to pursue my claims against the *Enquirer*, though. I wasn't about to quit that fight. For me, the issue was no longer about restitution for what they did to my reputation and me; it was about the fact that their disregard for both the facts and human decency had nearly killed my kid.

I felt like David fighting Goliath. As the lawsuit moved forward, the tabloid's attorneys pulled my medical records, starting from my first gynecological checkup when I was eighteen. They were threatening to use some of that information against me in court. I saw their gambit; they wanted me to meditate on the threat of not just public embarrassment but downright mortification. They couldn't have tried any harder to make the situation more ugly.

I tried to focus on the good stuff. At Michael's one-year checkup, I was told that I didn't have to bring him in once a month anymore. The doctor said he might still be a couple months behind developmentally, but he would catch up soon enough. To celebrate the good news, we threw a first-birthday bash for all of our family and friends who had prayed along with us for the past twelve months. Just before everyone arrived, though, I fell apart in our bedroom.

Bruce came in and found me curled up on the bed, crying and unable to catch my breath. When he asked what was wrong, I told him that I was suddenly and unexpectedly overcome by thoughts of all the things that could have gone wrong with Michael—the heart problems, the bleeding in the brain, the drama of those first twenty-four hours, everything. It was a delayed reaction to the worry I had kept bottled up for the past twelve months. The dam just burst.

I was feeling things and I didn't like it. That's when an occasional glass of wine turned into two at five in the afternoon. Three glasses was even better. My drinking escalated from there.

The lawsuit wasn't quite finished. At one point, after I won a small pretrial motion, I received a call from Screen Actors Guild president Richard Masur. He explained the union was working diligently on privacy legislation to curb the tabloids and paparazzi, and in exchange for speaking up on my plight, he offered me support from their government relations office and legal department. To thank Richard, I said, "Let me know if there's anything I can do for you." He would eventually take me up on that offer.

The suit would drag on for nearly another two years until finally we had to end it. The cost was staggering, in the hundreds of thousands of dollars, and by then all I wanted to find out was why—why they would print a story they knew was blatantly untrue and obviously damaging to my life and career, and my children's lives. My attorney arranged a meeting with the *National Enquirer*'s editor in chief, Steve Coz, and their attorney, at their headquarters in Clearwater, Florida.

We flew to nearby Miami and checked into the Delano Hotel. I was a nervous wreck. Before the meeting, Larry took me for a long walk on the beach. He knew that despite my uncertainty, I was anticipating the face-to-face with the fuck who had approved the story about me. Larry told me what to expect and urged me to remain centered, focused, calm, and to keep my wits about me. I took his counsel to heart. It enabled me to contain my anger so that I could focus it and use it with laserlike precision.

The meeting lasted several hours. We agreed the details would remain confidential. However, I can say that it was a remarkable experience for me. I had the opportunity to confront someone who I thought had wronged not only me but my family.

And I learned a great deal that day, starting with the revelation that the *National Enquirer*'s attack on me was not at all personal. It was purely business for them. Stories like the one they wrote about me sold magazines, period. It convinced me more than ever that gossip rags were a cancer on our culture and individual sensibilities. I wanted to run to every newsstand and grocery store checkout line in the country and tell people how much pain they were inflicting on people by buying those pieces of trash.

I also learned how to walk away from a fight. At one point during the meeting the lawyer for the *Enquirer* said something that caused me to almost explode. I wanted to fly across the room and rip that guy's head off. Fortunately, Larry squeezed my hand tightly and suggested that I go for a walk.

I did and went to my suite. I called Bruce at home and told him what was going on. He calmed me down and helped me see that the fight, whether or not I got everything I had wanted, was over. I had made my point. There was a deal on the table. As he said, it was time for me to agree to it and come home.

"In some victories, you don't always get everything you want," he said. "But this is a victory. It's over. Walk away. Michael is fine."

"He is fine, isn't he?" I said.

"He's better than fine," Bruce said. "He's exceptional. So are you. Now put your sword down and come home!"

twenty-six

INAPPROPRIATE BEHAVIOR

Six months later, in the summer of 1997, I was battling for my children again. But this time it was for a movie.

I was in Calgary shooting *Seduction in a Small Town,* the story of a woman who moves to a small town with her family and fights to regain her two kids from foster care after being falsely accused of child abuse. I had Michael with me, and about halfway through the movie Bruce brought Dakota and Lee up for the famous Calgary Stampede. Little did Bruce know what he was walking into.

Before I left for location, Bruce and I were getting along, but there was a distance between us that made sense only in retrospect. My inability to express my feelings or needs was at a peak. I was overly self-sufficient and full of resentment at everyone and everything. I dealt with these feelings by ordering a glass of wine or two . . . or three at the end of the day. A couple drinks took me to another state of mind. It was like changing the channel during a commercial.

The cast of the film bonded instantly with one another and our director, Charles Wilkinson. We were together constantly on set and off, barbecuing, singing, and drinking . . . a lot. I became especially close to my leading man. Inappropriately so. I'd always developed little crushes on my leading men, but this was different and it was fueled by alcohol, which allowed me to pour my heart out. The problem was, I was pouring my heart out to the wrong person. I should've been sharing all of this with my husband, but I was too afraid.

I guess you could characterize my relationship with my leading man as an emotional affair. Just as wrong and dangerous as a sexual affair . . . maybe more so.

The film wrapped and I came home for a bit, then went to Toronto to shoot *Christmas in My Hometown* with one of my favorite leading men of all time, Tim Matheson. I was in a slightly better place mentally, especially on days when I could end the workday with martinis or wine.

Several months later, I began another film, this time in L.A., called *Childhood Sweetheart*. It was great to be shooting back in L.A. again and also to be working with Ronny Cox, whom I adored. Everything was going smoothly, until one afternoon, about three-quarters of the way through the movie, when Bruce got ahold of me on my cell phone. I was in my dressing room, and as soon as he heard my voice, he began to scream.

"You did this to me! I should have seen it coming! I can't believe you did this to me. I hate you. I trusted you, and you abused that trust."

His voice couldn't have been louder or more full of rage and pain. At the same time, he sobbed in giant, wounded gulps. Panicked, I tried to get him to stop, take a breath, and tell me what had upset him. I started to cry, too. I could feel a giant seismic upheaval beneath my feet, and I didn't know why. Finally, he said there was a tape.

"What?" I asked.

"Someone left a tape in the mailbox," he said.

"So?"

"It was of you on the phone, talking," he said. "I know you had an affair with that guy in Calgary. I know this—"

I had heard Bruce in various emotional states, but never this upset. He was nearly out of control. Somehow I managed to calm him enough that I could finish my scenes that day, but he was still in a volatile state when I walked in the door hours later. He could hardly look at me as I set my things down and asked for more details. He handed me a tape recorder and said, "Listen to it yourself."

I looked down at the recorder and was about to ask which button to push to get it to play when I realized Bruce had left the room. I figured it out on my own.

Sure enough, the tape had me on the phone with various friends of mine—female friends and male friends—complaining about Bruce, complaining about our marriage, talking about how great I thought Calgary guy was, and asking why Bruce couldn't be more like my movie's leading man. Oddly, though, some of my conversations were intercut with other conversations that I couldn't remember. Nor could I recognize the voices. I thought I was losing my mind.

I listened again. Yes, half of the conversations were between my friends and me, but I realized the other half of the conversations were recorded off a TV.

I went upstairs to the bedroom and got on my knees in front of Bruce. Trembling as tears rolled down my face, I said emphatically that I did not have an affair with Calgary guy. There had been nothing physical between us, ever. On the other hand, I admitted the relationship I did have with him, as he had heard on the tape, was an emotional one and inappropriately intimate. It was, I said, because of things going on between us that we weren't addressing, which after a while Bruce understood.

"But this tape is more sinister than anything I did," I said. "Please, let's you and I figure out how we can get through this and move on together. I'm admitting this and willing to work on whatever I have to."

By this point, I was crying from embarrassment, shame, and humiliation—and sorrow for the hurt I had inflicted on Bruce. The lid had been pulled back on me and I was exposed; this part of me that was an inappropriate, desperate daddy-seeker had glommed on to another guy and now I was found out. Bruce calmed down a bit, and we held each other tightly and cried for a long time.

"We'll deal with this," I said finally. "But let's figure out what the hell this tape is, where it came from, and who would do this."

It turned out the tape had arrived in an unmarked envelope left in the mailbox. Bruce had brought it in earlier in the day with the mail. When he showed me the envelope, I noticed our address was wrong and realized it had been hand-delivered as there was no stamp; someone had gotten inside our gated community in Hidden Hills. Later that day, Bruce's friend Jerry called and told us that he had also received a tape in the mail, along with a note that said, "Better that you should tell Bruce about this. He should hear it from a friend instead of reading it in a tabloid."

"Something really creepy is going on here," I said to Bruce and Jerry. "This is freaking me out."

I sat down and stared at the envelope as I listened to the tape again. While listening, I realized two things: first, most of the conversations had taken place while I was cooking dinner and talking on the cordless phone as I moved about the kitchen, and second, the envelope was addressed to another house in Hidden Hills and had no return address. Feeling suspicious, I flipped through the local directory and realized that the address matched a house less than a mile from us. I was familiar with it. It had an apartment over the garage occupied by a woman who had been obsessed with Bruce for years.

Long before I came into his life, she would cross paths with him on the trails when he was running or walking. She continued to run into him after we became a couple. One day she approached Bruce's ex-wife, Kitty, and said she couldn't believe Bruce was dating "that Melissa Gilbert. She's fat and ugly and horrible." She scowled at me whenever Bruce and I saw her, which was, as I thought about it, pretty often; I realized then that this psycho stalker may have recorded our phone calls for nearly a year and sent the tape to Bruce to try to split us up.

I was absolutely terrified. I wanted to shut the blinds and lock the doors. If she was willing to go that far, what was to keep her from hurting one of our children or killing me?

I grabbed Bruce and said, "It's her."

"What?"

He knew exactly who I was talking about.

"Look at the address," I said.

I called my security expert and friend Gavin de Becker, who immediately went to work on the case. His people delivered flowers to her and saw she had a large antenna on her roof, which we surmised allowed her to tap into our cordless phones and pluck my conversations as they traveled through the air. According to the authorities, there wasn't anything we could do legally. Those radio waves were public domain. But we brought pressure on her in our own way until she moved out of the area.

Talk about your blessing in disguise. The crazy lady ended up doing Bruce and me a favor by forcing us to confront problems in our marriage before they grew too big to handle. We immediately started intensive couples counseling. In our first session, a three-hour marathon, we decided unequivocally that we were going to stay married, which, in our eyes, made our marriage the primary patient, and we moved on from there.

The biggest move was the work I did on myself in therapy to try to figure out what was going on with me. I was stuck in a pattern. I was always somebody's girl. After my father passed away, it was Michael Landon, then Rob, then Alan, then Bo, and then Bruce. I was like the little bird in the children's book *Are You My Mother?* Except my story was titled "Are You My Father?" I cozied up to a new daddy-substitute anytime I felt alone.

I was also desperately trying to prove myself to be lovable. My need to be loved and cherished was driving me to go out of my way to show people how "special" I was. I was the first to arrive during a crisis and the last to leave. If an acquaintance wanted to go toy shopping for their kid, I would get them a personal shopper at FAO Schwarz. I overextended myself for virtual strangers and at a cost to myself and my family: *Love me, love me, love me . . . aren't I lovable . . . I'll do whatever it takes.*

To top it all off, Bruce and I had only been married ten months when we faced a life-and-death situation with our son, and we came out of it relating to each other in a much different, more distant manner, not an uncommon thing after couples go through a traumatic event. We loved each other, but we didn't communicate. As a result, we misfired in a major way.

But I worked damn hard to turn that around. I wouldn't realize until later, after I got sober the last time, that much of my behavior was subconsciously influenced by efforts to fill a deep, psychic hole that went straight to the core of my being.

Unlike my kids, who had been handed to me as soon as possible after birth, who were immediately welcomed into this world by my voice and my loving face, I arrived quite differently: I didn't belong to anyone when I was born. For the first twenty-four hours of my life, I didn't have a name. Strangers passed me back and forth. As silly and clichéd as it sounds, I carried around the idea that my own mother, for whatever reasons, didn't want me. I'd be lying if I said it didn't torment me. If your own mother doesn't want you, who is going to want you?

Drinking took me away from these and other troubling thoughts. It was the calm from the daily storm inside my head.

My inner alarm clock rang at five on the dot, and I poured myself a glass of wine or a martini as I prepared dinner. By eight, I had the kids in bed and could sit down with Bruce in front of the TV to watch a movie. But my brain would still be racing from the groceries I needed, to what episode Bruce was working on, to his schedule the next week, to wondering what my parents had been arguing about that one time I heard them yelling thirty years earlier. I still needed that fourth glass of wine to quiet the racket and let me zone out in Bruce's arms.

In early fall of '97, we went to Dublin on a six-week shoot for *Her Own Rules,* a movie based on Barbara Taylor Bradford's melodramatic saga about a writer who returns to her native England to search for her roots after having been adopted as a child and raised in America. Like many of my movies, it touched a raw nerve. But the story was so over the top it was easy to ignore.

I was able to turn the trip into a family vacation. We rented a cute home in Sandymount and had a happy time. Bruce and I were extremely close throughout that shoot. There was definitely healing going on in our marriage. To this day, he would say he didn't notice anything inappropriate about my alcohol intake. But in hindsight, two or three Guinnesses, half a bottle of wine, and a couple of whiskeys over the course of an evening, that's a lot, right?

And it was every day. At the end of October, I was in Utah, shooting an episode of *Touched by an Angel.* Bruce and I took Michael trick-or-treating. Michael dressed up as a cowboy, Bruce went as Eddie Bauer (he wore jeans and an Eddie Bauer sweatshirt), and I dressed up as Dorothy from *The Wizard of Oz.* After I put Mike to bed, Bruce stayed with him and I went down to the bar with my friend Amanda, who at the time was the director's personal assistant/muse. I ended the night by getting ripped and singing backup with an amazing southern blues band on an overly emotive rendition of the Allman Brothers' "Whipping Post."

I couldn't see where I was headed. But it definitely wasn't Kansas.

Soon after Utah, I wound up in Austin for the movie *The Soul Collector,* a great project with Bruce Greenwood and an entire cast that fell madly in love with each other. Everyone was a foodie, and between

scenes, we planned our next meals. I grew especially close with actress Christina (Tina) Carlisi, who played my best friend in the movie.
She was sort of an Italian version of me, without the drinking.

She and her husband, Jay, were gearing up to adopt a baby boy
after having gone through the ups and downs of fertility treatments.
All of us were thrilled when the birth mother went into labor. Then,
at the last minute, she changed her mind and decided not to give up
her baby. Tina and Jay were devastated. Not long after, they were
notified of another adoption. They called me from Arizona, where
the mother was in labor, and two days later they left with a beautiful
baby boy.

I hung on every word as she described the birth mother handing
her son, Will, to her and saying, "This is your son." Everyone was crying, she said, as was I while listening to her recall the experience of
one mother letting go of her child and another taking hold. In fact,
that may have been the catalyst that would later allow me to heal a bit
and reconsider my own birth mother's decision to give me away.
Maybe she had wanted me to have a better life than she could have
provided.

Until then, I had no doubt that I was a good mother. My life
wasn't perfect or traditional, but motherhood was my top priority and
I worked my ass off to give my own two kids the best life possible.
But then something happened that put a major crack in my self-
confidence. Bo called to tell me that he was moving back to Texas,
and then he said the words that hit me like a sledgehammer: Dakota
wanted to go with him.

My immediate instinct was to say, "No effing way you're taking
my kid to Texas. Are you out of your mind?" But I held off and asked
him to give me time to have a conversation with Dakota and talk to
the rest of the family. I sat down with Dakota, and he assured me that
he did indeed want to go. I went into my therapist's office weeping,
wanting to know what was wrong with me that my kid wanted to
move to Texas.

"It's not what's wrong with you," she said. "It's what's wrong with his father that your kid feels he has to go to Texas to take care of him."

We talked through my options, all of which were going to hurt no matter what I did. Did I want him hating me for the rest of his life because I said no? Or did I want him hating me for a smaller part of his life because I said yes? I knew not to discuss it with my mother, who would have immediately read me the most devastating passages from *Sophie's Choice*. I talked it over with Bruce, who pointed out Dakota would be back for long weekends, holidays, and the summer, so it was just a different way of dividing up the visitation schedule we had already worked out.

By the time Bo actually moved, I had come to terms with letting Dakota go. I was fine as I took him to the airport and put him on a plane. I got about two miles up the freeway before I fell apart. Agonizingly sad, primal screams came out of me, and I pulled off to the side of the road and just wailed. As far as I was concerned, I was no better than my birth mother. I had just given my kid away.

I was convinced I had made the biggest mistake of my life. It sent me reeling into a depression that I had little time for. A small bright spot was when Bruce and I finally sold his Hidden Hills place and moved into my dream home: my own manor house with majestic views on Mulholland Highway in Calabasas. But then my grandfather's health took a turn.

Sometime earlier, Papa Harry had been diagnosed with prostate cancer. At eighty-four, he had refused the surgery his doctor had recommended, preferring not to endure the side effects. He made his wishes clear at a family dinner when he said, "When it's my time, I just want to go. No heroics."

Papa Harry knew his audience. All the women at the table immediately berated him for even hinting at such a time when he would be nearing his final breaths. You have to fight, they bleated. You can't ever give up. Blah-blah-blah-blah. Papa Harry shook his head; they didn't understand. But I saw no problem. I believed any adult who wasn't responsible for parenting a child had the right to end his life whenever he felt he'd reached the end.

"You call it. I'm there," I said to him. "Whatever you need, one way or another, it's up to you."

He leaned over and whispered in my ear, "That's why you're the jewel in the crown, kid."

I felt like more of a juggler than a jewel. I oversaw work on our new house. Then I gave Bo ninety thousand dollars after he called and said he wanted to give Dakota a better place to live than his apartment but didn't have the cash for a down payment. I also helped my mother, who was handling my grandfather's decline in her own way. While my mother tried to feed him tuna noodle casserole, banana pudding, and other fattening foods as if they were the cure for cancer, he had no appetite for anything except spending precious time with his family.

In the midst of all the turmoil, I had to go to Seattle for the movie *Switched at Birth*, but I flew back every weekend to be with my Papa Harry. One time when I had Mike with me, the two of us climbed into bed with him and snuggled up on either side. He would turn to me and kiss my forehead, and then he would turn and stroke Mike's cheek. He did that over and over again. No words had to be spoken.

After that visit I went back to Seattle to shoot another week. Bruce called me late that Friday afternoon. When I picked up, he asked me if I was at the hotel. I said I wasn't and he said for me to call him when I got there. I knew what had happened and there was no way I was going to wait. I was shaking uncontrollably and I begged him to tell me. I said, "Papa Harry's gone, isn't he?"

"No," said Bruce.

"Well, what is it?!" I begged.

Bruce told me that a few minutes earlier, my dear fifteen-year-old beagle, Sidney, had been running across the backyard and just fell over. He was gone. My firstborn pup. Sidney Bidney Kidney Bean. The Bean. Mr. Beanly.

I was completely unprepared for that. I was devastated but finished the day's work, then flew home the next day to see my family and visit Papa Harry.

In his final days, Papa Harry lost the ability to speak and grew frustrated by it. My mother encouraged him to relax; he'd already said everything that needed to be said. Soon thereafter he slipped into a coma. I went back to Seattle for the last week of shooting. About two hours after I arrived, my mom called and said, "He's gone."

I stared out the window into the nighttime sky and thought about Papa Harry. He passed true to form, on his own terms, with grace, dignity, and style. His ending was peaceful and serene, an end I wish for everyone.

At work the next morning, I thanked everyone for their concern and condolences and insisted I was fine. I wasn't. Between scenes, I hid in my trailer and cried. As soon as I was needed on the set, I dried my eyes and put on my game face. I didn't have to be told the show must go on. That was second nature to me. I could stuff away colds, broken bones, and even the death of my beloved grandfather.

Or so I thought. After two days of setting aside my grief, I was on the set and in fact in midsentence, speaking with my director and costars, when suddenly I started to hyperventilate. Then my hands began to shake and my fingertips tingled. The set medic came running over.

I had just experienced my first anxiety attack. I still get them, but much less frequently. They happen when I stuff away anger or pain.

I wrapped the film and came home the day before Papa Harry's funeral. Bruce was away on a trip he takes every year with his guy friends, herding cattle in Wyoming. To his credit, he wanted to come home but I told him to stay. So the night before the funeral, my friend Cordelia slept over and then helped me prepare for the service.

My Papa Harry's service was a remarkable celebration of his life. It was closer to a roast or a variety show than a funeral. Uncle Miltie spoke. So did Uncle Jan (Murray), Sid (Caesar), and one of my favorites, Red Buttons. Garry Marshall told great stories about Papa Harry. Sara and I delivered eulogies on behalf of my mother and my aunt Stephanie.

I sat there with my boys, Sam, Lee, Dakota, and Michael, and grieved with my family for the first time in my life. Dakota carried Papa Harry's ashes to his place of interment. It was fantastic and sad and healing. It was what grief should be, and it really made me miss my dad.

Later that night, I was reminded of a story about my grandfather and Jerry Lewis, who amused themselves by making crank phone calls back in the sixties. One day they were looking through the newspaper classifieds for people they could prank when they saw an ad that said "Parakeet Found." They called the number and told the man who answered that they had lost their parakeet and believed he had theirs.

"Is it yellow?" they asked.

"Yes," the man said.

"With an orange beak?" my grandfather asked.

"Yes."

"That's him!" Papa Harry and Jerry Lewis yelled into the phone. "That's him! You got him!"

"When you say Marvin, does he chirp?" my grandfather asked.

They heard the man talk to the bird. "Marvin! Marvin!" Sure enough, the bird made noises back.

"He chirped when I called him Marvin," the man reported.

"That's our bird!" Papa Harry and Jerry Lewis said. "God bless you for finding him."

"Do you want to come get him?" the man said.

"No, no, no, that's not necessary," they explained. "Just take him to the window, point him toward Highland Avenue, and tell him to fly to Orange."

"Really?" the man asked.

"Yes," they said. "He has a wonderful sense of direction."

There was a pause. Then the man got back on the phone.

"Okay, I did it," he said. "He's gone."

And so it was with Papa Harry. As far as I was concerned, he went to the window and flew toward Orange or wherever his next stop was, having made this life much better with his entertaining chirps.

twenty-seven

ALL KINDS OF CRAZY

I continued to suffer anxiety attacks after Papa Harry's death. They were like emotional earthquakes. Without warning, something would shift inside me and then the ground would shake with a fury that made it seem like life was about to end. They didn't happen often, but they struck frequently enough to keep me on edge.

I didn't know what was going on. All kinds of crazy that had built up inside me over the years started to bubble out. My head was full of conversations. I heard discussions from my childhood. I replayed fights I'd had with Bo years earlier. I went over the checklist I had created a few days earlier for the fiftieth birthday party I was planning for Bruce. The chatter never stopped.

I relied on alcohol to get me through the thicket of noise and anxiety. I drank through the making of *A Vision of Murder: The Story of Donielle* in Vancouver. I drank even more in Toronto when I worked on the movie *Sanctuary*. I tried to be strict about my drinking, though. My alcohol consumption did not invade my day before 5:00 p.m. But then it was like troops storming the beaches of Normandy. By the end of a typical night, I would have gone through two bottles of wine myself.

Bruce had no idea how much I consumed. At home, I had my secret system down to a science. I would pour a glass of wine, take a few sips, and as it would get lower in my glass, I would sneak back into the kitchen and fill it to the same level so it looked like I was barely drinking. Sometimes I would hide an open bottle of wine in other rooms so I could refill without going back to the kitchen.

One night our friend Archie was over for dinner. A former marine and Gulf War veteran, Archie had worked as Bruce's double on *House of Secrets* in New Orleans, and we had stayed close. He was like one of our kids. Neither Bruce nor Archie drank that night, but I had my glass of wine, which I secretly topped off throughout the evening until something happened. It was like a switch flipped; I don't even remember. From what I have since been told or put together, I put Michael to bed and joined Bruce and Archie in the family room. I sat down on the dog bed in the middle of the floor, began talking to them, and then fell asleep. "Fell asleep"—that was denial talking. I passed out facedown in the dog bed.

Bruce couldn't wake me up so I could say good-bye when Archie got ready to leave. He made an excuse about me being tired; he may have believed it, too. Then he tried to take me to bed. Apparently I went off on him for waking me up and struggled as he helped me up the stairs. Anger came out of me like steam from a vent on a street, noxious and foul—and I had no clue. To this day, I have no recollection of that night.

I woke up in the guest room. When I opened my eyes, Bruce was sitting on the bed, staring at me. I heard him say my name and I broke into tears.

"I have a problem," I said.

"Yeah, you do," said Bruce.

"I have a drinking problem," I said.

"Yeah, you do," he said, nodding.

I wiped the tears off my face and sniffled deeply.

"Holy shit," I said. "What do I do?"

"Get help," he said.

"I don't want to go to rehab," I said. "I can already see the whole thing in the tabloids: Half Pint drinks a half pint per day, blah-blah-blah."

"Melissa," he said emphatically, "let's start at the beginning. You just said you have a drinking problem. Go deal with it."

I got into an emergency session with my therapist and told her the deal. My situation was dire. I felt like it was life and death. Certainly, my marriage and ability to mother was on the line. I couldn't remember putting my kid to bed the night before. I had called my husband terrible names, words that had never come out of my mouth before. I had blacked out.

"A blackout?" I said. "Me?"

It had been awful.

"Look, I have a drinking problem," I said, talking a hundred miles an hour. "But I don't want to go to rehab and have this conversation in front of strangers and have to worry about one of them selling it to one of the rags. This is my life. I've done enough of it in public."

We agreed to try rehabbing at home and if it got to be too much, I would check myself in somewhere. I was surprised to learn my therapist was twenty-eight years sober. She said there was a saying in AA that wherever two alcoholics are gathered, there's a meeting. In fact, Alcoholics Anonymous began in 1935 with just two members, failed stockbroker Bill Wilson and Dr. Bob Smith, a surgeon. They talked, smoked, and drank coffee in Smith's kitchen, and a worldwide movement grew from there.

"The only way to get sober is with AA," she said. "How you choose to do it is up to you."

I stopped drinking that day for almost the last time. To offset my body's craving for sugar, she had me eat a spoonful of honey every hour till I went to bed starting at 5:00 p.m., the time I normally poured my first drink. I also drank fruit juice. My juice of choice was white cranberry peach. It took me almost two years to get off that stuff! But it kept me from having horrible physical withdrawals. I had a rougher time emotionally. All of a sudden I had to feel everything that I had been trying to avoid. I was insecure. I didn't want to go out. I didn't want to talk to anybody. I feared I wouldn't be funny anymore. I was irrational, short-tempered, paranoid, and angry, which was new for me. I hadn't ever been an angry person. I didn't recognize that part of me. All of it scared me to death.

Whenever you see someone in a movie or on TV going through their first thirty days of sobriety in rehab, they are socially inept, inappropriate, and angry at the world. They chain-smoke and chew gum. I was like that, except I was rehabbing at home under the supervision of my therapist. It was unconventional, but I got through it.

As I got into the second and third month I embraced my newfound clarity as a blessing. I didn't enjoy all the difficult emotional crap I had to feel, but I took ownership of my life. For the first time ever, I was forced to say out loud if I was unhappy. Or angry. Or cranky. Or craving a drink, so watch out. Or sad. Or if I needed to talk to someone about why my mother didn't love me enough to keep me. There was no running away.

But as I articulated these issues, I could start working on them. And that was a good thing.

I wasn't staying sober according to AA's Big Book. I wasn't going to meetings. I wasn't working the steps. I was sober, though, and that's all that mattered to me. I was present for my kids, present in my marriage, and present in my life. And that was a good thing, too.

In the fall I got elected to the Screen Actors Guild Board of Directors. I was completely naive when I started the position. I had served as an alternate once when Richard Masur had been president, and the meeting had been terribly boring.

Then the commercial strike of 2000 piqued my curiosity. At the time, I was the face (or the head) of Garnier. Say what you will about me, I've had good hair my entire life. But that account fell apart during the 2000 strike. I instinctively knew the strike was too long. I also knew that the reputation of SAG within the industry had taken a beating. Something had to be done to restore its image; so when Richard called and asked me to run for the board of the Hollywood division, I agreed.

I was excited when I came in among the top ten vote-getters, which was a win. My first call was to Anna. She had been a past president of SAG. She congratulated me and wished me luck, but I detected a slight edge to her voice. I would find out soon enough why. The first board meeting I attended was a Hollywood division board meeting and it was bloody awful. The strike had just been settled and a seemingly disinterested President Daniels sat at the dais while his vice president gave awards to people who had worked hard during the strike.

The meeting was supposed to run about three hours; it lasted six. Two hours was consumed solely by a discussion concerning one board member whose photo had been left out of the previous year's "class photo." There was screaming and yelling. There was even crying as the awards were handed out. I had never witnessed such a colossal waste of time and energy. I ran a very tight ship at home. This was crazy. I couldn't imagine what the national board meeting would be like.

I attended a dinner at Bill Daniels's house for new board members who were somewhat unaffiliated. Like the country, SAG was basically divided into two main parties. Bill Daniels and those at his home belonged to the neo-con Performers Alliance, later known as Membership First. They had taken the Guild into the commercial strike.

Before dinner, Kent McCord spoke. I knew he had been on a series I didn't watch when I was growing up, *Adam-12*. He spoke endlessly, quoting labor history and arcane rules like a walking encyclopedia. Valerie Harper, best known as Rhoda on *The Mary Tyler Moore Show*, sat next to me. She had the annoying habit of muttering "uh-hum," "yeah," and "uh-hum" as she listened to someone talk. Hers was always a second voice in the room. As Kent spoke, she muttered and stared like he was Lincoln, Churchill, and Roosevelt rolled into one. I thought, *Wow, this guy knows a ton of history.* I was impressed with his breadth of knowledge. Then, about twenty minutes into his soliloquy, I realized that nothing he was saying was applicable to the topic at hand. He spoke a good game but it made no sense whatsoever. If you look up the word "blowhard" in the dictionary, you will find a picture of Kent McCord.

By the end of the evening, I knew this was the wrong side of things. All these people were patting themselves on the back for running this great strike, which had crippled California's economy and ruined the commercial industry, which had partially migrated straight to Canada and never returned. Tremendous monies were lost that would've gone toward pension and health plans. How was that a victory?

I called Richard Masur and said I wanted to talk to his friends about this, because it struck me as weird, or wrong.

In April 2001, I attended my first national board meeting. It was in a top-floor conference room at the Sheraton Universal Hotel. There were 106 national board members. At the time, the entire union totaled 98,000 members, nearly 90 percent of whom did not work full-time as actors. New York board members Paul Christie and Paul Reggio, both close allies of Richard's, instantly embraced me, a move that would help shape my future. Some of the more moderate Hollywood division members as well as those from the Regional Branch Division also welcomed me. They were sane, rational, thoughtful people, who I quickly recognized as beacons of light in a thick fog of crazy.

Before the meeting, I fixed a cup of tea at a buffet in the back of the room. That's when I spotted Sally Kirkland, another newly elected board member. She was dressed in layers of multicolored Indian robes and had a rhinestone bindi in the middle of her forehead. She had come with an assistant who set up a special antigravity chair for her, and she had a foot-high stack of unwrapped, sliced American cheese on the table in front of her.

Zino Macaluso, who ran the agency relations department, caught me staring at Sally and her cheese.

"Welcome to the board, Ms. Gilbert," he said.

"Thank you very much," I said.

"You look perplexed."

"I don't think I've ever seen anything like that," I said, nodding toward Sally.

He laughed. "Just breathe."

Board meetings were known to be disruptive, what the *Los Angeles Times* later called "as peaceful as a food fight." A month earlier, the LAPD had been called to break up a fight at a meeting of the finance committee. However, this board meeting was about as exciting as a coma. It went on for two days. Kent McCord droned on endlessly about procedure and statutes, quoting *Robert's Rules of Order* and points from history that didn't seem to relate to anything. A timer would go off, Bill Daniels would announce that his time was up, and Kent would keep going. The arguments back and forth in the language of Robert's rules of parliamentary procedure were like Greek to me. Thank heaven for my friends who translated. I just listened, trying to learn as much as possible.

By the end of the two days, I was cross-eyed. I had no idea what we had accomplished other than passing Global Rule 1, and I still had questions. I was never called on during the discussion, though, because someone was quoting laws from 1976 and some other putz was talking about when he was on *Room 222*.

After the meeting finished, I gathered with Richard and others from the United Screen Actors Nationwide faction at Claudette Sutherland's home to strategize ways to move forward. A couple hours later, I felt like we had accomplished something; I wondered why it had been so difficult with the larger group. As I walked to my car, Richard intercepted me and said he wanted to talk for a minute.

It was a warm spring night, and we stood just beyond the yellow circle cast by the front porch light.

"There's a presidential election coming up this fall, and we want you to consider running," he said.

I took a step backward. He may as well have admitted seeing an alien spaceship zoom across the sky. This was the office Charlton Heston, the SAG president from 1965 to 1971, had called "a bitch of a job."

"Are you crazy?" I said. "I don't have a clue what happened over the past two days. It was a zoo in there. I can't be the president of this union."

He put his hand on my shoulder and said, "Just think about it. You've got our support if you're willing to do it."

Bruce laughed with me when I told him about Richard's entreaty. I had driven home thinking that Richard was as loony as the rest of them. We had a really good laugh that they would even ask me. I could run a household. I could direct an After School Special. But what the hell did I know about running a union?

After going to sleep that night still laughing my ass off, I woke up the next morning with an entirely different attitude. I wasn't even out of bed when I turned to Bruce and said, "Screw it. If James Cagney can be the president of the Screen Actors Guild, I can be the president, too."

Bruce didn't say anything. He already knew what had happened. Sometime in the night that little voice in me had said, *Oh no? You don't think I can do it? Well, watch this.* No one taught you how to become president of SAG. No one in Hollywood ran classes on how to become a labor leader.

"Patty Duke did it," I said. "William Daniels has done it for the last two years, and I don't think he's done a very good job. Why can't I do it?"

"Do you really think you can?" he asked.

"I honestly don't see why I can't."

"Do you want to?"

"Yeah, I'm thinking I just might."

I decided to explore the issue with people whose opinions I valued. My first call was to Anna, and she said, "Do it." Not so much because the Guild needed me, which she said it did, but more because she said it would teach me more about myself than anything I had done before. My manager and agents gave their endorsement and assured me it wouldn't negatively impact my career (*ha!*). Then I got a brilliant idea.

I called actor Kevin Kilner, another newbie board member and a supporter of mine. He was a big, tall, good-looking, very smart, and reasonable guy. We had already bonded and we would cling to each other in the future, or rather I would rely on him many times as a life raft. I called him and said, "You know who would be great for this job, far better than me? Warren Beatty."

"Call him and see if he'll do it," Kevin said.

"Yeah, I will," I said. "And I can be his vice president."

I phoned Warren, who had supposedly once mulled a run for United States president, and told him that I had been asked to run for the presidency of SAG, but I wasn't sure I had it in me. Then I made my pitch. After a long pause, which was common when speaking with Warren, he said, "Melissa, I would rather be the president of Cambodia."

However, he encouraged me to run. After some discussion, I said, "Okay, I'm going to run. But if it gets to be too rough or too much trouble, I'll quit."

"No, you won't," he said. "I've known you for a long time. You're tenacious. Once you get in there, you're going to want to see things change, and you're going to want to stay until those changes happen."

I laughed. "You don't know me *that* well."

I took a drag off a cigarette. He chided me for smoking.

"So I can count on your endorsement and support?" I asked.

"Well, I wouldn't go that far," said Warren.

"Are you telling me that you're not going to publicly support me in this?" I asked with an indignant tone.

"I probably will," he said. "But I don't like stepping out publicly on stuff like this."

"Why's that?" I asked.

"To be honest," he said with a chuckle, "it's because I want people to like me."

"Fine, don't support me," I said. "I completely understand." Then I jokingly added, "But I don't like you."

"Yes, you do," he said.

"Okay, I like you," I replied. "But I'm going to pretend I don't."

One by one, I called people and gained support and encouragement. The last call I made was to my mother. She expressed surprise that I could become the Guild's president and that pissed me off. I told her that I could run for SAG's presidency if I wanted, or Congress for that matter. I sounded like I was fourteen years old.

"Then do it," she said. "I'm behind you all the way."

So that was it. I called Richard and told him that I would run—and do my best to win.

twenty-eight

MADAM HALF PINT

Before I officially announced my candidacy or pulled the required paperwork, I realized Anna was right. I was already facing truths about myself, one in particular: I wanted to win.

I wasn't blinded by the fact, though. My own ego wasn't anywhere close to becoming more important than the cause, a flaw I had observed in many politicians. But it was an interesting revelation. It brought back memories from numerous epic games of Monopoly with my brother, and competing against him on *Battle of the Network Stars* specials. I liked to win.

However, this wasn't a made-for-TV game. I met with a circle of people whom I began referring to as my cabinet of advisors. We hired a campaign manager and then we began to raise money. There were two ways to run for office at SAG. I could either go in front of the nominating committee, which was then stacked with William Daniels's supporters, or I could pull a petition and get it signed by Guild members in good standing. Since there was no way I would get approved by the nominating committee, I pulled a petition and organized volunteers to gather signatures.

I was already familiar with the big issues facing the Guild, including the TV/Theatrical agreement coming up for renegotiation—the collective bargaining agreement that covered all things shot for television and feature films—and the ATA franchise agreement between SAG and talent agencies (this agreement set rules and boundaries for the relationships between talent agencies and their clients, for commission percentages, etc.), which had expired. I wanted to curb productions running out of the country, especially to Canada. All of that was very important, but at the very top of my list was merging SAG and her sister union AFTRA. I saw where the industry was headed with respect to digital rights and royalties. Digital was a jurisdiction that was still up for grabs, and I knew with two unions vying for it, there was the very real possibility of a jurisdictional war—a tremendous problem, considering that forty-five thousand SAG members were also members of AFTRA. No one benefits in a jurisdictional war, as it is possible for each union to lower rates by using waivers and thereby undercutting contractual provisions—what is essentially a "race to the bottom."

In addition, and perhaps naively, I wanted to try to rid SAG of the divisiveness brought about by the two warring factions: Restore Respect (mine) and Membership First (Valerie's). The constant fighting blocked any chance for progress. So when I heard that Valerie Harper was going to run against me, I decided to try something bold and unconventional. I called her up and reintroduced myself (we had met when I was a kid), and although I had seen her worship at the feet of Kent McCord, I proposed that the two of us unite SAG by running together.

One of us would be president and the other would be vice president. We would work together. I even offered to let her pick which office she wanted, something my supporters would've freaked out about if I'd told them. (I had advisors and a cabinet, but I was still a very independent thinker.)

"I don't care," I said. "Let's just bring everyone together from the top down."

She said she had to speak to her advisors before giving me an answer. A few hours later, she called and declined my offer. She said she was already committed to the people around her. I interpreted that to mean her handlers had said no. Ironically, those same folks would later call me a puppet who couldn't speak for myself. One of them actually said publicly that Richard's hand was so far up my ass they couldn't tell where his hand stopped and my mouth started.

My next task was to find someone willing to run with me, so I asked Mike Farrell to run for the board with an eye toward being my first vice president. Mike had been and still is an idol of mine; he's the kind of guy who never backs down from his beliefs. I figured anyone as smart and savvy as he was would probably tell me to go pound sand, but he surprised me by saying yes. I could barely speak after hanging up with him, I was so elated. I turned to Bruce and said, "Holy shit! I must be doing something right."

Bruce, who in the larger world has very different political views than either Mike or me, said, "Jesus, Melissa, that's huge. Congratulations."

In July, we began the campaign, which consisted largely of speaking at gatherings people hosted at their homes, sending e-mails to SAG members, and taking out ads. My day began at five in the morning and lasted late into the night. I relied on Mike, Kevin, Richard, Amy Aquino, and other allies in Hollywood. In New York I had the Pauls and Eileen Henry, to name a few, and in the Regional Branch Division I had Cece DuBois and Mary McDonald-Lewis, among others.

The hours were long, the work was hard, and all of it was exciting. Sometimes it was even fun, like the time Paul Christie conjured up a wise shaman from a drainpipe in his building who advised our tribe. The drainpipe, or DP, also gave us tribal nicknames. Mine was Fullpinttalkslikepauls because I cussed like the Pauls in New York.

The election, as the *Los Angeles Times* described it, was basically "a referendum on the Daniels regime," though I tried to inject my own vision by emphasizing the need to negotiate, using a strike as a last resort, and trying to unify the divisions that were hurting the union. My supporters included Debra Messing, Tobey Maguire, and my former beau Rob Lowe. Valerie boasted Marty Sheen, Gregory Peck, and Sarah Jessica Parker.

In the meantime, the national board met one more time, this time to decide whether or not to hire Bob Pisano as our new national executive director. The meeting, as usual, went on and on for needless hours as people discussed the pros and cons of hiring Bob. In the end, Bob was hired. His first day of work was to be that coming Tuesday. It would turn out that Bob's first assignment on that day would be to close the New York office.

Bob's first day was September 11. The events of that day changed the country and the world, and they changed my campaign into one about banding together and perseverance.

I got up that morning at six o'clock to read my e-mails. I had just clicked on a news alert on my AOL homepage about a plane crashing into the World Trade Center when Bruce came downstairs for breakfast. We turned on the TV minutes before the second plane crashed into the other tower. Like everyone else in America, we spent the rest of the day glued to the TV, in a state of shock and disbelief, crying and holding on to each other and watching the replays and reports over and over again. I thought for sure there would be strikes in Chicago and Los Angeles.

Our house was normally in the flight path out from Los Angeles International Airport. Planes taking off flew over our house all day and night as they climbed out across the ocean and made the sweeping turn back toward land. But in the hours and days after the 9/11 attacks, planes were grounded. There wasn't a sound in the sky. When I went outside to smoke a cigarette, I didn't hear anything but an eerie silence. That was the scariest part. Life had changed.

I had speaking engagements scheduled, but I didn't want to go; I just wanted to crawl into a shell and wait for the next disaster. Mike Farrell talked me out of canceling them by explaining that the point of terrorism was to terrorize people, cities, and an entire country to the point where they ceased to function. If I canceled, he said, they would win.

I more than understood and pushed through my fear, working harder than before while adding a message about working together through difficult situations. I hoped it would resonate to ordinary people who had felt the same way I had. I was disappointed when Valerie refused my invitation to debate the issues. Instead, she and her camp attacked me as a traitor for violating rule one when I had made *Ice House* with Bo in 1989. They also accused me of owning a Canadian production company named after a daughter I supposedly had. Insanity!

I went to Dave McNary at *Daily Variety* about the first charge, explaining I had starred in my former husband's movie out of love for him and ignorance of the rules. Not only had I been punished a decade earlier, I had chaired the Young Performers Committee to ensure other child actors turning eighteen didn't repeat the same mistake. As was typical, I was misquoted and Mr. McNasty made it sound like I had intentionally violated rule one because "we all do foolish things when we are in love." It wasn't the first time I had been a victim of yellow journalism and it wouldn't be the last.

My skin turned out to be pretty thick. I was worried, though, that the combination of inaccurate press and the attacks from "the Valiban," as we dubbed my opponent's team, would damage my credibility with the SAG membership. Fortunately, her bitter campaign didn't seem to register with members. On November 2, I captured 45 percent of the vote, versus the 39 percent my opponent received. It was a clear and convincing victory, which we celebrated late into the night.

By the next morning, though, the papers announcing my election also reported the elections committee, loaded with Valerie Harper supporters, was calling for a new election, citing irregularities in the voting process. Apparently, ballots mailed to New York members didn't have the same signature line as the ballots sent to members in Los Angeles. The elation I felt the night before after winning turned to anger. It took a while before a new election was officially approved and set for early March 2002. By then I was livid about the whole thing. Having heard Fred Savage from *The Wonder Years* refer derisively to me in a board meeting as "the maybe president" made my skin crawl. Soon after the election, I came into work and sat down at my desk in my SAG office at union headquarters to prepare for an ATA meeting when I saw John McGuire, the associate national executive director, walk by. I called out to him and asked if he had a minute to talk. He came in and shut the door.

A lawyer with movie-star looks, John was like the institutional memory of SAG. He represented the union internationally. He was a calm, reasonable man who rarely lost his temper, and when he did, it was for good reason.

"They're rerunning my election," I said. "What the hell? What is this about?"

I ranted for a few minutes, unloading a truckload of anger, frustration, and confusion while John sat across from me and nodded. When I finally paused for a breath, he asked, "Are you done?"

"Yes," I said.

"You're going to win," he said. "Don't worry about it."

Then he stood up and walked out of my office.

I focused on work. While helping to negotiate the ATA agreement between SAG and agents, which, if passed, would allow limited investment by advertising companies in agencies in exchange for putting money in SAG's health and pension fund, and a commitment to fight the exodus of productions from the United States, I was notified that Karl Rove, deputy chief of staff to President George Bush, was coming to Los Angeles to meet with the heads of the entertainment industry.

He wanted to discuss ways that Hollywood could help assist the country's mood as it recovered from the 9/11 attacks.

The secret meeting took place at the Peninsula Hotel in Beverly Hills. Attendees included chiefs from all the studios, networks, and agencies, as well as legendary titans like agent–power broker Lou Wasserman. It also included the presidents and national executive directors of the unions, including Bob Pisano and me. The room was somber and serious as Rove led the discussion. Ideas were floated from every corner. Jeffrey Katzenberg offered to send *Shrek* DVDs to families who'd lost loved ones in the attacks; other studio chiefs promised similar gifts to our soldiers. Then I offered the Screen Actors Guild's support and participation.

There was an awkward silence. Of course, everyone in the room was aware of my reelection situation; even the CNN news crawl informed viewers of the battle between Half Pint and Rhoda. Then Rove said, "Thank you very much for that input, Ms. Gilbert." Then, with a puckish smile, he added, "Also, if you need a good election attorney, we have one."

His reference to Bush's contested victory over Al Gore in the 2000 presidential election turned the room upside down with laughter. I was the only one who didn't find it hilarious. I thought about how much I hated the people who had embarrassed my union.

At the end of the year, Elliott Gould, who had been elected SAG's recording secretary, decided to have a kumbaya conference call with all of the candidates running for president, secretary, or treasurer. In addition to Valerie and me, the roster included law professor and labor activist Eugene Boggs, and Angel Tompkins, an actress who changed her name to Angeltompkins so she would be listed first on the SAG ballot, which presented candidates in alphabetical order. There was also Kent McCord, Kevin Kilner, and Amy Aquino, who were running for secretary and treasurer.

On the call, Elliott tried to set some ground rules for the campaign to keep it from spiraling down into the gutter. Valerie didn't help matters by jumping in and saying she didn't think I should be showing up at events and representing myself as the Screen Actors Guild president because, as she claimed, I wasn't really the president. She recited a laundry list of don'ts. She also had the audacity to claim I was giving out awards to performers with disabilities and appearing at other events merely to get myself elected. I countered by saying I was, in fact, the president, as the board had agreed, until the rerun election told us otherwise, and so for the next three months I was going to act accordingly.

I was professional on the line but I was in tears when I hung up the phone. I called Kevin Kilner right after the conference call and bawled into the receiver. Not very presidential, I knew. But tough. I could not believe the blatant questioning of my integrity. I would maintain my duties, but I made it very clear that the opposition candidates should steer clear of me until the election was over. I hung up and told Bruce it was too hard. Then I went upstairs to tuck Michael into bed. My six-year-old noticed my eyes were red.

"Mommy, have you been crying?" he asked.

I said yeah.

"Why?" he asked.

"Because I was on the phone with people from SAG, and the lady who wants to be president said some things that hurt my feelings."

Michael took a deep breath, gave me a hug, and said, "Mom, she's just jealous of you."

That was the last time anything SAG-related made me cry. For the next three months, I helped SAG wrangle its way through the ATA mess until there was an agreement. The election was at the beginning of March 2002. Ballots were counted two days before the SAG Awards, the union's annual celebration of outstanding performances of its members. Whoever won the election would attend the rehearsal the next day and then the awards show on Sunday, which meant I had to prepare for either winning the election and attending the awards show or losing and watching the gala from home.

Wanting to be closer to town, I decamped with my family to the Beverly Hilton Hotel, where its owner, Merv Griffin, a family friend, generously let us have a penthouse suite. On the day of the election, my family, friends, and supporters waited in the suite with us while the votes were counted. SAG's national executive director and CEO Bob Pisano let me know the turnout for the election was the largest in SAG history. He said the media had turned the headquarters into a zoo.

Ordinarily, results were announced around seven o'clock, but by nine that night we still hadn't heard anything. My mother and her husband, Warren, were attending a black-tie function downstairs for Rudy Giuliani, and they kept running up to the suite for news. The wait was nerve-racking. On the bright side, though, I was so stressed-out that I was the thinnest I had been in years. There's always a silver lining.

At close to two in the morning, my cell phone rang. It was Pisano. He asked what I was doing, as if I would be doing something at that hour other than waiting by the phone for the results.

"I'm standing here with everybody," I said.

"Well, congratulations," he said. "This is awesome news."

Normally, a member of the election committee would call with the election results. Since I hadn't received that call yet, I said, "What are you talking about?"

"Oh shit," he said. "You haven't gotten the call yet, have you?"

"No," I said, looking around the suite at everyone anxiously staring at me. "What do you know?"

"You won," he said.

"By how much?" I asked.

"About fifteen thousand," he said.

I calmly thanked him, then hung up. Everybody asked me whom I'd spoken to, and when I said it was Bob, they lost interest, since they knew he wasn't the official call. Then I said, "He knows. I won." This was met by a collective scream, and I burst into tears in a delayed joyful reaction.

I'd won!

Indeed, the official call came a minute later. As Bob had said, the results weren't close. I had taken 56.6 percent of the vote, compared to Valerie's 33.4 percent. I felt vindicated, drained, and elated all at the same time. For the next several hours, the phone rang off the hook. Later that morning, I gave a press conference, declaring the victory a mandate for change.

"I'm upset we had to go through this again," I said. "It was a big waste of money, time, and effort. But the silver lining is that so many members voted in the election. I hope that's a sign the members can put aside differences, come together, and accomplish some great and necessary things."

If the previous weeks had been awful, the SAG Awards made up for it. My dress was an unusual off-the-shoulder brown full-length gown. It was also leather, which was a conscious decision on my part: I wanted to look pretty, yet tough. The red carpet was nuts. My victory had made headlines all over the world and now every media outlet wanted to talk to me. It was actually kind of scary, but I was on the arm of my incredibly strong and handsome husband, who kept gently nudging me forward.

The SAG Awards is a cozy affair; actors fill the front tables, eat dinner, and visit between commercials. And trust me, if you want to have a good party, invite two hundred actors and put a couple of bottles of wine on each table.

At one point I left to have a cigarette. When I came back, Bruce had an odd look on his face. Apparently while I was gone Kiefer Sutherland, who was also at our table, had leaned over to him and confessed that he was in love with me, and had been in love with me since we were kids, but he'd never had the courage to tell me.

"He said I was a lucky man," said Bruce.

"Are you okay with that?"

"Of course. I know how lucky I am."

I'm the lucky one, I thought. *I married an amazing man.*

As the SAG president, I was scheduled to give a speech, and I was uptight about delivering it. I made a sarcastic crack to Bruce during dinner about this being a fine time to be sober. Moments later, I was dragged backstage and then I heard myself introduced. Nervously, I walked onstage, where I was met by thundering applause that turned into whoops and chants, and finally a standing ovation led by Joe Pantoliano, followed by Jack Nicholson. I was so overwhelmed I almost fell apart on live TV. But I delivered my remarks and held it all together.

Back at my table, I leaned into Bruce and said, "This may be one of the biggest things I've done in my entire life." He put his arm around me and said, "I'm so proud of you. I can't believe you did this." Neither could I.

Apparently neither could James Gandolfini, who I hadn't seen since we acted together in the basement theater beneath the Trocadero bar in New York. At the after-party, he barreled across the floor, scooped me into his arms, and tossed me in the air like I was a beach ball. He put me down and said, "Congratulations, Grandma!" Grandma? I don't know what he meant by that. I didn't care either. It was the best election party ever.

At the next board meeting, I banged my gavel and opened discussions on the ATA agreement. It was immediately combative, and I had to repeatedly call the room to order. Kent McCord actually challenged my friend Peter Onorati to step outside and fight. It was surreal. Staff members were brought to tears, some asked where their thirty pieces of silver were. Esai Morales capped off the classy gathering by saying, "It's like I'm bent over this desk and I can feel the tip, man." Charming!

After this final salvo, I thought about calling in a shrink or my son's kindergarten teacher to give the worst offenders a time-out; we needed more than me as Madam Half Pint banging a gavel. During a break, I stepped off to the side and Valerie Harper sidled up to me and said, "Isn't it just awful the way people are fighting?"

"Yes," I said.

"Well, better you than me, kiddo," she said.

I turned my head to the side and looked at her with absolute shock and more than a little disrespect. If she felt that way, why had we just put our union through the cost, effort, and embarrassment of a second election? Had she even wanted the presidency? Or had she truly been a puppet?

Then came the debate before the membership. What a circus that was! Kent McCord and Scott Wilson presented one side. Kevin Spacey and I were supposed to speak on the other side, but Mike Farrell had to step in for Kevin after his mother took ill. Afterward, Kevin called me and asked how it had gone. I described the insane debate during which Kent had, at one point, recited the Boy Scouts oath while I had been loudly booed every time I opened my mouth, and how in the end, I felt, we lost.

"Shit," Kevin said.

"I have never seen people behave more horribly in my life," I said.

Kevin apologized for not being there.

"There is a silver lining here, though."

"What's that?"

"I must finally be rid of the Half Pint image because these people really hate me!"

Not everyone hated me, though. One day I was in my office when an assistant came in looking flustered. She said Marlon Brando was on the phone for me. I glanced at the phone on my desk; the light indicated a call was on hold. I glanced back at the redheaded woman as if to say, "Really? Marlon Brando?"

"I think it's really him," she said.

I picked up the phone and said, "This is President Gilbert."

The man on the other end introduced himself. He was indeed Marlon Brando. He said he thought it was great I was the new president.

"God, I couldn't stand that other guy," he said.

"Thank you very much," I said. "Your confidence means a lot to me."

Then he said he needed some help tracking down several residual checks from *The Godfather*. I knew there had been a problem with getting residual checks to people in a timely fashion, but I still couldn't help myself from blurting out, "You've got to be kidding me."

"Oh, no, no, no, no," he said. "I'm very serious."

I walked down to the residuals department and explained that Marlon Brando had just called to say he was behind and we needed to figure it out as soon as possible. It turned out he was right. Three days later, I received another call from Mr. Brando. He thanked me for getting him the dough.

"The other guy never helped me," he said.

"Well, I try," I said.

"That's why I like you."

twenty-nine

A PAIN IN THE NECK

I still had to work, and I couldn't have felt more comfortable when I made the pilot *Then Came Jones* in summer 2002. It was a twisted Western that starred Sean Patrick Flanery as a small-town whore-house owner turned sheriff with a nervous stomach, and me as his reformed alcoholic sister. I loved the script, the Western-style clothes felt familiar, and best of all, we shot at the Big Sky Ranch, the same place we had used to shoot exteriors for *Little House,* so it felt like home.

On the first day, I stepped out of my dressing trailer, turned the corner, and heard someone shout, "Hey, Half Pint, you old rat ass." I instantly recognized that voice. It was Jack Lilly, the man who had taught me how to ride a horse on *Little House.* Denny Allen, our former wrangler, was next to him. They had been training the guys on the show to ride and shoot and act like cowboys. I half expected to see Mike around the corner with his shirt off.

We enjoyed a warm reunion and laughed as I read from a press release I had in my hand about the show taking place in Texas at the dawn of the twentieth century—"when men were men, and women loved them anyway." Unfortunately, when ABC tested the show, the results came back saying that TV audiences didn't want to watch a Western. I thought that was a lot of horseshit. I was disappointed; I had enjoyed the job and everyone involved, and it would have been a joy to work with them for an extended period of time.

In hindsight, my life may have already been too busy to take on a full-time acting job. The SAG presidency consumed way more time than I had ever imagined, but I didn't know how to do it or anything else halfway. Bruce resented the intrusion into our lives—the phone rang constantly, and there were always meetings to attend, trips out of town, or strategies to plot. He was only half joking when he said he would run for a spot on the board of directors to ensure he saw me regularly. He did, and he won.

Thanks to a rule change, all hundred-plus seats on the board were up for reelection that year, and I ended up with a super majority in the boardroom. As a result, meetings that had routinely lasted from six hours to two days were completed within two hours. Mike banged the gavel in Hollywood Division meetings in record time.

Everything from work to my home life, including my sobriety, was in pretty good running order, except for one major pain in my neck. It really was a pain in my neck, too. Ever since the fall I took nearly ten years earlier on *Sweet Justice,* the discs in my neck had been degenerating and causing an increasing amount of pain. I had been under the consultation of renowned spinal specialist Dr. Robert Bray, and we'd been doing everything to avoid surgery. Acupuncture, physical therapy. But over the years my neck got worse and worse. Tired of flare-ups that would paralyze my left arm and leave me couch-bound, taking Vicodin like Pez when I was trying to stay sober, I went in for tests, which revealed several leaky discs as well as bone spurs that clamped down on the roots of nerves coming out of my spine.

I went in for surgery feeling confident in Dr. Bray, but scared of the possible side effects, since the doctors would be going through the front of my neck to get to my spine. In the operating room, as the anesthesia began to take effect, I grabbed Dr. B.'s shirt, pulled him toward me, and said, "If you screw this up, my husband and my sons are going to kick your ass." Then I was out like a light.

Luckily, he was a good sport—and an even better surgeon. I woke up several hours later in the recovery room, and after the grogginess began to wear off, I realized something extraordinary. My neck didn't hurt. Nothing hurt. I had been living with a low-grade level of pain that was so constant I had grown used to it.

When my doctor came in and asked how I was doing, I started to cry. I told him that I had pain from the surgery, but it was different than I was used to. The pain that brought me to him in the first place was gone. I could also hear better, which was weird. He laughed knowingly and said, "Yeah, you were a mess."

After recovering, I dove into the process of trying to merge SAG and AFTRA. A meeting developed into committees that explored the issues for both sides and eventually led to a plan for consolidation and affiliation that I really thought we could get passed. While working on the plan, I attended an AFL-CIO and AFTRA event at Ron Burkle's home, kicking off the Working Families campaign. A number of high-profile SAG and AFTRA members were in attendance that night.

Bruce was out of town, so I asked Kevin Spacey to be my date. We met for tea at the Ivy in Beverly Hills and then Kevin drove both of us up to the Burkle mansion. He drove like a maniac through back alleys to escape paparazzi that had chased us after we left the restaurant. He very calmly turned to me at one point and said, "Don't worry, I've taken an evasive driving course."

I walked into Burkle's house and came face-to-face with a marvelous van Gogh painting, a real one, which enchanted me for about twenty minutes. There was a van Gogh inches away from me. I was standing in some pretty rarefied air there. Indeed, the event's headliner was former president Bill Clinton. Kevin engineered a quick introduction beforehand, and then at the end of the evening we were cracking jokes in the corner about some poor schmuck's toupee when Clinton sauntered over and began talking to us.

Actually, he talked to Kevin. I just nodded, trying really hard not to say anything stupid. I figured I had to nod, smile, and keep my mouth shut for about ten minutes, and then Clinton would move on. Instead, looking right at me, he asked, "What are y'all doing after this?"

"I'm in Kevin's car," I said hurriedly. "So I go wherever he goes." Clinton looked over at Kevin.

"Why don't you guys come with me?" he asked.

He was heading to a fund-raiser for Senator Thomas Harkin at Haim Saban's house and then another at the Beverly Hills Hotel. Kevin blurted out that he was in, and I said, "Sure, whatever." Before we left, my pal John Connolly, AFTRA's president, said that AFL-CIO president John Sweeney wanted to take us out to dinner. The political move would have been to accept, but I said no thanks and explained I was about to leave with President Clinton.

"Kevin and I are going," I said.

I was trying so hard to be cool. Now I wonder if I came off that way. As Kevin and I climbed into the backseats of a large black Suburban—Clinton and a Secret Service agent were in the middle row, another Secret Service agent drove, and an assistant sat beside him—I could sense myself quickly running through my reserves of coolness.

We got about a half block down the street when I saw flashing lights from cop cars behind us. I immediately thought, *Oh my God, the Beverly Hills police are pulling us over. Wait till they find out whom they're going to ticket.* I was about to say something, then thought better of it, and I was glad I did. It turned out not to be the police but the police escort. There went my last ounce of cool.

We were chatting when Clinton received a call from Senator Tom Daschle. From what I was able to hear, Daschle wanted to talk through strategy about how to deter President Bush, Vice President Cheney, and Secretary of Defense Rumsfeld from invading Iraq. I looked at Kevin nervously; I was unsure if we should be eavesdropping on this conversation. It wasn't like listening to someone talk about getting a plumber to fix a leak. They were talking about how to get people on board to block the country from going to war with a country that had nothing to do with the September 11 attack on the United States. It was power personified.

When Clinton hung up, he swung around, and without mentioning a word about his previous conversation, he told stories about his childhood. He said he was working on his autobiography. He was delightful, charming, smart, funny, easy to talk to, and thoroughly, disarmingly magnetic. I had seen his charisma work its magic in a room full of people. One-on-one in the back of a car, he was almost overwhelming. I could see why people fell all over him.

We were late to the fund-raiser at Saban's magnificent house, but apparently Clinton ran on his own time schedule. It was nothing for him to be an hour or two late. The Secret Service guys told me it was called "Clinton time." Whenever he got to an event was when it started for him, and everyone was thrilled he was there. Afterward, on our way to the next event, we somehow got on the subject of nose jobs. I described a letter I'd recently received from a girl who wrote how much alike she thought we were.

"Get this—she said, 'I am also the victim of a botched nose job,' " I said.

Both Kevin and Clinton laughed. The former president then told a story about former supporters of his who had strongly advised him to get his nose done before he ran for president. They didn't think he could win with his real nose. He laughingly said, "They thought it was functional, but not presidential."

We were having a good time when we pulled in front of the Beverly Hills Hotel for the last event. The walkway leading into the hotel was lined with a crowd five deep on both sides. People screamed his name. It was like being with all four Beatles rolled into one. As we walked in, Marty Sheen came walking out of the hotel. He said hi to Kevin; then he looked at Clinton and said, "Mr. President"; and then he looked at me and said, "Madam President." Since Marty occupied the top office on *West Wing*, I quickly picked it up and said, "Mr. President." Then I looked at Clinton and said, "Mr. President." Though amused, Clinton put out his hand to indicate he wasn't going to enter into our Marx Brothers–like silliness. But he added, "Actually, Melissa is the only real president among us, the only one who's actually in office."

After that, Clinton, Kevin, and I were taken into the kitchen behind the stage of the ballroom where the former president was set to speak. While he waited for his introduction, he shook hands and posed for photos with the kitchen staff, from the chefs to the waiters to the busboys. He took time to acknowledge everyone. I was impressed with his ability to connect with people. But then, that's what made him Bill Clinton.

At some point, Kevin, who was getting ready to start filming *Beyond the Sea*, started singing "Mack the Knife," and the next thing I knew, the two of them were singing and bopping along. I chimed in, too. Around one in the morning, we finally rolled back up to Burkle's house. They invited me to stay and play cards. But frankly, I was out of cool, and moments away from saying or doing something totally dorky. I let a Secret Service agent drive me back to my car and went home replaying the whole evening in my mind.

I was fully rehabbed from neck surgery and feeling strong and fresh when I flew up to Calgary to work on *Hollywood Wives: The New Generation*, a TV movie event based on Jackie Collins's best-selling novel. On and off camera, the movie, whose cast included Farrah Fawcett, Robin Givens, and my longtime friend Jack Scalia, was full of Jackie's trademark excess. At the first photo shoot, Farrah took one look at Robin and me, then ran back to her trailer, sobbing, "They're so much younger than me." We waited three hours while she redid her makeup. But waiting for Farrah, who was listed number one on the call sheet, became part of the routine. Every day I came in and asked, "How's Number One today?" Let me just say I read three novels while shooting the movie. Still, I adored Farrah. There was something about her vulnerability that made me want to protect her.

If Farrah was fragile, there was one person on the set with the strength of ten: Jackie Collins. I loved and admired her. She was a real dame—a strong woman who existed successfully in a man's world without sacrificing an ounce of her femininity. In fact, she oozed femininity. Jackie had everything figured out, including men and women, sex, money, and power. She shared her expertise on wardrobe, jewelry, and looking sexy, and the stories she told on the set were better than her books. She knew the most delicious dirt about everyone. She told me about a superstar singer turned actress who would check into the Peninsula Hotel in Beverly Hills to get a manicure and pedicure, strip off all her clothes, and then order room service so she could see the reaction on the waiter's face when he walked in and saw her nude while getting her nails done.

I was afraid to ask what she knew about me. But then again, if I had, she might have warned me about the role I slipped back into on that movie—that of alcoholic. Bruce and Michael were with me during most of the production, and one night we were at dinner, along with my brilliant assistant Kari, and after they ordered drinks, I said, "You know what? I'm going to have a martini."

As the waiter wrote down my order, the others at the table—not Michael, but Bruce and Kari—looked at me with shock and confusion.

"Why can't I have a martini?" I said. "I'm not in pain anymore, not since my neck surgery. I'm not covering that up anymore. I'm no longer traveling with a box of painkillers and muscle relaxants. There's nothing going on. I'm fine. I can have a drink."

I was doing cartwheels inside as I sipped my martini. I could hear my brain say, "Yeah, I'm drinking again." The next day I called my shrink and told her that I'd broken my sobriety, but I felt confident I could have a drink here and there. She said, "Okay. If you say so." Of course, that didn't last long.

Nor did the stability in my life. In July 2003, I decided to run for a second term as SAG president. I knew my job wasn't finished after my effort to unite SAG and AFTRA barely missed. Although 58 percent of the membership voted for the merger, constitutionally it nceded 60 percent to pass. In any other world, 58 percent would have been a mandate. In the world of SAG, it was a defeat. The theatrical contract between actors and studios was also up for negotiation. We had extended it the previous year in order to study what new media was going to look like in the future, and to avoid a possible lockout over issues we weren't sure about, but the contract needed to be addressed.

As I threw myself into both the contract and my campaign, Bruce landed a starring role in the series *Young Blades*. The series shot in Vancouver, requiring him to move there and be gone for large chunks of time. It was rough, and I handled the stress and strain by drinking more.

In September, I won reelection to a second term, and Membership First once again took a stronghold in the Hollywood division. While my return to the union's starring role was a vote of confidence for my platform, it wreaked havoc on my personal life. Bruce would come home on a break and resent me for being consumed by negotiations; and I would, in turn, resent him. We weren't communicating well, if at all; our biorhythms ran in opposite directions.

That Bruce was in Canada shooting a movie when I celebrated my fortieth birthday didn't help. I had a slumber party the night before with my closest girlfriends and then a larger bash the next night with all my favorite foods, dancing, and a screening in the backyard of my all-time favorite movie, *My Favorite Year*. It was a sort of last hurrah in the house; shortly thereafter we realized we needed to downsize, since one of us was not working as much as she had in the past as a result of the SAG presidency.

There was other fallout from the presidency. The TV/Theatrical negotiation was taking a toll on me emotionally. It is very difficult to take a package of proposals into a negotiation and then begin the back-and-forth of deciding what goes and what stays. It's almost like deciding which child will live and which will die.

I spent many nights distracted, sleepless, tossing and turning with worry. One night, I fell asleep on Bruce's side of the bed, which was wrought iron, with four large posts that had decorative vines and roses wrapping around them. In the middle of the night, I got up to go to the bathroom and on my way back I walked straight into the bed. I knew from the immediate pain I had done major damage. I just didn't know how bad.

Afraid to look, I went back into the bathroom and turned on the light. I saw that I had a gash across my forehead and a cut across my nose; in fact, there was a flap of skin hanging open next to my nose. Blood poured down my face and neck. After washing my face, I decided to call my dermatologist in the morning rather than wake Michael up and go to the emergency room. So I put butterfly Band-Aids on the flap next to my nose and somehow I managed to fall back asleep. In AA one would call that self-will run riot. In my world it was a perfect example of my constitutional incapability to ask for help.

At seven the next morning, I dropped Michael off at school and went to the dermatologist, who put 15 stitches in my face, bandaged me up, and gave me a prescription for pain pills, and then I drove to the AMPTP headquarters for that day's round of negotiations. Later, my car wouldn't start and I needed a tow, which only added insult to injury.

I felt like the world was trying to thwart me with one frustration after another. In reality, I brought on the problems myself. I didn't see what should have been obvious when I looked in the mirror and saw myself covered in bandages: I was overwhelmed, fighting the world, taking on too much, and trying to do it all myself. I couldn't bring myself to ask for help—not even the night before when I had stared into the bathroom mirror and seen my face covered in blood.

How much more of a clue did I need till I woke up?

More.

My final act as president of the Screen Actors Guild was to get the theatrical agreement negotiated, out to the membership, and passed—and by the end of my term we would do that. Bruce was still traveling back and forth shooting *Young Blades*, and our marriage was in deep trouble.

Things just weren't right. My face wasn't healing properly. Then I started having trouble with one of my implants. I went to the doctor who had put them in ten years earlier, and he recommended changing them immediately. It was a tricky situation because we were at a crucial part of the negotiations and I knew I would need four days to recover from surgery.

I pulled Pisano and AFTRA's national executive director, Greg Hessinger, aside and informed them that I needed to have some surgery and would be unavailable from Thursday through Sunday. Pisano worried the surgery must be pretty intense for me to need four days off. I tried to slough off his desire for more info by explaining it was a girl thing, but after seeing he was genuinely concerned, I decided the hell with it and said, "Guys, ten years ago I had breast implants put in and now I'm having some problems. They need replacing. I'm not making a big deal."

"Understood," Bob said.

Greg nodded uncomfortably.

I came through surgery fine. Whether my marriage would fare as well was still up in the air. I harped on Bruce when he was home and made him feel like he couldn't do anything right. I was overly capable, and he had become extremely self-sufficient again from living on his own in Canada. We fought so badly that he started to use the D-word. We loved each other, but we knew something had to change or we couldn't go on living together, which I found unacceptable. So did he.

When *Young Blades* ended and Bruce was home for good, we went straight to the therapist, who asked us point-blank if we were telling her that our marriage was no longer her primary patient, that we were done. Two hours later, after a long, hard look at the twelve years we had spent together, we left having made a pact. We weren't just going to work out our differences. We were going to make our marriage work. We had a child, a home, and a life together. I must give Bruce a tremendous amount of credit. He is a very rare and special man in that he has always been willing to go to therapy to make our marriage and our family work. In fact, in my family we are all great believers in therapy and go in any number of combinations: Bruce and me; Bruce and Lee; me and Dakota; Bruce, me, and Michael. It has softened and healed Bruce's relationship with Sam and Lee. It has made us a solid family unit, and none of it would have been possible if Bruce hadn't been willing.

There was still a wild card—me. While I worked on my marriage, I failed to acknowledge the entirety of my own self-destructive behavior and its effect on my family. If I had, I would have dealt with my alcohol consumption. I clearly had a drinking problem and wasn't facing it. I had already ripped my face apart in the middle of the night. My body had fallen apart from stress. I was a mess.

What was I waiting for? Why didn't I recognize the obvious? As Laura Ingalls Wilder wrote, "Once you begin being naughty, it's easier to go on and on and on, and sooner or later something dreadful happens."

In my case, I went to New Orleans to make the movie *Heart of the Storm*. I was already close with director Charles Wilkinson and bonded quickly with my costars, especially Brian Wimmer. We shot from sunset to sunrise and then went back to our hotel in Covington, where our tightly knit cast and crew unwound by playing guitar and drinking. Our cocktail hour was at eight in the morning.

My drinking was out of control. Though I never drank at work, I consumed twice as much as everybody else when we were off. I was probably hungover 85 percent of the time, but I thought I was having a blast. I had no idea how much stress and strain I was trying to suppress.

Then I returned home. On August 8, I was in the kitchen making dinner, drinking wine, and going through my motions of trying to secretly keep my glass full. I was up to three bottles a night at this point. After opening the fridge and topping my glass off inside so no one could see, I shut the door and saw Michael standing there, looking up at me.

"Momma, you're not going to drink more wine, are you?" he asked.

My heart stopped. That was my bolt of clarity from out of the sky, my spiritual awakening. It scared and humiliated me more than anything I had ever experienced. My nine-year-old kid had asked me to stop drinking. I was sick that he knew I had a problem. I didn't wonder how many other people knew. The pain and guilt flooded over me in a tidal wave. I immediately went upstairs to my room and collapsed in a heap on the floor, sobbing.

The next day I showed up at my therapist's office. I may as well have crawled in on my hands and knees. She already knew what had happened. I simply said, "I surrender. I will do it the right way this time. I will do whatever I need to do to stop drinking. I have to stay sober."

To keep myself on course, I began attending AA meetings. Private, women-only ones. I realized I needed help, and it ran counter to my nature to ask for it. But I couldn't do it alone. Not much later, I ran into my friend, Michael Des Barres, whom I hadn't seen in years. We talked for a while and he suggested I go to a meeting that he regularly attended. I went and immediately felt at home. The meeting was small and closed to people who weren't alcoholics, but it was still a public meeting. I ran into more friends there, some from as far back as childhood. I had found my home and still maintained my precious anonymity.

Soon after, I faced my greatest fear about such gatherings when I agreed to speak at a much larger meeting in Beverly Hills. As I was standing outside waiting for my friends, a woman came up to me and said that as a longtime fan of *Little House*, she was excited to see me at her meeting. Then she caught herself, apologized profusely, and said, "Wait. How do you do anonymous?"

I shook my head and said, "I don't—and come to think of it, it really doesn't matter compared to the alternative."

I had never spoken truer words. For years, I had been afraid of people judging me harshly if they knew I had a problem, even though it was almost de rigueur in Hollywood to have a drug or drinking problem. In reality, I only feared one person finding out the truth: me. And as soon as I came to terms with that, well, facing the facts of my life was a lot easier and less tiring than running away from them.

THE SWEET, SIMPLE THINGS

In the fall of my last term as SAG president, I received a call about an eleven-year-old boy named Dustin Meraz. Dustin was a patient at Children's Hospital in Los Angeles, and he was dying of an exceptionally horrible form of cancer called neuroblastoma. After being told he wanted to be an actor, I arranged for Dustin to receive an honorary SAG card. Then I decided to turn the presentation into a full-fledged ceremony.

If I couldn't use my powers as president for good, what good were they? So I made a few calls and showed up at Children's Hospital with Will Smith, Leonardo DiCaprio, and Stephen Collins. They helped me give Dustin his SAG card in front of his family, his roommate, and the hospital staffers. It was an afternoon that none of us will ever forget. Dustin passed away just a few weeks later. Not a day goes by that I don't think of him. His words are engraved on a bracelet I wear on my left wrist: "Today is a gift, have fun." Could there be better advice?

Later that year, I was invited back for a Christmas party with the kids on Dustin's unit. I brought Leo, *Spider-Man*'s Tobey Maguire, and my sister Sara. During the party, Lori Butterworth, the founder of the Children's Hospice & Palliative Care Coalition, took me aside and said she noticed that I had an aptitude for relating to these extremely sick children.

I had visited sick children in hospitals since my first season on *Little House,* and somehow I always wound up on the pediatric oncology floor. But my so-called aptitude may actually have been my curiosity as an adult to learn how to live from these children.

I went out to lunch with Lori, aka "the blond tornado," and her cofounder, Devon Dabbs. They explained the massive amount of resources and money needed to take care of terminally ill children and then pitched me on helping them raise awareness for the Coalition's work. I immediately agreed. Just putting together the words "hospice" and "children" seemed wrong. But they had my commitment with the first mention of a single statistic—that 92 percent of children that die in the United States die in uncontrolled pain.

As far as I was concerned that figure was disgusting, frightening, and thoroughly unacceptable. Part of the problem was silly law. Children had to qualify for hospice care. They often fought their illnesses harder and longer than adults simply because they were children. Hospice was suddenly taken away if they showed any improvement; there was no transition. I promised to do whatever I could to help lower that statistic and change the law, even if we had to do it one child at a time.

In February 2005, I said my good-byes as president of the Screen Actors Guild at the union's annual awards show. Bruce was out of town, so I took Sam and Lee, who looked incredibly handsome in their tuxedos, Gucci shoes, black shirts, and pink ties, which they gamely wore to match my pink dress with black flowers.

My stepsons were especially impressed when my gorgeous pretend daughter Jennifer Garner mentioned in her thank-you as winner for Best Actress in a Drama that I had once played her mother (I could see everyone in the auditorium quickly doing the math; we're eight years apart). Then at the after-party Kiefer Sutherland literally swept me off my feet with a giant bear hug, and while holding me in his arms, he pressed his lips to my ear and whispered, "You look so beautiful."

"Watch it, those are my stepsons standing to my side," I said, blushing.

He put me down, stepped back, and then, while looking directly at Sam and Lee, said, "Boys, I'm in love with your stepmother."

"Awesome," Sam said.

"Cool," Lee chimed.

It was a wonderful night and I made it through sober.

Three weeks later, members of SAG and AFTRA voted to accept a new three-year contract with studios covering theatrical and TV production. The $200 million deal I had spent years helping to craft and negotiate had passed. I considered it the crowning achievement of my two terms as SAG's chief elected officer.

My joy was tempered when my dear friend and colleague Bob Pisano decided to resign as executive director. As he put it, he had become part of the problem. The board hired Greg Hessinger in his place. I would miss Bob horribly, but I was pleased the Guild would be in Greg's very capable hands.

Unable to slow down, I managed to set sane limits and boundaries. I promised Bruce no SAG-related work before 8:00 a.m. or after 8:00 p.m. Between those hours, the family had me to themselves. I was also sober—six months and counting at that point—which put the kibosh on whooping it up at parties and events. Without a drink in my hand, I felt uncomfortable in social situations.

We stayed home most nights. Bruce and I would read, watch TV, and have friends or family over for dinner. The closest I got to life in the fast lane was the express line at the grocery store. But I was okay with driving carpools and helping with homework. Laura Ingalls Wilder once said, "It's the sweet, simple things of life which are the real ones, after all." She was right.

After nearly forty years in show business, I devoted time and energy to figuring out myself. Sobriety was one facet, and I took it more seriously than ever. Knowing that my life depended on avoiding alcohol, I committed to working on the fourth step in AA's twelve-step program. I had never done that before.

I was able to tackle the first three steps without any difficulty. I could admit that I was powerless over alcohol. I could believe a power greater than myself could restore me to sanity. And I could turn my life over to God as I understood Him. But I had always procrastinated when it came to the fourth step—making a searching and fearless moral inventory of myself. Who wants to face up to all the darkness and bad things she has done in her life?

For me, it wasn't a matter of whether I wanted to do this anymore. I *needed* to take a long, honest look at myself. One could say that all the time I had spent looking at myself in the mirror or on-screen, whether it was at my nose, my boobs, a fancy gown, or my face after bloodying it on the bedpost, were either missed opportunities or a gradual lead-up to this more crucial assessment of the way I looked on the inside.

With help from my therapist, I went to work trying to understand why I had made various choices throughout my adult life and what had driven me to this point. For months, I tackled the big questions that seemed to define me: Why was I so overly competent? Why was I constitutionally unable to ask anyone for help? Why was I unable to say no? Why, why, why was I the way I was?

The answer was like a nasty joke. Thanks to a lifetime spent on TV, I had been popular, admired, and loved my whole life by everyone except myself. Inside, I couldn't get past the first twenty-four hours of my life, when my mother and father had given me away. I was made to see and accept that the motivating factor behind many of my decisions was feeling I had to prove I was worthy and lovable.

I worked through that with exercises. My therapist had me imagine myself as a five-year-old and write a letter to my birth mother, Cathy, asking why she hadn't kept me, why she had gotten pregnant in the first place, and if she ever wondered what had happened to me. Then she had me answer those questions. I was shocked when I found myself in the guise of my birth mother, writing back that she had put me up for adoption to give me a chance at a better life than she could provide.

"Why hadn't I ever thought of it in that way?" I asked my therapist.

"Here's a better question," she said. "How are you going to go forward now that you have thought of it?"

There was no short, simple answer. My healing was an evolving process of recognition, awareness, and understanding. I didn't have to look for fixes outside of myself, not in work, men, or alcohol; I could find them in myself. I didn't have to worry about proving that I was lovable; I was already lovable. I could even love myself. I didn't have to be perfect; there was no such thing as perfect. I didn't have to worry about getting someplace; I was always exactly where I needed to be.

I had always been afraid that if I started to let out some of that pain, fear, and betrayal, I would start to cry and never stop. But finally confronting those wounds, whether through writing letters or just talking, helped. Sure, I cried—but not for long. And I felt better afterward.

I learned that a feeling is just that—a feeling. I didn't have to stay sad my whole life. Nor did I have to stay mad. Likewise, I wasn't able to stay happy all the time either. I was better off when I experienced everything life dealt me and then moved on to the next thing— whatever that turned out to be.

I also learned how to ask for help when I needed it. I was blessed to have a great circle of girlfriends around me, my own league of extraordinary women: Sandy, Amanda, Cordelia, Tina, Leilani, Colleen, Ali, and Kari, girlfriends I could call on when I needed help, and they were always there. I also had a very close relationship with my sister Sara. By then our age difference seemed virtually nonexistent. We have all been through so much together—marriages, divorces, births, deaths. Each one of them has contributed something unique to my life. Each of them has been a part of my history and I have been a part of theirs. What a miracle for someone like me who trusted no one, especially other women, to have a circle of women who share my secrets and in turn share theirs.

After a couple years, I could see both therapy and sobriety paying off. I stayed open and aware in most situations, if I got down I didn't stay down, and above all, I tried to behave as if my number one goal was to return in my next life as a fat, happy house cat whose only task would be to look for the warm spot.

In October 2006, I was elected president of the board for the Children's Hospice & Palliative Care Coalition. Six months later, I testified in front of the California state senate about the need to change hospice eligibility requirements. I also took a course in pediatric end-of-life nursing and got involved with kids and their families. That's where I felt like I was at my best.

I know it's where I have been able to do my most memorable work, as I am able to make a difference in a child's life. If I can help a child die pain-free and with dignity, then I've done something extraordinary.

Take sixteen-year-old Nick Snow. On the day we met at Children's Hospital, he had battled and beaten neuroblastoma, and I couldn't stop staring at his Afro. It may have been the world's biggest. Leo DiCaprio was with me that day and he said what I was thinking: "Dude, that's a hell of an Afro." Nick explained he grew it for all the years he didn't have hair.

His will was like the Energizer bunny. He didn't know when to stop. He flunked hospice twice—both times he rebounded slightly after new treatments. He was aware of what was going on each time hospice was pulled from him. His belief was that kids should be able to have hospice in palliative care whenever they needed, not just when the rules allowed. As he aptly said, it was cruel to make parents choose between curing and caring.

Nick eventually died not from cancer but from a perforated bowel.

I think he was tired from years of fighting and he just needed to rest. Thanks to him and others like him, though, we were able to pass the Nick Snow Act in California in 2009. This was the first big step in abolishing the hospice eligibility regulations for children, and the first step in creating a comprehensive, compassionate hospice bene-fit for children; the idea will sweep across California in stages. Now the goal is to spread that enlightened policy change across the United States.

In Akron, I met David, seventeen, who, without being able to speak a word, let me know that although he was scared as he battled leukemia, he was determined to win. He emanated courage. Then there was Jessica, a little girl who had bone cancer. When I asked her if she was afraid, she said, "No, not for me. But I worry about my mom and dad." She squeezed my hand and said, "I believe that a thousand years on earth is one day in heaven. So by the time I'm sit-ting down for my first lunch, my mom and dad will be there."

I had a friend whose baby died suddenly and unexpectedly. I dis-cussed this tragedy with my son Michael. My little philosopher rea-soned that this baby had been an angel. He went even further, postulating that all children start out as angels, flying down from heaven. At some point, their wings fall off. But my friend's baby hadn't lost his wings, and so he had to fly back.

I decided that all kids who died were angels who hadn't lost their wings. As for why they had to die in pain, I could only ask, who would do that to an angel?

These courageous children reinforced my belief in heaven. I'm not sure there is a hell, but there absolutely has to be something bet-ter. There has to be a pony in this barn full of crap. It just has to get easier. Which begs the questions, why is life so complicated, why is it such a puzzle, why do most of us find it such a struggle on so many different levels?

My therapist shared a theory she had come across, and I liked it. It held that before making your next journey in this life, your soul sits at a large, circular conference table and chooses the souls who are going to be part of your life. As for which particular people would be chosen, I figured they would be individuals from previous lives with whom there was still unfinished business.

My son, Michael Boxleitner, is definitely one of those people. His arrival into this world taught me about the miracle of life, and every day thereafter has been a reminder to me to appreciate it. Other people provided different lessons. Sam and Lee taught me that siblings do not have to be connected by blood to truly love and care for one another. More important, I learned that my love for each of my children is equal, whether they grew under my heart or in it.

Bo was the catalyst who pushed me to confront my own birth and taught me to begin to set boundaries, and I dragged Rob into my life to show me it was okay to be free with myself. Michael Landon showed me the most important thing was family and home. So he had three families and three homes—he tried. Bruce has enhanced my personal growth; we have taught each other to stay and work out situations rather than run away and miss the stuff that matters, the sweet, simple things.

It's interesting that the two most significant relationships in my life before Bruce were both with men who were cheats, as was I, and not for a second have I ever thought Bruce has been with another woman. To me, that's an example of healing and growth.

Why did I pick my mother, Barbara? I think I brought her into my life to teach me how to love unconditionally and, most important, to forgive. I have come to feel the same way about my birth mother, too. Forgiveness is a big theme in my healing process. After any type of emotional pain or distress, it's the only sure pathway to love again.

There's a sense of relief in forgiving people. Take my father, who chose to smoke, drink, and not take care of himself properly instead of spending more time with me. Do whatever you want to your body as long as you don't have a child. But once you're a parent, it's not your life anymore. You have to do everything you can to stay alive. My daddy didn't.

He was the last person with whom I wanted to be mad, but I had to learn to let myself be angry with him—and then to forgive him. Once that happened, the real reason he was in my life became apparent. It was so I could dance.

If there's one person I have had a hard time forgiving, it's myself. Clearly, that's what this journey has been about, at least thus far. I can think I'm making progress until I get to my son Dakota, who looms as both a mystery and a challenge. I am still trying to forgive myself for not being the mother I thought I could have been by letting him go to Texas. He reminds me of the work I still have left.

That's the point. The more people who enter my life and challenge me to learn and grow, the closer I get to the house cat in the next life.

By summer 2008 my mind and heart were in the best place of my life. I had over three years of good, solid sobriety under my belt and a support group in AA that was like a second family to me. My first family provided me with an immeasurable sense of safety and courage. I remember one Sunday afternoon when I was sitting with my sister Sara, watching Dakota and Michael play with her two little children, and I was imbued by a satisfying sense of warmth, closeness, and growth.

It was the kind of feeling a woman gets when she feels the passage of time, sees the lines in her face, and knows every bit of life that happened was worthwhile. Not coincidentally, I began an exciting new chapter soon after doing something that had terrified me all my life: I signed on to do a musical version of *Little House on the Prairie* at the Guthrie Theater in Minneapolis.

I've always been terrified of singing in front of people. It scares me to the very core of my being.

Ability is not the issue. As a child, I sang all the time with my dad. Apparently, I had perfect pitch, too. I grew up wanting to be a triple threat—an actor, singer, and dancer, like Shirley MacLaine, Patti LuPone, Ann-Margret, and Liza Minnelli. They are women who can do it all, and do it all so well. I just needed the opportunity, and then I had to get over the fear.

To prepare for the show, I spent nearly a year taking weekly voice lessons with my voice coach in L.A., Eric Vetrow. He got sound to come out of my voice that I didn't know existed within and taught me little tricks, like saving my throat by sipping Ricola cough drops steeped in hot water. Before leaving for Minneapolis, I took a signed photo of my father (it said, "To Missy-do, Love Dad"), shrunk it down, and had two copies made.

At the first rehearsal, I put one of those photos in my pocket and waited for my turn. One by one, the principal cast members stood and sang their numbers. I admired the wonderful, seemingly effortless sound they made. They seemed to disappear into a whole other person, or rather, their person seemed to expand into a greater being, this being who was transformed by music, inflated and imbued by a feeling they were able to express confidently, joyously, and pleasingly with their voice. They were singers.

As I waited, my heart thumped nervously, uncontrollably, almost like it does when I have an anxiety attack. I worked feverishly to gain control of my nerves so I could sing. Finally, my turn came, and I stood up, chest out, hands clasped behind my back so no one would see them shaking. I was like a courageous soldier marching into battle. Then, standing rigid and still, I began to sing.

I'm getting anxious just remembering the moment. Despite all my coaching and hard work, I heard, as did everyone else, a tiny, soft, and scared voice come out of me. It was mortifying. I got angry at myself. My brain screamed, "Dammit, pull yourself together!"

I don't exactly know what happened next, other than I reached down into my pocket and touched my hand to the picture of my father, and per my therapist's instruction I pictured him sitting in the front row. Then I stepped a little bit forward and felt my singing voice grow stronger and stronger. The rest is a blur except for the very end of the song, when I heard myself belting out the lyrics not only with confidence but also on pitch!

Just like that, it was over and everybody was applauding, and I thought, *Okay, I can do this. I have a voice.*

As for the rest of the rehearsal process, I immersed myself in it. There was a lot to tackle, and I felt excited and blessed. Normally, opportunities for actresses my age begin to wane, and yet there I was at forty-four starting a whole new facet of my career.

I was equally blessed to have such a wonderful cast and creative team around me. All of us bonded instantly, and I grew especially (and appropriately) close to Steve Blanchard, who was playing Pa. He and Bruce hit it off immediately. Before he returned home, Bruce even asked Steve to take care of me, something that would have been unheard-of in the past. But our marriage was now that solid.

The strangest part of the whole experience for me was grappling with the idea of playing Ma instead of Laura. Talk about an identity crisis. Early in rehearsals at the Guthrie Theater, I would answer whenever someone called for Laura or Half Pint. Later, during the scenes when Pa and Laura (Kara Lindsay) were onstage, I stood in the wings and wept, remembering Mike and me and watching the two of them create that bond in a whole new and beautiful way.

Rehearsals flew by. During the daytime, we added new songs, changed scenes, and moved things around. At night, we performed in front of a live audience willing to risk their money on a work-in-progress. My brain was boggled by all the information I needed to digest. It was dizzying, challenging, and scary to know the audience would be coming in expecting to see something special. I had so much to learn. I also felt the pressure of the *Little House* legacy. Would we be able to catch lightning in a bottle again?

On the day tickets went on sale for the official run, the Guthrie's website crashed. Hundreds of fans stood in line at the theater. I greeted people and marveled at the dozens of girls who showed up dressed as Laura, their hair in pigtails. For opening night, Bruce flew in with all the kids except for Dakota, who stayed home with strep throat. He would have come, but I vowed to make it through the run without getting sick.

After the two-and-a-half-hour performance, Bruce and the family engulfed me backstage. All of us were sobbing from joy. Elated and relieved, I sighed, "Oh man, I did it. This is really good." A few weeks later, I was backstage before a show and heard someone call out, "Caroline!" I automatically said, "Yes?" When I learned they had meant a girl in the company named Caroline, I thought, *Well, I guess I'm over the Laura thing now.* But as I left the theater that night I walked into a crowd of autograph seekers who shouted, "Laura! Laura! We love you, Laura!"

Ultimately, it didn't matter what people called me. I didn't have to be one person to anyone, including myself. Instead of worrying about who I was, the key was to focus on who I could become. I could have many different identities, including wife, mother, stepmother, friend, ex-wife, daughter, scared little girl, actress, former child star, Half Pint, former SAG president—and on certain occasions when everything was working in my favor, I heard guys whistle, "Hey, sexy." That was okay, too.

Somewhere on my journey from Baby Girl to grown woman I had discovered myself. I had also become the triple threat that once seemed possible only in my dreams. I could act, sing, and dance. I could also laugh, cry, and forgive. I didn't worry as much about who I was compared to who I could become.

In October, about two weeks before the play closed, I went with the kids in the show—Kara Lindsay, who played Laura, Jenn Gambatese, who played Mary, and Kevin Massey, who played Almanzo—on a five-hour drive to Walnut Grove, Minnesota, and De Smet, South Dakota, the real-life homes of Laura Ingalls Wilder and her family. Despite numerous invitations, I had not visited either place. The timing finally felt right now that I was old enough to appreciate it.

We arrived unannounced in Walnut Grove and visited the museum, where one display included the fireplace mantel from the set of the TV series. When no one was looking, I smelled it to see if it still contained any of the familiar scents from the set. It didn't, but memories of my girlhood flooded my heart and mind. We later ate lunch at Nellie's Café and walked along Plumb Creek.

In De Smet, our next stop, the owners of our bed-and-breakfast arranged a tour of the town. We walked through the house Pa had built, where I marveled at the cabinets he had made for Ma, and then we were ushered into the Laura Ingalls Wilder museum, where our guide opened a vault containing the most special items. She pulled out a nightgown and several handkerchiefs.

"These were Laura's," she said.

I instinctively reached out to touch them, then pulled my hand back and asked, "May I?"

"Yes," she said.

We sped back to Minneapolis, where all of us felt we put on one of the most inspired performances of the entire run. I climbed into bed late that night, exhausted but unable to fall asleep. I kept thinking about the flood of memories I had experienced after touching Laura's nightgown and handkerchief. While my fingers ran over the cotton fabric, I relived everything from my first audition for *Little House* to the present: happiness, sadness, heartbreak, and love. For someone who grew up not being allowed to feel anything, I now felt so much.

Indeed, in those sweet, simple things I felt the heft not of a career but of a life—an authentic life.

I looked forward to more.

ACKNOWLEDGMENTS

When I buy a new book, the first thing I read is the author's acknowledgments. I'm not sure why. Perhaps it's because I can get a sort of composite of who the author is by knowing who they feel has touched their work.

Well, now I am the author and it is my turn to thank those who have touched me and supported me throughout the writing of this book.

When this process began, I really had no idea where it would lead or how it would end. I felt a tremendous sense of responsibility: first to myself and then to all those who have been a part of my life thus far. Especially those whose names appear in this book.

I have to start by saying that none of this would've been possible, none of it, were it not for the friendship and guidance of my former agent/current manager, Marc Schwartz. Marc, your encouragement, humor, and ability to dismantle my inner time bomb when it begins to tick are invaluable to me. Because of your vision and faith in me, I have been able to reach beyond myself and really luxuriate in all the possibilities ahead. No small feat for an actress of a certain age. I can only imagine what will come next.

Thank you to:

Dan Strone, my literary agent, who upon hearing snippets of my life story ran with the seeds of a book and delivered me yet another hyphen: "author."

Emily Westlake and Jennifer Bergstrom at Simon & Schuster,

whose encouragement, excitement, and emotional connection to my story made me feel free enough to actually tell it.

Todd Gold!! Sculptor extraordinaire. Without you I am simply a formerly effed-up child star with a lot of stories to tell but no real blueprint for how to string them together.

Jonathan Howard and everyone at Innovative Artists for giving me the opportunity to keep stretching and growing in my other job.

Ame VanIden at PMK/HBH for keeping me relevant. No small feat in these days of the fifteen-minute celebutard.

My dear friend Greg Gorman, who always manages to bring out the very best of me. Thank you for my beautiful cover and all the magnificent images you have captured of me over the last twenty-five years. Here's to at least twenty-five more!!

Dr. Dan Zucker of the Institute of Health and Sports Chiropractic, and Richard Giorla, founder of Cardio Barre, for keeping my spine straight and my butt up where it ought to be.

Lord Torgue Ward, only you can make the gnomes and broccoli disappear and write movies!!

Daniel, Joanie, Chaz, Jeffrey, Vivian, Linda, Dr. D., Tina M., and all those who work so hard keeping my outside looking as glowing as my inside.

Bob, Seth, David, Greg, Mike, Jamie, Kevin, Paul C., Paul R., and all of you who stood beside me through my SAG presidency. You made the unbearable not just bearable but challenging, and sometimes even fun!

Marta, my spiritual advisor, counselor, sponsor, confidante, and friend—for holding my heart and my marriage and my family in your wise and gentle hands.

My girlies!! Friend Owl, Princess, Lei, Fance, Ali, Colleen, Rocket, and Speshy. You are my lifesavers. I love how we hold one another so close and no matter what, when, or where, when the call goes out, you all come running.

Ned-Nelson-Noodle-Flossie, my right hand for these last four years. I will miss our working relationship but am so happy that now we can just hang and be friends!

Lori, Devon, and everyone at the Children's Hospice and Palliative Care Coalition for giving me a purpose.

D.G. Always there. Always making me laugh. Always safe. Always . . . always.

Ms. P., how many lifetimes we have shared and through it all we remain side by side, adding pearls to the necklaces that make up our lives. Ours is a friendship that was predestined and transcendent. I do love you so.

My family at "Kraproom" for keeping me grounded, sharing your strength, and always giving me hope. That goes doubly for you, Marquis Michael Des Barres!!!

My P-dawgs: Sara, Jenn, Kara, Kevin, Maeve, and most especially, Steve and his lovely Meredith.

My amazing family: Mitzi, Charlie, Aunt Stephanie, Nanny Julia, Jenny. You have seen every moment, shared every tear, plotzed with every laugh. No matter where I go or what I do, I take you with me.

Sara, my baby love. The day you were born, you filled my heart with astonishment. Every year I have watched you grow, becoming the woman you are today, amazed by your mind, your heart, your essence. Thank you for my beautiful and brilliant nephew and niece. I love you.

Mom. We have been through so much . . . so, so much, and at the end of the day, here we are. I love your hands, your smell, your whimsy, and your heart. No matter what we have gone through, side by side or sometimes on opposite sides, our bond is unbreakable. All this time you thought it was me, but you are the ballerina, the beauty, and the real princess.

My boys. Not a day goes by that I don't thank God for allowing me to have you in my life. Each of you, with your own ways, your own strengths, fills me with pride. Sharing the journeys of your lives is my greatest joy.

Bruce, love of my life. There are no words for you. All you need to do is look in my eyes.

Finally, I must say that I had the hardest time finding a title for this book! It was a real struggle. So I had a contest among my very wise and very funny friends. I thank all those who participated. You know who you are and which suggestions were yours!

Thank you to Charlie Adler, Ann Andrews-Morris, Alison Arn-grim, Leilani Baker, Nancy Banks, Robert O. Berdahl, Lee Boxleitner, Dean Butler, Mitzi and Charlie Brill, Sidney J. Burgoyne, Tina Carlisi, Tira Christensen-Scott, Paul Christie, Amanda Cizek, Stephanie Crane, Katie Daly-Dancy, Michael Des Barres, Tayloe Emery, Krista Erricksen, Iva Franks-Singer, Bill Funt, Michael Gully, Tom Hanks, Mary McDonald-Lewis, John C. McDonnel, Peter Onorati, Charity Ozarowski, Jim Ramlet, Robbie Rist, Colleen and Charlie Schlatter, Oliver Scott, Vernon Scott IV, Jayne Spears, Mark Steinberg, Angela Teresa, Kerri Torrance, Daniel Wachtenheim, and Brian Wimmer.

Only you could come up with such eloquent, sweet, and twisted titles. I love you all!

I Told You So
Half Pint Goes to Hollywood
Prairie Blossom
Little House, Big Heart
Take a Walk on the Wilder Side
Lights, Camera, Blackouts
The Summer to Forget
Big Girl
From Half Pint to Sag-ging Adult?
Half a Pint of Trouble!!
How My Mom Dated Bill Funt's Dad?
My Life on the Brink, Man
Life, Love, and Hollywood
The Joys of Working with Robert O. Berdahl
The Highs and the Lowes?

Battle of the Network Stars

Don't F*** with America's Sweetheart!

Prairie Home Companion

Some of Melissa's Favorite Foods

Half Pint; Full Quart!

The Large Pint Giveth and the Small Pint Taketh Away

I Never Tripped on That Hill (But My Little Sister Did, Bwaaaaaahhh)

Little Ho on the Prairie

Bruce's Babe

Half Pint and Half Lit

There's *Fire* under That Gingham Dress!

Mankato, Here I Come!

Mr. Edwards, Your Lap Sure Is Uncomfortable

Me, Myself, and Why

Save the Whales: The Story of Melissa Gilbert

Nellie's Not a Bitch, Mary Is

Sylvester and Me, A Secret Love Revealed

Prairie Girl

Ha-ha! I Never Went to Jail and You Did!

I'm Not a Bunny Boiler

Wild Child

Little Pint in the Big World

Melissa Ellen Gilbert: Just a Kid with a Career

Baby Girl

Melissa Gilbert: Pulling No Punches

Melissa Gilbert: Growing Up Sweet, Living Strong

Walking in Laura's Shoes . . . Living in Mine

Big Lights, Little House: The Melissa Gilbert Story

How I Learned to Love Gingham

This F*****g Book Should Be about Paul Christie But I Made It about Me Instead

Little Girl, Big Dreams: Melissa Gilbert

Corn Beef and Kreplach

A Sale of Two Titties
And You Thought Charlie Adler Was Pretty!
A Whore in the Temple of the Arts
The Carpet Does Match the Drapes
I Am Not Elaine Stritch
Don't Read This Book
A Little Prayer on the Housie
The Mackerel Worker
Mind Your Business
Enough About Me . . . What Do You Think About Me?
I Am My Own Stalker
My Pet Cemetery Is Bigger Than Yours
Laura Ingalls Became President of the Movie People
All This and I'm Only Half Done!
Fully Me: My Journey in and beyond the Prairie
Fill the Pint
The Prairie Moves
Melissa Gilbert from Pigtails to Politics
Melissa the Chosen Child
Half Pint . . . a Day
Does This Gingham Dress Make Me Look Fat?
I F****d Rob Lowe on the Skyway to Tomorrow Land
Things I Have Stuck Up My Nose
Fear and Loathing in Walnut Grove
Waaaah Waaaaahh
Melicious Gilbert—My Prairie Tale Life
Acting's One Thing. Actors Are Another.
The Kid Slays in the Picture
Half Pint and Other Measures
Shaking (Off) the Prairie Dust
Little House, Big Secrets
The Autobiography of Melissa X
I Am Not Sara
Half Pint . . . Fully Loaded

Half Pint . . . After Dark
I Love Charlie Schlatter
Little Whore on the Prairie
I Gave My Friend Dying from Leukemia a Fart Box
I Am Not My Pigtails